A STUDY

OF

MARRIAGE-LOVE AND WOMANKIND

IN

THE ARAB RACE

The Book
of
Exposition

P. AVRIL. DEL   A. BESSE. SC

The Secrets of Oriental Sexuology

THE

Book of Exposition

(Kitab al-Izah fi'Ilm al-Nikah b-it-Tamam w-al-Kamal)

LITERALLY TRANSLATED FROM THE ARABIC

BY

AN ENGLISH BOHEMIAN

WITH TRANSLATOR'S FOREWORD,

NUMEROUS IMPORTANT NOTES ILLUSTRATING THE TEXT, AND
SEVERAL INTERESTING APPENDICES

DARF PUBLISHERS LTD
London
1987

ISBN 1 85077 901 5

Printed in Great Britain by
Butler & Tanner Ltd, Frome and London

CONTENTS

"There is no need of entreaties, gentlemen, where you can command; and therefore, pray be attentive, and you will hear a true story, not to be equalled, perhaps, by any feigned ones, though usually composed with the most curious and studied art."

El cura y todos los demas se lo agradecieron y de nuevo se lo rogaron, y él viéndose rogar de tantos, dijo que no eran menester ruegos adonde el mandar tenia tanta fuerza; y asi estén vuestras mercedes atentos, y oirán un discurso verdadero, à quien podría ser que no llegasen los mentirosos, que con curioso y pensado artificio suelen componerse.

DON QUIXOTE. Primera parte, XXXVIII.

L-il-Abrár kull shei Barr.
TO THE PURE ALL THINGS ARE PURE.
(Puris omnia pura).

ARAB PROVERB.

Niuna corrotta mente intese mai sanamente parole.

"DECAMERON" — Conclusion.

"Mieux est de ris que de larmes escripre,
Pour ce que rire est le propre de l'homme."

RABELAIS.

Nought is so vile that on the earth doth live,
But to the earth some special good doth give,
Nor aught so good, but, strain'd from that fair use,
Revolts from true birth, stumbling on abuse.

Rom. and Jul., ii, 3.

TABLE OF CONTENTS

FOREWORD

THE BOOK OF EXPOSITION

EXCURSES

FOREWORD

"Love took up the harp of life, and
smote on all the chords with might;

Smote the chord of Self, that trembling
passed in music out of Sight."

TENNYSON.

Alexander Dumas justly says:—"The question
of Love is a grave one, because Love
represents the Animal aspect of our nature,
when it does not represent the Sublime aspect.

Love means either Heaven or Mud. It is a Need
of Nature which demands the continuation of the
species for an end unknown to us.

. . . . "You are looking out for *your* Female: that is
the Law of the Body; You seek for Love: that is
the Law of the Soul. Of Females you will find as
many as you desire, more than you may desire. Love
is another thing."

Love of Woman is the mightiest passion [1]) in the

---

[1]) Perfectly ideal as it may sometimes seem, Love is yet,
consciously or unconsciously, based on purely physical sym-
pathies which seek their normal outlet and expansion in
physical acts.

heart of Man.—Poets of all lands and of all times
have sung in immortal verses its praises and enchant-
ments. Novelists have exhausted their wit and ingenuity
to unravel the varied webs of noble heroism or criminal
conspiracy woven on the ever-busy shuttles of Human
Passion. From the days of Adam until now, Woman
has played the leading, if inconspicuous, rôle in all
the changeful drama of the world's history. In a
famous mystic book there occurs 'a fine phrase, which
is as true as it is well-expressed:—"Love is strong
as death. Many waters cannot quench love, neither
can the floods drown it." [1]) Letourneau says: "This
is not exaggerated; we may even say that love is
stronger than death, since it makes us despise it.
This is perhaps truer with animals than with man,
and is all the more evident in proportion as the
rational will is weaker, and prudential calculations
furnish no check to the impetuosity of desire." [2])

Napoleon well said that men are but grown-up
children, influenced mainly through the imagination.
The heart prompts the intellect, and the intellect
rules the will, and the will chisels out the rough-
hewn block of life. Sexuality plays the supreme rôle
in all phases of human experience. In striking contrast
with the sentiment of Tennyson quoted at the head of
the present Chapter, Shakspeare has remarked: "Love
is a familiar; love is a devil: there is no evil angel
but love. Yet was Samson so tempted, and he had
an excellent strength; yet was Solomon so seduced,

---

[1]) "Solomon's Song," VIII, 6, 7.
[2]) "The Evolution of Marriage," chap. I. part. IV.

and he had a very good wit ". (" Love's Labour
Lost ", I, 2.)

In the blindness of its passion, Love for the
bewitching daughters of Eve has wrecked empires, [1])
overtoppled statesmen, and sapped the strong foundations
of the proudest thrones, the pillars of the most ancient
temples. Silent and invisible, it is yet like a mighty
sorceress that mesmerises the most rebel will into
obedience. It is, in brief, the vital heat of life. This
is proved by Philosophy ; illustrated by the Romance
of everyday existence, and Science steps in to confirm
previsions and reasonings of both. " Man has two
powerful instincts, which govern his whole life, and
give the first impulse to all his actions : the instinct
of Self-preservation, and the instinct of Race-preserv-
ation. The former reveals itself in its simplest form
as hunger, the latter as love .... The result of love,
the union of the youth and the maiden into a fruitful
pair, has always been surrounded by more ceremonies
and festivities, preparations and formalities than any
other act of man's life ; in primitive times by customs
and etiquette, and later, by written laws confirming
these formalities ..... Love is the great regulator

---

[1]) In case this may seem too strong, we cite Helen of Troy,
Cleopatra, Empress Eugénie as amongst the more salient of
many others that will occur to the historical reader.

By the term " love," we, of course, mean the influence of
sexuality, what Haeckel calls in scientific jargon, " the elective
affinity of two different cellules—the spermatic cell and the
ovulary cell " (" Anthropogenia," p. 577.)

Goethe's " Wahlverwandtschaft" expresses more meaning than
could be conveyed in exhaustive volumes.

of the life of the race, the impelling force which promotes the perfecting of the species and tries to prevent its physical decay.... The propagating impulse alone is blind, and it needs the reliable guide, love, to enable it to reach its natural goal, which is at the same time the perpetuation and improvement of its kind." [1]

The book before us is an Ode in praise of Priapus. Here it breaks out into the finest panegyric; there it gives way to a freedom of speech that astonishes by its very lubricity.

Speaking of the works of Baffo, [2] Octave Uzanne, the famous French man-of-letters, refers to the Italian poet as "this great cynic overflowing with erotic genius, that is to say: the pleasure of physical love."

Almost precisely similar terms may be employed with reference to the work we have translated. Praise of the Physical love of Woman is its main object. Interspersed with Invocations to Allah—for the Moslem is nothing if not profoundly religious, even in those acts of human life where Deity in an European mind is generally least thought of,—come Anecdotes, Snatches of poetry, Reminiscences of famous Orators, Writers and Kings of the then Present or Bygone times.

If, as Balzac said, "the Books of Rabelais formed

---

[1] Max Nordau in "Conventional Lies of our Civilization," London, 1895, pages 256-263.

[2] Vide "Nos amis les Livres", p. 56 and 61, Paris, 1886. Baffo enjoys in Italy about the same unenviable reputation for utter obscenity as the Marquis de Sade in France.

a Bible of Incredulity," the present little *brochure* may aptly be termed the "Song of Songs of the Flesh." For never was pen put to paper with so undisguised an object as that had in view by the learned Sheikh who devoted his mastery of Arabic to its composition.

The reticence shown by the newly-married young Englishwoman who, calling on the butcher, ordered "stomach of pork" instead of using the term "belly," by which that article is known to the "trade," would be utterly incomprehensible to an Arab.

He sees no harm, even when highly educated, in "calling a spade a spade," and referring to a thing by its right name. Yet, precisely the people who wade sedulously through the filthy columns of garbage that adorn the great English Dailies—the latest spicy Divorce suit; Seduction and Paternity case, Oscar Wilde's vagaries; Revelations of the Erotic tendencies of Massage; or an affair of Rape on girl, or child,—are the first to condemn a book issued in a limited edition to a select circle of private subscribers.

Burton has well pointed out that the Oriental fails to grasp that it is improper to refer in straightforward terms to anything Allah has created, or of which His revelation, the Holy Quran, treats. But, on the other hand, in his conversation as in his folk-lore, there is no subtle corruption, or covert licentiousness as is too largely found in writers of many classes to-day: none of the leering suggestions or false sentiment that pervade the productions of the Catulle Mendés and Zola school, and their milk-and-wateryEnglish imitators.

We must be on our guard here, however, to avoid plunging into any egregious blunder. There *does* exist in the Moslem mind a sentiment of shame and modesty, but it is not for precisely the same things as in Europe. It is the sentiment that forces an *Orientale* to conceal her face before the stranger, even though she be only clothed in a simple chemise, and obliged in the act of covering her features to leave open to indiscreet eyes those other parts of her person, of which the modesty of *European* women suggests the hiding up, or at any rate, does not usually permit her to show, except under the domination of amorous excitement in the prudent obscurity of the boudoir. ¹)

In Moslem morals, nakedness of words and nakedness of form do not count, and yet the philosophy of Islam, large and generous in all that is natural, stamps onanism and other sensual irregularities whether legitimate or otherwise, with a severity unknown in occidental communities.

---

¹) It is to this highly moral practice of decency that the Turks allude in giving to the Sultaness Validé the honorary title of *Taj-ul-Mastourat,* or " Crown of Veiled Heads," thereby meaning that one honours in her the first of veiled and self-respecting women, as opposed to the women of the " infidel Christian " who, in not going covered, are regarded as shameless. (See " Turquie Officielle," by Paul de Régla, 4th ed., 1891, p. 269.)

Turkish women would find perhaps still more foundation for their opinion with regard to their western sisters if they could see them perspiring, and half nude, dancing round with other women's husbands, who may be utter *strangers* to them, at some of our great *Society Balls.*

THE AGE AND AUTHORSHIP OF THE BOOK.

The writing of this outspoken treatise is credited
to Jâlal-ad-Dîn as-Siyuti, although it is only fair to
add that the authorship is much disputed.

But, the fact of Jâlal-al-Dîn having been a sober
Divine, and a historian who could rank in the lists
with the best, does not of itself detract from the
probability of his having given birth to the work.

In Europe, in this hypercritical Nineteenth Century,
it would be considered very improper if, for instance,
men like Canons Farrar, Wilberforce or, to go to
France, a Cardinal of the Catholic Church, were to
put their name to a treatise, which had for express
object the praise and glorification of the carnal pleasures
to be had from women's intercourse, even though
their aim, in so doing, were to counteract certain
unnatural vices.

Such men as these may be allowed to inveigh in
general terms and covert manner against sexual sin,
providing they offend nobody in particular, while
tickling every one's ears with rhetorical embellishments.
Society *must* not be shocked. Now, in the East
people are more honest and outspoken on these
matters. No false shame prevails, and consequently,
far less uncleanness. No "SOCIETY FOR THE PREVENTION
OF VICE" exists, and men of Mr. Stead's stamp would
have to seek some other trade entirely unconnected
with the "*Maiden Tribute*" line, or faked-up "Exposures
of Modern Babylon." In the East, men of great social
standing, and high religious dignitaries, did not think
it beneath them to compose works upon sexual

questions. Thus, d'Herbelot attributes one of the most outspoken, a 4to of 464 pages, called the "*Halbat al-Kumayt*", or "Race Course of the Bay-Horse", a poetical and horsey term for grape wine, to the Hadj-Shams al-Din Muhammad.

To give an idea of its contents we extract a story from this delightful classic:—

THE PERPLEXED PEASANT-WOMAN.

One day at Cairo, an Arab met in a deserted bye-street, a fellah woman, or peasant. She was standing between two large leather bottles of oil, awaiting a customer. He approached her, inquired the price of her merchandise, and asked to taste it. The woman undid the mouth of one of the bottles; the customer tasted it and found it good. "Let us see," he said, "if the other bottle is of the same quality." The woman held with one hand the neck of the bottle that was already open, and the Arab undid the other. "Hold the neck of this one," he said to the oil-seller, "whilst I compare the two oils." So saying, he poured a little oil from each bottle into each hand, attentively examined the two samples, then mingled them together in his left hand, then suddenly drew out his tool, rubbed it with oil, then pulled up the woman's clothes. She, being occupied in holding the necks of the bottles, could not defend herself. He pushed her against the wall, inserted his weapon in her, accomplished his design, and went away without fear of being pursued, on account of her embarrassment.

"I see," he said, as he went away, "that the

proverb is true which says that "a woman takes more care of what is in her hands than of what is between her legs."

The learned Sprenger, a physician as well as an Arabist, says ("Al Mas' udi", p. 384) of a tractate by the celebrated Rhazes in the Leyden Library, "The number of curious observations, the correct and practical ideas, and the novelty of the notions of Eastern nations on the subjects which are contained in this book, render it one of the most important productions of the medical literature of the Arabs."

It is generally said abroad, points out Burton, that the English have the finest women in Europe, and the least know how to use them. In the East, this branch of the fruitful knowledge-tree is not neglected. Modern education in Europe insists, as a rule, upon keeping from boy and girl all knowledge of sexual subjects, leaving them to glean and acquire this part of life's training as best they may. With what entailment of unspeakable misery and needless shame the truth is, in many cases, arrived at, is too well-known.

Physiology, it is true, is pretended to be taught, but that section treating of what the Turks call "*la partie au-dessous de la taille*", is avoided with precious care, as though the organs of generation were unworthy of notice, and we ought all to be ashamed of our existence. A system like this has its results, the bitter harvest being reaped in the after-years of the broken life, the blighted family, or mournful procession of diseased generations. You may affect to ignore that water will drown, or fire burn, but falling into a sufficient quantity of the one, or thrusting your head into a blazing furnace of the other, will quickly put an end to such ostrich-like hallucinations.

THE SAJ'A—RHYMED PROSE.

Some parts of our translation, particularly at the commencement of it, have been thrown into a kind of rhymed prose. A word in explanation of this is, probably, for some readers necessary. Otherwise one may be condemned unheard on a charge of affectation. " Al-Saj'a, as scholars are aware, the fine style, or *style fleuri*, also termed Al-Badi'a, or euphuism, is the basis of all Arabic euphony. The whole of the Koran is written in it, and the same is the case with the *Makàmàt* of Al-Hariri and the prime masterpieces of rhetorical composition: without it no translation of the Holy Book can be satisfactory or final, and where it is not, the famous assemblies become the prose of prose. Burton, writing further in his usual exhaustive manner on this subject, says: " English translators have, unwisely I think, agreed in rejecting it, while Germans have not." M. Preston [1]) assures us that " rhyming prose is extremely ungraceful in English, and introduces an air of flippancy:" this was certainly not the case with Friedrich Ruckert's version of the great original, and I see no reason why it should be

---

[1]) Rev. F. Preston, translated the Mak'am'at, or Rhetorical Anecdotes of Abu'l Kasem al Hariri, of Basra into verse and Prose (1850). He illustrates his rendering with annotations. The style is certainly easy, but the great *freedom* he has taken with the original is regrettable.

so or become so in our tongue. Torrens declares
that "the effect of the irregular sentence with the
iteration of a jingling rhyme is not pleasant in our
language:" he therefore systematically neglects it, and
gives his style the semblance of being "scamped,"
with the object of saving study and trouble. M. Payne
deems it "an excrescence born of the excessive facilities
for rhyme afforded by the language, and of Eastern
delight in antithesis of all kinds, whether of sound or
of thought; and, aiming elaborately at grace of style,
he omits it wholly, even in the proverbs." Burton
then goes on to state his reasons for the employment
of this peculiar style as applied to our own tongue,
questioning Payne's dictum that the "Seja form is
utterly foreign to the genius of English prose, and
that its preservation would be fatal to all vigour and
harmony of style." Antony Munday, who translated
"The History of Prince Palmerin of England,"
attempted the style in places with considerable success,
and Edward Eastwick, in his version of the "Gulistan"
from the Persian, made artistic use of it.

A kindly critic and reviewer of Burton's translation
of the "Nights" where the Saj'a has been transferred into English with matchless effect and brilliancy,
writes; "These melodious fragments, these little eddies
of song set like gems in the prose, have a charming
effect on the ear. They come as dulcet surprises,
and most recur in highly-wrought situations, or they
are used to convey a vivid sense of something exquisite in nature or art. Their introduction seems due
to whim, or caprice, but really it arises from a profound study of the situation, as if the Tale-teller felt

suddenly compelled to break into the rhythmic strain. "

This rhymed prose, to which the Arabs gave the name of Saj'a, from a fancied resemblance between its rhythm and the cooing of a dove, is the peculiar diction of the race, and indeed, part and parcel of the genius of the Arabic language itself.

This is no place to go into the history of the growth and development of this remarkable linguistic peculiarity, which indeed bears a striking likeness to the form of composition employed in the Hebrew. The poetical literature of both languages was built up, we may assume, on the common foundation of the Semitic life, and they certainly, amid all their diversity, bear traces of this primitive union. Compare the curse and blessing of Noah on his sons, the answer of Jehovah to Rebekah when she enquires concerning the struggling children in her womb, the blessings of Isaac upon Jacob and Esau, the curse of Moab in Numbers XXI 27, and the Song of Israel at the digging of the well, verse 17. The rhymed prose of the Arabs may therefore be placed as the analogue of Hebrew poetry, and the origin of both referred to the primitive ages of the Semitic Race. The history of rhymed prose is the history of Arabic literature.

I can do no more than add in the words of Sir Richard Francis Burton: " Despite objections manifold and manifest, I have preserved the balance of sentences and the prose rhyme and rhythm which Easterns look upon as mere music. This Saj'a has in Arabic its special duties. It adds a sparkle to description and a point to proverb, epigram and dialogue: it

correspondends with our artful alliteration, and generally, it defines the boundaries between the classical
and the popular styles. This rhymed prose may be
"un-English" and unpleasant, even irritating to the
British ear; still I look upon it as a *sine qua non*
for a complete reproduction of the original " [1]).

WOMAN AND AL-ISLAM [2]).

Nothing is more remarkable than the perfectly
mistaken notions held, mostly by Englishmen, who,
by the way, represent the mightiest Mohammadan
Power in the world, respecting the Position of Woman
among their fellow-subjects professing the Religion
of Islam in India. Such notions are *far* more dangerous
than utter ignorance, as they serve to place many
millions of people in a false light, and create an
animus that has no right to exist. Otherwise the
preposterous legends that get handed down from
father to son anent this subject would deserve ridicule

---

[1]) It is only loyal to say that we are indebted for a large
part of the information here set forth to the late Thomas
Chenery's learned introduction to his able translation of the
first twenty-six "Assemblies of Al-Hariri" (London 1867);
and Burton's article on "The Saj'a" in the X. vol. of his
marvellous version of the "Nights". Chenery was Editor of
the "Times" newspaper, as well as a profound Arabic Scholar,
and a Barrister.

I hope this frank avowal will save me from impeachment for
piracy on the high seas of literature.

[2]) Islam means "*Surrender*," one of the grandest names
for a Religion', says even *wary* Prof. Max Müller, that has
ever been invented!

and derision rather than serious answer or argument. Much of the stuff about the Polygamy of Moslems is, no doubt, due to the pious inventions of parsons and missionaries not blessed with the luxury of an over-cultivated conscience, and more solicitous for the supposed *" Glory of God "* than the consecration of the Truth. Their lies and subterfuges, fabricated with the intent of vilifying one of the noblest religions current amongst men, have been refuted by able writers over and over again: but, with that powerful vitality displayed by falsehoods in general, and *half-truths* in particular, they are constantly re-springing into existence, either in the same or another form, seeming indeed to possess—*unlike the proverbial cat*— not merely nine, but Nine Hundred and Ninety-Nine lives.

Now this subject has been ably argued by many learned men, in particular by John Davenport [1]), and, for fear lest we should be ourselves suspected of too much bias, we prefer to quote him *in extensô*. No other writer has handled the question, to our knowledge, with more clearness and common-sense.

ON THE SENSUALISM OF THE QURANIC PARADISE.

"Another charge brought against Mohammed is the sensual character of the joys promised by him in his Paradise to those who receive his Law, and conform their lives to the precepts it contains; but,

---

[1]) *An Apology for Mohammad and the Koran*. Lond. 1882.

upon reflection, it will be found that there is nothing so absurd in this as is generally imagined by Christians, when it is considered that our bodies will, as we are told, assume at the resurrection a form so perfect as infinitely to surpass all that we can conceive, and that our senses will acquire so extraordinary an activity and vigour as to be susceptible of the greatest pleasures, each according to the difference of their objects, for, indeed, if we take away from those faculties their proper exercise, if we deprive them of the fit objects to please and gratify them, it cannot be otherwise than supposed that they have not only been given us to no purpose, but even to inflict upon us continual disappointment and pain. For, in fact, by supposing that the soul and body are restored to us, as must be necessarily the case if our bodies are restored in perfect state, it is not clear upon what grounds it can be supposed that the senses should not have objects to exercise upon, in order to be capable of bestowing and of tasting all the pleasures which they may be capable of affording. Can there be any sin, crime, shame or degradation in the enjoyment of such pleasures? And as to that pleasure more particularly denounced—that of the sexes—did not the Almighty institute and grant it to the most perfect creatures who ever appeared in the world? And as the Almighty had freely and liberally provided for them whatever was necessary for the preservation of life, so He made them susceptible of the most rapturous delight in the act and duty of multiplying their species.

That Mohammad, in his Quran, promises the faithful

the use of women, and mentions delightful gardens and other sensual delights, is true, but that he places the chief happiness in these things is a mistake. For as the soul is more noble than the body, so he was willing to allow the body its own pleasures, that by the reward he promised he might the more easily allure the rude Arabians, who thought of nothing but that which was gross and sensual, to fall into the worship of the one and only true God as expounded in his doctrine.

But Mohammad always assigned to the soul its own peculiar pleasures, viz, the beholding the face of God, which will be the greatest of all delights, the fulness of joy, and which will cause all the other pleasures of Paradise to be forgotten, they being common to the cattle that graze in the field. He that beholdeth his gardens, wives, goods and servants, reaching through the space of a thousand years'journey, is but in the lowest degree among the inhabitants of Paradise; but among them he is in the supreme degree of honour with God, who " contemplates His divine countenance every morn." It is therefore false that the pleasures of the Moslem's Paradise consist exclusively in corporeal things and the use of them; it is false, also, that all Moslims believe those pleasures to be corporeal; for many contend, on the contrary, that those things are said parabolically and are considered as of spiritual delight, in the same manner as the Doctors of the Christian church maintain that " *Solomon's Song* " is not a mere Epithalamium, but is to be understood in a spiritual sense as typical of Christ's love for his church.

The famous Hyde [1]) writes: That those sensual pleasures of Paradise are thought by wiser Believers in Islam to be allegorical, that they may be then better conceived by human understanding, just as in the Holy Scriptures many things are said after the manner of man. For writing to the ambassador for Morocco, when I mentioned a garden pleasant like that of Paradise, he checking me, wrote back that Paradise was such a place to which nothing could be likened; such as "neither eye hath seen, ear heard, neither hath it entered into the heart of man to conceive." To this may likewise be added the testimony of the famous Herbelot, who after having shown [2]) that Moslems place the chief good in the Communion of God, and the celestial Joys in the fruition of the light of the Divine countenance, which make Paradise wherever it is, writes thus;—It is not therefore true which many authors who have opposed Islam have asserted—that the Moslems know no other happiness in Heaven but the use of pleasures which affect the senses.

From what precedes it follows that much more than is just has been said and written about the sensual character of Mohammad's religion. No doubt, that from a Christian point of view, and taken in the abstract, certain usages of the people of the East present themselves to European criticism as real defects and as great vices, but with a little more of evangelical

---

[1]) In his *Not: ad Biboi, Turcar Liturg*, p. 21.
[2]) In his "*Bibliotheca Orientalis*".

charity we should treat them less severely. We should take more into account the influence of origin and the material necessity of social obligations.

Equally mistaken, if not wilfully unjust, are those who find in Mohammad's sensual Paradise, a reflex of his own character and represent the Prophet— ("Impostor" they call him)—as a sensual Voluptuary, for so much to the contrary, he was a poor, hard-toiling, ill-provided man, careless of what vulgar men so eagerly labour and contend for.

ISLAM'S PROPHET AND POLYGAMY. [1]

Polygamy was a custom general throughout the East so long back as the days of the Patriarch Abraham, and which, 'tis certain, from innumerable passages in scripture, some of which we shall quote, could not in those purer ages of mankind have been regarded as sinful.

Polygamy was permitted among the ancient Greeks, as in the case of the detachment of young men from the army, mentioned by Plutarch. It was also defended by Euripides and Plato. The ancient Romans were more severe in their morals, and never practised it,

---

[1] Syed Ameer Ali says justly:—"In certain stages of social development polygamy, or more properly speaking, *polygyny*,— the union of one man with several women is an *unavoidable* circumstance. The frequent tribal wars and the consequent decimation of the male population, the *numerical* superiority of women, combined with the absolute power possessed by the chiefs, originated the custom which in *our* advanced times is justly regarded as an unendurable evil." *The Spirit of Islam*, Lond. 1891.   (Trans).

although it was not forbidden among them: and Marc Antony is mentioned as the first who took the liberty of having two wives. From that time it became pretty frequent in the empire till the reigns of Theodosius, Honorius, and Arcadius, who first prohibited it by an express law, A. D. 393. After this the Emperor Valentinian permitted, by an edict, all the subjects of the empire, if they pleased, to marry several wives; nor does it appear from the ecclesiastical history of those times that the Bishops made any objection to its introduction.

Valentianus Constantias, son of Constantine the Great, had many wives. Clotaire, King of France, and Æribartus and Hypercius his sons, had a plurality also. Add to these, Pepin and Charlemagne, of whom St. Urspergensus witnesses that they had several wives. Lothaire and his son, as likewise Arnolphus VII, Emperor of Germany (A. D. 888), and a descendant of Charlemagne, Frederic Barbarossa and Philippe Theodatus King of France. Among the first race of the Kings of the Franks, Contran, Caribert, Sigebert and Chilperic had several wives at one time. Contran had within his palace Veneranda and Mercatrude and Ostregilde, acknowledged as his legitimate wives; Caribert had Merflida, Marconesa and Theodogilda.

Father Daniel confesses the polygamy of the French Kings. He denies not the three wives of Dagobert I., expressly asserting that Theodobert espoused Dentary, although she had a husband, and himself another wife, named Visigelde. He adds that in this he imitated his uncle Clotaire, who espoused the widow of Creodomir, although he had already three wives.

With respect to the *physiological* reason for polygamy, it has been observed by the celebrated Montesquieu that women in hot climates are marriageable at eight, nine, or ten years of age; thus, in those countries, infancy and marriage almost go together.

They are old at twenty. Their reason, therefore never accompanies their beauty.

When beauty demands the empire, the want of reason forbids the claim; when reason is obtained, beauty is no more.

Thus woman must necessarily be in a state of dependence; for reason cannot procure in old age that empire which even youth and beauty combined could not bestow. It is therefore extremely natural that in these places a man, when no law opposes it, should leave one wife to take another, and that polygamy should be introduced.

In temperate climates, where the charms of women are best preserved, where they arrive later at maturity and have children at a more advanced season of life, the old age of their husbands in some degree follows theirs; and as they have more reason and knowledge at the time of marriage, if it be only on account of their having continued longer in life, it must naturally introduce a kind of equality between the sexes, and, in consequence of this, the law of having only one wife. Nature, which has distinguished men by their reason and bodily strength, has set no other bounds to their power than those of this strength and reason. It has given charms to women, and ordained that their ascendancy over men shall end with those charms; but in hot countries these are found only at the beginning, and never in the progress of life.

Thus the Law which permits one wife is *physically* conformable to the climate of Europe, and not that of Asia. This is the reason why Islam was established with such facility in Asia, and extended with so much difficulty in Europe; why Christianity is maintained in Europe, and almost destroyed in Asia; and in fine, why Moslims have made such progress in China and Christians so little.

In appears from Cesar, that in early times our ancestors practised polyandry, ten or twelve husbands having only one wife among them. When the Roman Catholic missionaries came among these primitive people, they encouraged celibacy, and held that the marriage of a man with a widow was bigamy, and punishable canonically. At length we subsided into monogamy, as appears to have been the practice of the ancient Germans, according to Tacitus (De Moribus Germanorum).

As to the lawfulness of polygamy, it will be seen by referring to the following passages in the scriptures, that it was not only approved but even blessed by Jehovah himself. Genesis XXXV, 22; Exodus XXI, v. 2; Deuteronomy XVII, v. 17; 1 Samuel V, v. 13; Judges VIII, v. 30; Judges XII, v. 9. 14.

St. Chrysostom, speaking of Abraham and Hagar, says. "These things were not then forbidden." So St. Augustine observes that there was a blameless custom of one man having many wives, which at that time might be done in a way of duty, which now cannot be done but from licentiousness, because, for the sake of multiplying posterity, no law forbade a plurality of wives.

Boniface, Confessor of Lower Germany, having consulted Pope Gregory, in the year 726, in order to know in what cases a husband might be allowed to have two wives, Gregory replied on 22nd November of the same year in these words—If a wife be attacked by a malady which renders her unfit for conjugal intercourse, the husband may marry another; but in that case he must allow his sick wife all necessary support and assistance.

Many works have been published in defence of polygamy even by writers professing Christianity. Bernardo Ochinus, general of the Order of Capuchins, published about the middle of the sixteenth century, dialogues in favour of the practice, and about the same time appeared a treatise on behalf of a plurality of wives; the author whose real name was Lysarus, having assumed the pseudonym of Theophilus Aleuthes.

Selden proves, in his *Uxor Hebraica*, that polygamy was allowed not only among Jews, but likewise among all other nations.

But the most distinguished defender of Polygamy was the celebrated John Milton, who in his " Treatise on Christian Doctrine," after quoting various passages from the Bible in defence of the practice, says: " Moreover, God, in an allegorical fiction (Ezekiel XXIII), represents Himself as having espoused two wives, Aholah and Aholiah, a mode of speaking which Jehovah would by no means have employed, especially at such a length even in a parable, nor indeed have taken upon Himself such a character at all, if the practice which it implied had been intrinsically dishonourable or shameful.

On what grounds, then, can a practice be con
sidered as so dishonourable or shameful which is
prohibited to no one even under the Gospel; for that
dispensation annuls none of the merely civil regulations
which existed previously to its introduction. It is
only enjoined that elders and deacons should be
chosen from such as were husbands of one wife
(I Tim III, v. 2). This implies, not that to be the
husband of more than one wife would be a sin, for
in that case, the restriction would have been equally
imposed on all, but that in proportion as they were
less entangled in domestic affairs, they would be more
at leisure for the business of the Church. Since
therefore polygamy is interdicted in this passage to
the ministers of the Church alone, and that not on
account of any sinfulness in the practice, and since
none of the other members are precluded from it, either
here or elsewhere, it follows that it was permitted, as
aforesaid, to all the remaining members of the Church,
and that it was adopted by many without offence."

Lastly, I argue as follows from Hebrews, XIII,
v. 4.—Polygamy is either marriage, fornication, or
adultery. The apostle recognises no fourth state.
Reverence for so many patriarchs who were poly-
gamists will, I trust, deter every one from considering
it as fornication or adultery, " for whoremongers and
Adulterers God will judge," whereas the patriarchs
were the objects of his especial favour, as he himself
witnesses. If then Polygamy be marriage properly
so called, it is also lawful and honourable: according
to the same Apostle, marriage is honourable in all,
and the bed undefiled."

Mohammed, therefore, did but legalize a practice not only honoured but even blessed by God Himself under the old dispensation, and declared to be lawful and honourable under the new one; and, consequently, he must be exonerated from the charge of having santioned Polygamy, and thereby encouraged licentiousness.

The chief arguments adduced against polygamy are that it introduces into the matrimonial state a despotic usurpation which destroys the equality of rank between the sexes; that it is destructive of real love and friendship; that it is the parent of jealousy and domestic dissensions.

The belief that the possessor of a harem of wives, in those countries where polygamy is permitted, exercises a despotic sway over them, is one of those errors which Western people adopt from their ignorance of Asiatic manners. Where marital discipline prevails in the East it is, on the contrary, amongst those whom poverty condemns to monogamy. It often happens that, where there are many wives, one will rule the rest, and the husband into the bargain. Those who have looked into the works written by natives of the East, which give true particulars of Oriental manners, will at once perceive that the notion of women being the objects of domestic tyranny in that part of the world is merely ideal. " Little," says Mr. Atkinson. " is understood in England of the real situation of women in the East beyond the impression of their being everywhere absolute slaves to their tyrant husbands, and cooped in a harem, which to them, it is supposed, can be nothing better than a prison."

But this he denies, and he shows how much power and how many privileges Muslim women possess.

So far from the harem being a prison to the wives, it is a place of liberty, where the husband himself is treated as an interloper. The moment his foot passes the threshold everything reminds him that he is no longer lord and master; children, servants, and slaves, look alone to the principal lady. In short, she is paramount; when she is in good humour, everything goes on well, and when in bad, nothing goes right.

Mirza Abu-Talib Khan, a Persian nobleman, who visited England between sixty and eighty years ago, paid great attention to our domestic habits. In the account of his visit which he afterwards published, and which was translated into English, he assigns reasons to show that the Moslem Women have more power and liberty, and are invested with greater privileges than European ones, and he annihilates at once the notion of the marital despotism of polygamy, by observing. "From what I know, it is easier to live with two tigresses than with two wives."

The celebrated traveller, Niebuhr, is of the same opinion. "Europeans," he observes, "are mistaken in thinking that the state of marriage is so different amongst the Moslems from what it is with Christian nations. I could not discern any such difference in Arabia. The women of that country seem to be as free and happy as those of Europe can possibly be. Polygamy is permitted, indeed, amongst Mahommedans, and the delicacy of our ladies is shocked at this idea; but the Arabians rarely avail themselves of the privileges of marrying four lawful wives, and entertaining at the same time any number of female slaves. None but rich voluptuaries marry so many wives, and their conduct is blamed by all sober men. Men of sense, indeed, think the privilege rather troublesome than convenient. A husband is, by law, obliged to treat his wives suitably to their condition, and to dispense his favours amongst them with perfect equality! but these are duties not a little disagreeable to most Mussulmans, and such modes of luxury are too expensive to the Arabians, who are seldom in easy circumstances."

Then as to its being destructive of real love and friendship, it may be doubted whether amongst the higher classes, in the sphere to whom polygamy, if permitted, would be chiefly confined (owing to the expenses it would entail is establishments), there would be less real and less reciprocal friendship in a second or third connection than at present in the first. The cold formality of marriage settlements, pin-money, the separate carriages, and other domestic arrangements common among the upper classes, must destroy all the tender sentiments which belong to pure, disinterested love; and women in our fashionable life are more frequently bought and sold than in polygamic countries. [1])

As to polygamy being an extinguisher of love, this

---

[1]) " The conventional marriage, nine times out of ten, as contracted among the civilized peoples of Europe, is (therefore) a deeply immoral relation fraught with the most fatal results for the future of Society." Max Nordau " *Conventional Lies of our Civilization*" p. 272, Lond. 1895 (Trans).

is a notion springing from the same source of absurd prejudices as that which suggests " Old England " to be the only land of liberty and happiness. If polygamy deserved all the hard things said of it, if it were the source of so many evils and the spring of so few enjoyments, we should scarcely see it in vogue throughout so large a portion of the world, where refinement has made so little progress.

Note by Trans.—For further information on this very debateable question, which it is beyond the limits of our book to discuss more fully, we recommend the interested to refer to the able article on the " Status of Women in Islam " by Syed Ameer Ali (*Life and Teachings of Mohammed*); Hughes' *Dictionary of Islam*, Allen, Lond. 1885; *Mohammed and Mohammedanism* " by Bosworth Smith; Lane's " *Arabian Society in the Middle Ages*" edited by Lane Poole, Lond. 1883. Both the latter are prejudiced and short-sighted.

Over against the priggish piety preached about Islamic Polygamy, we suggest a candid comparison of the cruel evils created by the Christian doctrine of " *Sacerdotal Celibacy*," taught, countenanced, and carried out by the church that was for centuries the *only* church in Christendom, and is still the *most* powerful. See Henry C Lea's " *History of Sacerdotal Celibacy*," Boston, *Houghton Mifflin et Co.*, 1884; also the able realistic " *Roman du Curé* " by Hector France, and since done into English under the title of the " Grip of Desire." This work was brought out in Brussels, the *catholic* France of Voltaire and Rabelais refusing to sanction its appearance.

COPULATION AND ITS ETHNICAL VARIATIONS.

The Hymen and its Rupture.—Diverse importance attached to Virginity among diverse Races.

Human speech seemed to the Metaphysicians to be so miraculous a phenomenon as not to admit of explanation by the physiology of the nerve-centres. Consequently they made a Supreme Being intervene in order to teach Language to us featherless bipeds; who, without this miracle, would to this day be as dumb as fishes. I do not know whether these same metaphysicians find the intervention of the Deity equally necessary to teach men and women the way to unite together in a fruitful embrace. Anyway among the negroes of Loango a quaint tradition exists, explaining how man and woman first learned the art of Love.

Nzambi (the Creator) commended the woman because she had resisted the temptation of eating of the fruit of God, but he was displeased to see her stronger than the man. Accordingly he opened her and took out the bones, so as to make her smaller and weaker. When it came to sewing her up again, he ran short of thread; so that he was obliged to leave a little aperture in the skin. This annoyed the woman extremely; and the man, to console her sought means to close the hole, and .... but the rest had better be left to the imagination. This is how men and women learned to love.

Such traditions would seem to show a man may be

---

[1]) *"Amour dans l'Humanité"* by PAUL MANTEGAZZA:—(Ch. III).

at one and the same time a negro of Loango *and* a Metaphysician. But we are neither Negroes nor Metaphysicians, and we hold that man needed no master to teach him how to unite with a woman. Copulation is a reflex automatic movement, an act transmitted and performed similarly to that of respiration, or that of sucking the mother's breast by an infant. A man and a woman, of adult years and in love, though innocent as Adam and Eve before the Fall, if shut up together in a room, or left free to wander in a forest, after first touching and kissing and pressing each other's bodies, would find out without intending it, one may say even without knowing it, the right road of sensual gratification whereby a new being is engendered.

I have positive knowledge of a circumstance that is of great rarity among Europeans. A young peasant, pure and unsullied as the fount that gushes from the living rock, found himself alone in a stable with a maid as pure and innocent as himself, and felt an irresistible impulse to attempt her possession. The girl let him have his will in everything. The boy feeling a mysterious liquid flowing from him, which in his ignorance he supposed to be the marrow of his bones, ran with tears in his eyes to his mother, and told her what had happened to him, imagining something had broken inside him.

Such things may very well happen more frequently among savage peoples than with ourselves, who are not in the habit of going naked. In Paraguay, I have seen with my own eyes, children of both sexes playing together completely naked and in perfect liberty; and

I think not seldom from curiosity and by way of diversion, they attempt copulation long previous to the age of puberty. This little by little dilates the genital parts of the female, resulting most likely in eventual defloration, but gradual, and unaccompanied by any violent rupture.

No visitor to the Museum of the Louvre at Paris but must have stopped before the figure of a youthful Satyr (no. 276.), with thin lips over which plays a wanton, cynical smile. The mouth is curled upwards, the nostrils dilated and the eyes strained towards some ardently desired object. The expression is most lifelike, and instantly recognizable as one of those that precede copulation; any woman seeing herself so looked at cannot but experience an irresistible fascination that throws her involuntarily in to the lover's arms. Again I know of a case where a young girl, a child absolutely innocent, on holding in her hand a male member which a debauchee had offered to her, experienced such a fierce rush of desire that she began to utter the same cries the females of many animals give vent to on the first onslaught of the male.

Facts such as these, and many others of the same sort attest only too eloquently the spontaneousness of sexual conjunctions at all times and in all countries. Would the fact were duly recognized by all parents, many of whom, while adepts in theology and metaphysics, have never once opened the book of Nature.

Parents should take precautions to shield their child from sudden surprises of the senses; for many a time the human is mastered by the brute that is latent in every woman, and a girl's virginity is lost in a sudden shipwreck that no barometer or meteorologicel observatory could have given warning of.

Still in civilized society, provided as it is with so many religious and moral extinguishers, we do more or less succeed in hiding the activities of the organs of sex ; and so the need arises of lessons in love, and the woman, more timid and more ignorant than ourselves, has to learn from the man how men are made. Sometimes, on the other hand, it is the mercenary handmaids of love who teach the young man how to pluck the fruit of the knowledge of good and evil. I once knew a young man of virtuous and religious character who was fain to carry his virginity to the marriage altar. Eight months did the silly fellow remain virgin by his wife's side. The latter, frightened at the pain attendant on the beginnng of the act of defloration, had persuaded her husband, who was so ignorant as to believe her, that he could not have taken the right road, or if he had, that he had not pursued it properly. As a last resource he had to apply to a doctor, who laughed at his innocence and gave him the necessary information.

Any man of any race whatever, provided of course he had reached puberty, may have connexion with a woman of any race whatever. Modern science has made a clean sweep of the mistaken notion that certain races existed sterile when brought in contact.

Count de Strezelecki states that an Australian woman, after conceiving by a white man, is incapable afterwards of having children by a man of her own race. [1] Brough

---

[1] "Description physique de la Nouvelle-Galles du Sud et de la terre de Van-Diemen", (Description of the Physical Peculiarities of New South Wales and Van Diemen's Land), p. 346.

Smyth combats this idea,—one adopted by other Ethnologists on very insufficient evidence,—citing the following highly significant facts. The Rev. Mr. Hartmann, of the Mission-station of Lake Hindmarck, noted an Australian woman of pure blood to have two half-breeds by a white man, then subsequently a pure-blooded Australian by a man of her own race. Another had a half-breed by a European, and directly afterwards a pure-blooded Australian boy by an Australian.

Green knew a Bocat woman of the Yarra tribe who had a half-breed, and subsequently two pure-blooded Australian children; the same observer knew a woman of the Goulburn tribe who had a half-breed child which she killed, and later on a family of four pure-blooded Australians.

The Reverend H. Agenauer, of the Mission-Station of Lake Wellington, knew a woman who in the first place had two half-breeds, then six pure-blooded Australian children; while in two other cases he saw Australian women have in succession half-breeds or Europeans, according as they had had a connection with Europeans or natives.

The half-breeds themselves are fertile, equally with other half-breeds as with Europeans or with natives.

It is very uncommon, but still such a thing has happened, for European women to have given themselves freely to Australians, and to have had sons by them, and Brough Smyth gives examples of it (p. 97.).

Observations on the form and dimensions of the genital organs in the different races are still far from numerous; but it has been proved conclusively that Negroes in general have the virile member of much

greater volume than other Peoples, and I have myself
verified the fact during several years when I practised
medicine in South America. This greater volume of
the genital parts in the male negro is matched by a
correspondingly greater size and width of the vagina
in the negress. Falkenstein found that the negroes
of Loango have a penis of very great size, and that
their women scorn us for the smallness of our European
organ. He contradicts the curious notion of Topinard,
to the effect that it is only in a state of flaccidity the
penis shows this enormous volume, whereas in erection
on the other hand its bulk decreases. The same
traveller also observed that among the negroes of
Loango, as with ourselves, the commencement of
menstruation offers wide individual differences, — from
twelve to seventeen, or even twenty years of age.

There is no doubt of the fact that man of all
animals is able to practise love in the greatest number
of different ways, thanks to the flexibility of his
powers of motion and the high mobility of his
member.

The *figurae Veneris* (modes of Love) given by Forberg
reach a total of 48, thus surpassing by twelve Aretino's
36 postures; but this is abject poverty in comparison
with the ancient Books of India, in which it would
seem, if we are to trust certain travellers, hundreds
of erotic postures are given! The question is of
importance not only from the point of view of the
Anthropologist and Ethnologist, but even from that
of religion and theology. Certain positions according
to the Casuists are permissible, whilst others again

are sinful! "Excessus conjugum fit, quando uxor cognoscitur retro, stando, sedendo, a latere, et mulier super virum." (It is a sinful excess as between married people, when the wife is known backwards, standing, sitting, sideways, or the woman on top of the man).

A great specialist in these questions of the metaphysics of love for the use of father confessors, says in the chapter headed: "De Circumstantia, modo vel situ:— Situs naturalis est ut mulier sit succuba et vir incubus, hic enim modus aptior est effusioni seminis virilis ac receptioni in vas foemineum ad prolem procreandam. Unde si coitus aliter fiat, nempe sedendo, stando, de latere, vel praepostere (more pecudum), vel si vir sit succubus et mulier incuba, innaturalis est." (On Circumstance, Mode or Posture;—The natural posture is for the woman to lie underneath, the man on the top, for this mode is better fitted for the outpouring of the virile seed and its reception into the female organ for the procreation of offspring. Accordingly if coition be accomplished otherwise, for instance sitting, standing, sideways, or from behind, (as cattle do), or if the man be underneath and the woman on top of him, it is unnatural.)

And elsewhere:—"*Sed tamen mineme peccant conjuges si ex justa causa situm mutent, nempe ob aegritudinem, vel viri pinguedinem vel ob periculum abortus: quandoque ait S. Thomas, sine peccato esse potest quando dispositio corporis alium modum non patitur.*" (Nevertheless man and wife commit little or no sin if they vary the posture for just cause, for example on account of disease, or of the obesity of the man, or because of the risk of producing abortion. For St. Thomas says, it may be so done without sin, when the condition of the body admits no other mode.) [1]

In another very curious book, dedicated *to His Holiness our good Lord Benedict XIV.*, Girolamo dal Portico, Priest Regular of the Congregation of the Mother of God, devotes 770 quarto pages to the theological study of Love, and dwells at length, in a series of subtle distinctions on caresses permitted and caresses forbidden. [2])

What a contrast between these petty instructions, ridiculous in their mean precision, and the advice offered by the celebrated French physician, Ambroise Paré, not indeed a Theologian but a good Christian for all that: "The husband being got to bed with his mate, should now coax, tickle, caress her, and rouse her senses, if he find her unready to answer the spur. The cultivator shall in no wise enter into human Nature's seed-field without due preliminaries, without having first made proper approaches; the which shall be made by kissing her.... as well as by handling her genital parts and titties, to the end that she be pricked with longings for the male (and that is when her womb twitches), that she may take good will and

---

[1]) Craisson, "De rebus venereis ad usum confessoriorum" (On Love and Marriage, for the Use of Father Confessors), Paris 1870.

[2]) "Gli amore tra le persone di sesso diverso disaminato co' principi della morale teologica, per instruzione di novelli confessori." (Love between persons of different Sex discussed in connexion with the Principles of Theological Ethics, for the Instruction of young Confessors), Lucca 1751.

appetite to cohabit and so make a little creature of God, and that the two seedings may meet in unison at one and the same time; for some women there are not so ready to this game as men are." [1])

I have enjoyed opportunities of seeing in many Indian and Japanese paintings, as well as in the precious ivories that were the adornment of a King of Tanjore's golden throne in the XVIth. century, the strangest and most ingenious erotic postures represented. To believe them, one would suppose all mankind to have employed their fancy on nothing else but the invention of novel forms of lust, and new acrobatic groupings of Love's accomplices. For the theological casuits of the Middle Ages these are one and all so many mortal sins, seeing that the ideally moral mode of copulation according to them is the one accompanied with the minimum of pleasure and the smallest possible contact of body with body consistent with attaining the sole and only object of the act,—the procreation of children.

Mankind have suffered their imagination to run riot, and exhausted the dictionary to find words to answer the needs of licentious nomenclature. In every tongue, the sexual organs and the act of coition are extremely rich in synonyms; the French language of the XVIth. century alone had more than 300 words to express copulation, and 400 names for the genital parts of man and woman.

The position most generally adopted in copulation is that where the woman is thrown on her back, and

---

[1]) A Paré, Œuvres Complètes, édition Malgaigne, Vol. II. 10.

the man comes between her thighs. On the vases of old Peru, in the Pompeian frescoes and the Hindoo paintings, the classical form of cohabitation may be seen over and over again. The ingenious Tuscans named it the *angelic* mode, to distinguish it as at once the most convenient and the most agreeable of all.

Doctor O. Kersten informed Doctor Ploss that he had often seen the Swahili of Zanzibar put themselves underneath their wives, who then move their bodies as if they would grind flour. This movement of the body increases the man's pleasure; it is called *digitischa*, and the girls are instructed in it by the old women of the tribe. The apprenticeship would appear to be arduous, for the course of instruction lasts 40 days. In the country in question it is counted as a dire offence to tell a woman she cannot do *digitischa*. Ploss adds that the same practice is known in the Dutch East Indies.

In the Soudan, Dr. A. Brehm assures us, the woman prefers to love standing; she bends forward, resting her hands on her knees, while the man takes up his station behind. This erotic posture is frequently found depicted in the Pompeian wall-paintings. The Esquimeaux also practise it, and the Konjagi would seem to do the like.

The inhabitants of Kamschatka hold copulation in the ordinary or *angelic* mode to be a great sin, considering that the man ought to lie with the woman side by side, because this is the way fishes do, and they feed principally on fish.

Péchuel Loesche says the negroes of Loango prefer the act of love sideways, adding that in all probability they adopt this posture because of the enormous size of the male organ; but it should be noted that the Tschutschis and the Namolos also prefer this position without the same excuse. [1]) At Loango sexual intercourse is never accomplished but with closed doors, never on the ground, but on a raised bed, always at night and without witnesses.

In the same country, the man who seduces a girl before she has reached puberty brings ill-luck on his tribe, and an expiatory sacrifice is required. Again, such as have intercourse before the legal age of twenty are punished; but copulation with a woman during pregnancy is not forbidden.

Little is known of the particular tastes of different races in these matters, but there is no doubt about the fact of the Australian natives making love in a very curious manner. Several travellers have been enabled to see them perform thus *coram populo*. It is enough to promise a man a glass of spirits; he gets a woman and with her goes through the desired performance. It would be an impossible mode of connection for Europeans, or at any rate highly inconvenient. Miklucho-Maclay relates one of these scenes, where the man, impatient to win his glass of gin, suddenly quitted the national posture, saying. " I going to finish English-fashion." He stretched the woman on the ground and got on top of her. [2])

---

[1]) Péchuel Loesche, " Les indigènes de Loango" (The Natives of Loango)—Zeit. für Ethn.—1878. II. 1. p. 26.

[2]) *Zeit. für ethn. Verhand.* 1881. p. 57.

According to Gerland [1]) the Australian women have the genital parts more behind than ourselves; and for this reason the men accomplish coition from behind. [2])

Mons. Meunier, Curator of the Museum at Havre, has kindly sent me two copies of drawings by Lesueur, made by Mons. A. Noury, a distinguished artist of that town. These drawings taken from the MSS. of a Voyage round the world made at the beginning of the present Century, depict coition as performed by the Tasmanians after Nature. This People, which has now died out, did the act of love in the same way as the Australian natives of the present day,—yet another argument proving the ethnic relationship of these two peoples.

We possess no statistics affording a general ethnographical survey of the degree of genital vigour belonging to the different races of mankind. But we may say with a degree of probability amounting to virtual scientific certitude, that, speaking generally, the Negroes are the most vigorous of all, and that the polygamous peoples by reason of the large amount of exercise their genital organs enjoy, possess these both stronger and ready for action. [3]) Turks, Arabs, Hindoos, as a rule expend less intellectual force than do Europeans, and

---

[1]) *Antrop der Natur. Völker.* Part VI. p. 714.

[2]) George Fletcher Moore states that the Australian mode of copulation is known as *mu-vang*, and Ploss describes it with copious detail, Vol. I. p. 230.

[3]) On the question of genital vigour among different individuals, see Mantegazza, " Hygiène de l'Amour," 4th. edition, Milan 1881, pp. 89 sqq.

having in their *harems* a rich and varied assortment of women, are able easily to surpass us in the lists of love.

The first act of coition is marked in females of the human race by the curious phenomenon of defloration, that is to say the rupture of the hymen, a membrane closing more or less completely the entry of the vagina. [1])

It seems that all women possess the hymen, but we do not know how far racial differences impress a special character on its shape and the resistance it offers. Taking European women alone into consideration, it is sometimes semi-lunar in form, sometimes circular, at times extremely fragile, at others offering sufficient resistance to call for the intervention of surgery. Occasionally again it may be altogether wanting, and I have noted complete absence of the hymen in a little girl of six or seven years of age. This would seen to be a phenomenon of no excessive rarity, for A. Paré, Dulaurens, Graaf, Pinoeus, Dionis, Mauriceau, Palfyn have denied its existence to be an integral and necessary condition of completeness in the sexual apparatus of women.

Let us consider in some little detail this fragment of tissue,—as to which human love and human pride have suggested ideas surely the strangest that have ever taken up their abode in the human brain. The hymen is placed transversely in the upper part of the vagina; this it closes completely behind, while in front it displays a gap or partial discontinuity on a level with the urinary meatus. It

---

[1]) On the question of virginity from the psychological point of view, see Mantegazza, " Physiologie de l'Amour," p. 102.

generally has the shape of a half-moon, the convex boundary of which is united to the inferior and lateral wall of the vagina; anteriorly it presents a concave front towards the urethra, leaving an opening communicating with the lower part of the vaginal orifice.

In the anatomical Museum at Heidelberg may be seen all the varieties of shape assumed by the hymen; these Dr. Gerimond reduces to three classes:

1. *Hymen with central opening.*—This opening may be circular and be found either on the medial line or more to one side; or again it may be oval or quadrangular in shape.

2. *Hymen of half-moon shape with anterior opening.*— Occasionally this opening is subdivided into two smaller ones by a perpendicular membrane, the extremity of which is inserted above the meatus.

3. *Hymen either imperforate altogether or pierced by a number of small passages.*—A variation is when the hymen is divided from front to rear along its whole length by an irregular slit; at times the orifice is double; and so on.

This is the little membrane, so fragile and so indeterminate in shape, on which jurisconsults and savants have expended oceans of ink, in order to decide questions of rape, of cohabitation, even of masturbation. And all the while we have around us numbers of young woman who have prostituted every orifice of their body save and except the gateway of Venus, and yet are anatomically virgins, just as we have seen cases of pregnancy where the hymen has been intact! [)]

[)] Consult in this connection: Guerard, " Sur la valeur de

Our task is not to write a treatise on medical jurisprudence; so we need concern ourselves solely with the varying importance attached to virginity by different Peoples.

At one time it has been given such a preponderating weight as to be taken for the sole and only guarantee of woman's purity, while at another it has been regarded merely as an inconvenient obstacle standing in the way of the gratification of love, and the effort involved in its rupture has been delegated to others by the husband.

I am of opinion that were it possible to gather exact statistics of the various Peoples who have respectively held one or other of these views, we should find the number of such as attach a high importance to virginity to be the greater. Indeed it is only natural such should be the case; man is proud and happy to be the first to enter the Temple of Love, satisfying at one and the same time his two ruling passions, pride and love. Besides, he thinks he thereby wins a greater degree of security; that what he has possessed the first will not be possessed by others afterwards.

---

l'existence de la membrane hymen comme signe de virginité" (Ann. d'hygiène, 1872, 2nd. series, vol. XXXVIII., p. 409); Bergeret, "Des fraudes dans l'accomplissement des fonctions génératrices", Paris 1873.; Court, "Traité pratique des maladies de l'utérus et de ses annexes", p. 35.; Taylor, "Jurisprudence médicale 3rd. éd., p. 807.; Rose, "De l'hymen", Strasburg Exercises no. 862, 2nd. series, 1865.; Toulmouche, "Mémoires sur les attentats à la pudeur et le viol" (Ann. d'hygiène 1864); Dr. Garimond, "De l'hymen et de son importance en médicine légale" (Ann. d'hygiène publique).

This cult of virginity among Peoples of a high degree of ideality has been transferred by them even to the heavens, and all Christians adore a *Virgin* Mother of God. Jenghiz Khan again was believed to be the son of a virgin,—a being beyond and above humanity. In the Bible, we read how the husband might repudiate a bride who had not been found intact, and if the charge was confirmed by the elders of the tribe, the woman was stoned to death. If, on the contrary, she had been falsely accused, the husband had to pay a fine and could afterwards repudiate her.

In Persia, the bride must be virgin, and the husband who has not found her to be intact the first night, may repudiate her by a simple declaration. To get over this danger, the family of a girl who has gone wrong marry her to some poor man or to a mere boy, whose task is to declare her a virgin; then she may be married again to some suitor of higher rank. On other occasions maidens (so-called) re-make for themselves, a few hours before the wedding, a factitious virginity by means of a couple of stitches drawn across the *labia majora*. They then triumphantly present the credulous husband with the blood of their sham virtue. [1])

It would seem, however, all husbands are not so easy

---

[1]) Quartilla in Petronius, appalling to relate, could not recall a time when she had been a virgin: "Junonem meam iratam habeam, si unquam me meminerum virginem fuisse!" (Juno my Patroness confound me, if I can remember ever having been a maid!)

as this. Sometimes, in Egypt, the husband wraps the index finger of his right hand in a piece of fine muslin, inserts it in the vagina, and withdraws it to the relatives as an irrefragable proof of virginity. The same practice is followed moreover by the Nubeans and the Arabs, but while with the former it is the husband who thus deflowers the bride before witnesses, among the Arabs the operation is performed by a matron.

Ploss [1]) states that the Catholics in Egypt deflower the bride by actual coition before the mothers of the newly married pair. Pallas relates it to be a custom with the Ostiaks and Samoyeds for the husband to make a present to his mother-in-law when she presents to him the signs of her daughter's maidenhood.

The Slav race holds virginity in high honour. In Southern Russia, the bride, before joining her husband, is obliged to show herself perfectly naked to witnesses, in order that she makes use of no artifices to simulate a maidenhood she does not possess. Likewise it is customary to call in some friend to deflower the bride the first night after the wedding, supposing the husband unable to succeed.

There exist some other tests of virginity which appear to have been devised to gratify the sensuality of inquisitive spectators, as may be seen for instance in the marriage customs prevalent in the Morea and in the principality of Wales. [2])

---

[1]) Ploss, "La femme dans la nature et chez les differents peuples," Leipzig 1884, vol. ɪɪ, p. 217.

[2]) Pouqueville, "Voyage en Morée et en Albanie," 1805.

In Africa, in the case of many tribes, the bride is returned to her parents on being found not to be a virgin. Among the Swahilis of West Africa, if the girl is virgin, half the money paid by her family is returned to them. The Bafiote negroes, as we have already noted, call the hymen *nkumbi* or *tscikumbi*. These terms likewise serve to designate a girl from the time when she first becomes marriageable to her first going with a man. According to some travellers however, the husband attaches no importance whatever to the virginity of his wife; and this fact is curious, for the Negroes of Loango reprobate prostitution, and yet a *nkumbi* may indulge in amorous intrigue without incurring any loss of general esteem.

In America likewise we find peoples that put a high value on the integrity of the hymen. Thus the natives of Nicaragua used to send back to her relatives a bride who was not a virgin, and it seems the Aztecs also made a point of the same thing. At Samoa, previously to the termination of the marriage feasts, the husband was accustomed to explore the virginity of the bride by means of his finger; the *virgo intacta* received numerous presents from the bridegroom, while on the other hand the woman discovered to have been already deflowered was beaten by her parents and relations.

In Lapland, a great deal of liberty is allowed young girls, but the husband is fortunate who finds his wife virgin. As a mark of satisfaction he breaks a glass on the morning following the first night,—a symbol that in his first embrace he had had something to destroy. If on the contrary the finds the road unobstructed, he throws a shower of feathers over the bride's parents in token of his contempt. At any rate such is the tale Alquit reports.

In Europe, young women, even those who are not over virtuous, but have studied the various forms of flirtation, are more often than not virgins when they marry. [1]) When such is not the case, means are not lacking to produce a factitous maidenhead, which is sold again and again by adroit procuresses. For example, shortly before going to the nuptial bed, the girl introduces a few drops of blood into her vagina by means of a quill, besides choosing for her wedding

---

[1]) The debauchees of ancient Rome were willing to pay a high price for a maidenhead, and various methods were known for making up such over and over again. To verify the fact of virginity, the custom was to tie a thread round the maid's neck; then if after the first night the thread has grown too short, the fact of defloration is manifest. This is the test Catullus alludes to in his *Epitadamium:*

> *" Non illam nutrix orienti lusi revisens*
> *Hesterno collum poterit circumdare collo."*

(Nay! the nurse revisiting the maid at break of day shall in no wise be able to encircle her neck with the necklet she wore yesterday.) The precious thread that had thus afforded proof of virginity was hung up in the temple of *Fortuna Virginadis*, and similarly the other bloody tokens of maidenhood were also consecrated to the *Virginensis Dea*. In old Rome, the death penalty could not be inflicted on virgins till after they had been violated by the executioner. Suetonius says: "Immaturatae puellae, quia more tradito nefas esset virgines strangulari, vitiatae prius a carnifice, dein strangulatae." (Young girls who had not known a man, inasmuch as traditional custom forbade virgins to be strangled, were first violated by the executioners, and then strangled.)

the last day of menstruation. Then a sponge applied at the right time and place shows the blood again just at the instant of the catastrophe, when a well-timed ah! ah! tells the credulous bridegroom the temple is violated for the first time and the veil of the " holy of holies" has actually been rent by him. Add, moreover, the employment of astringent injections, so powerful as to give the most hackneyed prostitute, stretched by a thousand lovers, a narrowness of aperture far surpassing that of a veritable maid. [1])

If only in the choice of their life's companion men laid more stress on virginity of heart and purity of soul, instead of looking with so much ill-applied curiosity for the blood-stain on sheets or underclothing, how much fewer disillusions they would find in marriage, and how much more true happiness!

More logical by far are those Peoples who, feeling no certainty of their women's virtue, guard them against all possibility of assault by stitching the two *labia* stoutly together; in other words by the practice of infibulation. But of this we shall speak more particularly in connection with other mutilations to which mankind have submitted their own as well as their companions' genital organs. [2])

---

[1]) A famous Parisian courtesan of the present day used to boast of having sold her maidenhead 82 times over!

[2]) See Dr. Jacobus's *The Ethnology of the Sixth Sense;* (Paris, 1899); also ("Untrodden Fields of Anthropology," (Paris, 1898).

THE

BOOK OF EXPOSITION IN THE SCIENCE

OF

COMPLETE AND PERFECT COITION

THE

BOOK OF EXPOSITION

IN THE SCIENCE

OF COMPLETE AND PERFECT COITION

In the Name of Allah,
the Compassionating, the Compassionate.

Reverence towards Allah and Obedience, I enjoin upon ye, O Servants of the Powerful both ye and myself, with Warning against Rebelliousness and Contrarifying His Command. And I charge ye without cease to pray for Grace and Prayer-blessing upon our Prophet, Lord of Apostolic men and the Silencer of Blameworthy Unbelievers. May the Safety of Allah be upon Him and upon His Family and Noble Companion-train.

––––––––

Alhamdolillah—Laud to the Lord who adorned the Virginal bosom with breasts, and who made the thighs of Women anvils for the spearhandles of men.—Who lance's point devised for attack of clefts and not of throats.—Who made the active worker cushioned coynte to correspond with nice fit and perfect measure all the space that lies betwixt the still unstormed-breach, and the maiden-

1

head unreached.—Who caused the brothers twain at the rose-lipped gates to refrain what time the [1]) awakened-one sleeping face had clomb upon, and for well-made mouths of slits [2]) javelin-head did fashion it.—

Who moved Man over boys Girls the preference to give, while graciously permitting gentle tap on stout lip soft upswelling, as on twice-tip-toe outstretched and exciting purpose bent, he opens wide his legs the prostrate one to mount upon with certain fell intent, and shoulder pressed 'gainst shoulder by the ever-willing hand, he sucks fair lip with his two lips while ivory thigh thrown over his in careless luxury rests, and underneath his bosom slide the lovely pair of breasts.

And as arms close round the yielding neck in joy's mad rapture and love's tight-clinging strength, there

---

[1]) Arabic—" *Al-Qā'im fih Nā'im* " i. e. the erect, standing-up in the dormant or reclining.

[2]) Arabic—" *Afwāh al aksās*," the latter word being what is called the broken plural of kūss—the crudest word for woman's private parts.

Al Kuss (the vulva). " This word serves as the name of a young woman's vulva in particular. Such a vulva is very plump and round in every direction, with long lips, grand slit, the edges well divided and symmetrical and rounded; it is soft, seductive, perfect throughout. It is the most pleasant and no doubt the best of all different sorts. May God grant us the possession of such a vulva! Amen. It is warm, tight and dry, so much so that one might expect to see fire burst out from it. Its form is graceful, its odour pleasant! the whiteness of its outside sets off its carmine-red middle. There is no imperfection about it." Shaykh Nafzawih, in Chap. IX of " The Scented Garden."

2

stand at belly's door ajar the never-parted Brethren, while Strong-yard raketh the Sleeperess with all his power and length.

We pray [1]) that Allâh may pardon you, whose mercy is not shortened, while you will not fail profit to cull in working His commandment. His will that is added to by such pleasurable excitement.

Favoured is he to whom is given fresh cheek's caress and fine form's press, with mount of slit mature and large, which hastening on and without shrink, he inpoureth the honey-like flow of life's stress, while in the breach and to the last hair, he bravely rides in vigorous charge.

To Allàh [2]) the praise I now repeat, who Woman's form has made so sweet; the praise of one who shagging slowly, thereby getteth down to love-depths more lowly. And with red wine flushed soon turneth red hot, and thereupon runneth out his rod, which outswelleth right round and boundeth up straight and gently tappeth at love's hidden gate, the while soft warbling low cry of happy state.

It is related of certain friends and acquaintances and futterers of their neighbours' wives through the holes of walls [3]) that Madame Slit called out: " Oh

---

[1]) The mingled piety and passion of the Oriental see so little indecency in the act of copulation that he invokes the name of Allah at every interbreath.

[2]) Another characteristic outburst of religiousness, the usual herald here of a revelry of passion.

[3]) The burning sexual desire of Egyptian women as of those of other damp countries, is proverbial. In spite of the precautions of the Harem and the severe laws respecting adultery, these

what torture! Thou art slaying me! Oh what pain!
Thy poker is settling me! Go away!"—But Mr. Tool
maketh answer and quoths :—" I do not kill, nor do
I seek to kill, as Al Hajj ¹) Eggs for me will testify ".
Then respondeth Al Hajj Eggs: " To nothing witness
I, nor to witness do I wish. Thou alone, Old Friend
workest in the corridor, and into the same like a
lance thy way dost wend, the whiles I and my brother
keep watch without the door-like bend. At the portals
loudly bang we, but no answer dost thou deign us
to send."

O Men! Marry from amongst the whites those
women that are tall, and of those that are brown the
short. And of both white and brown those that cry
out with gentle joy under pressure, and give forth
happy sobs of desire, and whose Opening is narrow.

But take good care and beware of the lean, and
of those who in aspect are ugly and unclean, and of
those in whose feet and hands distended veins stand
out like bands ²), even as the dogs that yelp in the
Market-Place and bark.

The delicate ones and preferable are distinguished
by their charm and attraction and character-beauty;

---

ladies invent schemes and stratagems that would outwit the
cleverest. A hole in the wall or door is one of them. The
unusually long penis of the Arab compensates for the distance.
Vide Lane's " Modern Egyptians," London, 1890, p. 279—80.

¹) *Al-Hajjaj* = the Pilgrim. A fairly accurate title descrip-
tive of the semi-passive part played by the testicles = *arabicé*,
Al-Machâsi.

²) The reference here is of course to Varicose, or distended
Veins, the danger of which to man and woman alike is
well-known.

but the one-eyed by muchness of talk and jealousy and tongue-slipping—then, Oh take care!

Look out for the fair of face—May Allah be merciful to her—and upon her whose cheeks are crimsoned with apple-bloom;—and Oh what happiness to remain always with them, whom Allah has made attractive to the sight and a very power of passion to the lover-wight! Then be of those who seek and covet them, for amongst all men is their reputation bright.

The mounting and riding ¹) of the brown-colored produces lively movement in the bodies. The tall white ones incline like the glory of a supple poplar which bends over other trees as the bending of branches, while the short are pretty of step, and facile of speech. Then Marry, O my brothers! the women that are good for you, either two or three or four ²).

---

¹) It is curious to note how quickly the learned Shaykh-author changes the subject. This is done purposely, the booklet being intended to divert. The Arabic text has been closely followed.

²) Allusion is here made to the Koranic verse (Vide " *Sūratu-'n-Nis* "): "But if ye cannot do justice between your orphans, then marry what seems good to you of women, by twos, or threes, or fours; and if ye fear that ye cannot be equitable, then only one, or what your right hand possesses" (i. e. female slaves).

Much has been said for and against this Islamic doctrine. For those who fanatically think that the religion of Islam is an unmixed evil, we invite a comparison between the relative decency of oriental polygamy, and the profligacy and filthy trade of prostitution of European cities.

Tooth-gape, He of the White Forehead and fine Renown [1]) has said:

"Who has need to marry then let him marry of them four; and whoever desires peace and calm and companionship must take an Abyssinian [2]) woman with feminine qualities, and for you should be Virgins with well-mounted breasts and of good family. These are better than women divorced, or widows.

And beware of marrying old women for they are no good to you; but rather take from amongst the marriageable the choicest and most amiable. In your Copulation with a woman hit upon a good way [3]): and of the whites marry the tall, but from the brown pick out the short, whose age is no more than 14

---

[1]) Literally "who has the front teeth disparted"—Arabic, "Al-Athnâ Al-Aflâj".

This circumstance is supposed to bring good luck.

The "White forehead" would indicate capacity. The terms are employed to hide the identity of some well-known sheikh of the time.

[2]) The slaves of the Arabs were chiefly from Abyssinia and the negro countries; a few coming from Georgia and Circassia. Many of the Abyssinian women are very beautiful, and instructed in embroidery, music and dancing. Some could even quote largely from celebrated poems. Besides these advantages they prove fairly tractable.—Hence the advice as to wiving them.

Vide p. 250—253, LANE's (E.W.) "Arabian Society in the Middle Ages." London, 1883.

[3]) The shaykh here refers to Postures, of which, in the work "The Old Man Young again", now being prepared in Paris for the press, as many as 60 different ones are tabulated.

OVID (Ars Amat. II. v. 680—1). "They join in venery in a thousand forms; no tablet could suggest more modes."

years, for she who exceeds that limit must be reckoned already old and amongst the be-shelved-ones.

Pass life in eating and drinking, and joy, and the sound of mirth and laughter, and freedom from care, and the dance and merry jest. Oh what pleasure is his who uncovereth the Grotto, and causeth to rise up the Father of Veins [1]), the One-eyed, the Strong and Pitiless, and sportively toyeth with him until like a Column he standeth straight and knoweth not how to bend,

Quoth the Author: " Do no forget to practise O Brethren! kissing and cuddling, and the interlocking

---

CATULLUS, carmen xxxii, speaks of Novem continuas fututiones.

" Sweet Hypsithilla, passion's delight,
My gleeful soul, bid me to come ;
Noontide is nearing, bar not the gate—
Hence roam ye not, stay close at home
Prepare our pleasures in nine fresh ways.
Thighs joined with thighs, nine bouts we'll try ;
Instant the summons, dinner is past,
Heated with love, supine I lie,
Bursting my tunic, swollen with longing ;
Leave me not thus, dear, your lover wronging."

In the " *Dialogues of Luisa Sigea* " examples of a great many attitudes are shown : and the reader who wishes to explore the subject further is referred to " *The Manual of Classical Erotology* " (De figuris veneris) by Forberg, who gives as many as 90 erotic postures (including spinthriæ bracelets, a group of copulators).

See Excursus to the present book.

[1]) Arabic: *Abu-l-'Orooq*—father of Veins. Appropriate title for the member in active condition.

7

of leg with leg, and to suck delicate lips: at what
time the Mounter now bites with passion and rapturous kisses, and then pats and taps with his sword-
like weapon, which anon he draws forth, but only
again to thrust into the expectant sheath, seeking
out all the nooks and crannies, and holes and corners,
while not losing sight of the walls and roof.

"And, O Ladies! To you I counsel a good counsel.
Then bear it well in mind, and to its constant nightly
practice be not blind.

"Take good care of your genitories, and in pulling
out the hair from off their face be not dilatory [1]),

---

[1]) The wolf-like shagginess on the mount of Venus is not
prized so highly by the Arabs as by the generality of their
European brethren, who esteem a luxuriant growth in that
locality as adding interest to their enjoyment.

All women in the East make use of a sort of paste, made
from a mixture of must and oil, to remove the down, which
is deemed a shame, especially by women of pleasure.

The men use a small pair of tweezers.

In the baths there is a special man kept to apply the paste
to the stomachs of the male clients.—The paste used by the
men is called *dowa'* and composed of quick-lime and arsenic.
It is left for a few minutes on the hairy parts, which are then
vigorously scratched. The *mukeyyis*, as he is termed, afterwards completes the operation by cleaning the spot with
warm water.

All Musulmans follow this habit, which is carried out likewise by many Christians. The women consider the operation
very important. This strange custom is reported to possess
hygienic value. It is said that a man on complaining to the
Prophet of being smitten with inordinate concupiscence, was
ordered to get himself depilated, when the passions became
curbed.

and their ramming do not prevent. For every woman whatsoever should permit herself to be rogered by her husband without let or stint, since unto such as these greatest recompense shall certainly be sent.

"Especially if she combeth and maketh fine her hair, letting negligently hang down her forelocks [1]), and attireth herself in the finest robes she owneth, and also beginneth amorously to coo and heave and to moan with desire. This is liked both by friends and foes; for cadenced amorous groaning slumbering prickle causeth to continue in size and dimension increasing.

"It is related of Satan — may the curses of Allah be rained upon him — that he spread it about that a good woman on the day of judgment came up riding on the back of a Bear; and her sweat was running down her, when a Crier cried out unto her:—"This is thy reward, O Thou who, all thy life, remained satisfied with a single prizzle."

It is further told of the Evil One that he noised it abroad that a harlot came along on the Last Day mounted on the back of a Mare, and wearing a green garment, when the Crier cried out unto her:—"Go

---

[1]) Arabic: *Magasees*—curled, or plaited, locks; compare the French "se coiffer à la chienne".

"Arab ladies are extremely fond of full and long hair; and, however amply endowed with this natural ornament, to add to its effect they have recourse to art. Over the forehead the hair is cut rather short; but two full locks hang down on each side of the face, these are often curled in ringlets, and sometimes plaited."

Lane's "*Arabian Society in the Middle Ages.*" (p. p. 216—217).

into the Garden of Paradise, because of the abundance of thy Compassion and solicitude, O Thou who left none unsatisfied, nor raised regret in the heart of whoever loved thee; nor prevented their mounting and shagging thee, No, not for one single moment."

May Allah make both you and me of the blissful circle who stretch their arms around Virgins' necks, and cause them then to unlock their close-locked lips of coral, and who, throughout all the night's length, and during every interspace of the day, do hugger and fuzzle. For this is my faith and my ancestor's, and the profession of my father before me—the faith of the amorous and the religion of the love-tossed.

We beseech thee, O Allah, to prevent us from grief and botheration, and to make us combatants in the campaign of these passion-puffed slits.

O Men! take to yourselves wives from those that are fresh and of surpassing beauty.

Happy is she who hath naught to attend to besides herself; and passeth the greater part of her days in visiting the baths [1]), or else bathing herself in the

---

[1]) Whether as an amusement or mode of passing the time, the bath—*hammam*, is a favorite resort of both men and women of all classes among the Muslims. Mohammad gave several precepts concerning it. In all large mosques, and in most respectable dwellings in Muhammadan countries, there are bathing rooms erected, both for the ordinary purposes of bathing and for the religious purification.

Vide Hughes' *Dictionary of Islam* "The women are especially fond of the bath, often have entertainments there; taking with them fruits, sweetmeats, etc., and sometimes hiring female singers to accompany them. An hour or more is occupied by the process of plaiting the hair, and "the depilatory." LANE.

house; combing herself with a comb, anointing herself with oil, and quick-liming the hair from off her privy parts:

—She doth not neglect her genitory's care, nor leave any stray hairs anestling there, and scenteth her clothes and fine head's hair, what time man's yard from her chink giveth her leisure enough to spare.

Who maketh agreeable movements, and perfumeth herself with various kinds of perfumes, even after the manner of young demoiselles and the daughters of the night; and entwineth ribbons in her beautiful black hair.

Buttoning up her buttons, she mounteth upon an ass, and unto the meeting-place place directeth his face. Arrived at the door of the house, and coming into the room, she lighteth a light, and unveiling her veil, calleth her husband, whom she addresseth with the softest of words. And sitting herself down upon his thighs, she presseth her bosom up close against his breast, until his heart beginneth to gladden and become merry, and his rod rigid.—She thereupon, uncovereth the lower part of her arms [1]), and he getteth further excited, and, losing his passion's control, his prizzle up-flameth clamouring to enter the rose-bud vestibule of her garden. Which done, the husband will no longer listen to aught against his wife. May Allah Bestow mercy upon his slave who so kindly

---

[1]) Arab women are said to have very round, beautifully-made arms and wrists; in which, it may be said, they resemble the generality of Parisian *belles*.

treateth his wife, and to her Passion's lust respondeth with equal delight of Love-desire. He receiveth her with welcome kindness, putting, for her sake, his clothes, and linen and dress in pledge; and is faithful to his word; and lavisheth, promiseth, and fulfilleth; for he who doeth these doings will become of those who are passionately loved by women. Again he bestoweth upon her sweetness of tongue, and every day taketh her out and showeth her a new and different garden.

O Allah! Grant that under such description may fall every son and daughter of man, whoever he may be. And be gracious unto the secluded lady, the proprietress of love-provoking coquetry, who attired in green of brightest colour [1] weareth upon her lips a gentle, honeyed smile—the quick-witted and elegant dame.

Be gracious likewise, O Allah! unto the Princess of Lovers, who peereth out from the door and the balcony with her dark black eyes and bound-up hair—the good-charactered princess—the Lady Farhanah [2].

Be kind to her also who is the Mistress of thick buttocks, a glance of coal blackness [3], and a stout

---

[1] :—The Arab colour of predilection, and, according to Muslims, the favourite colour of Paradise. The Sandschaki-sherif the sacred banner of the Mussalmans is of green silk.

[2] A celebrated beauty no doubt, of the period.

[3] Arabic: *makhool* = literally whose eyes have been orna-mented with kohl. Lane says: "The eyes of the Arab beauty are intensely black, large, and long, of the form of an almond: they are full of brilliancy, but this is softened by a lid slightly

coynte, and whose fame is spread about for her generosity. Her belly containeth fold upon fold, her navel is filled with musk, and down below it there nestles something that is swollen up, puffed out—awful—stupendous—and excellent. It is white and stout; whoever frequents its company forgets his other aims and cares.—The proprietress of a clear-sounding pronounciation, who is called the Lady Salihah.

We pray that Thou wilt likewise be gracious to Um ul-Kheir, the Basriyan; to Khadijah the Sa'eedenah; and Halimah, the Alexandrian; and Balqis the Meccan [1]). —The blessings of God be upon them all!—I have said my say.

May Allah All-great extend his pardon to you, and to Muslim men and women, and to true believers male and female, the living among them and the dead.

If Satan command you to do shameful things and what is forbidden [2])—refuse to do them.

---

depressed, and by long silken lashes, giving a tender and languid expression that is full of enchantment, and scarcely to be improved by the adventitious aid of the black border of kohl; for this the lovely maiden adds rather for the sake of fashion than necessity, having what the Arabs term natural kohl."

[1]) These are the names of certain celebrated courtesans of the day.

[2]) Arabic: *al munkir* = forbidden things. This is one of the key-passages of the work. St. Paul glanced at the same thing: "Wherefore God also gave them up to uncleaness, through the lusts of their own hearts to dishonour their own bodies between themselves.... for even their women did change the natural use into that which is against nature: and

It is asserted [1]) that Women have need above all of chasteness of character; and in the wife is required the love-provokingness of a daughter of Yaman; the amorous sobbing of an Abyssinian; the passion-warmth of a Soudanese; the wide thigh-stretching of an Aleppian; the symmetrical neck of a Circassian; the wide-awakeness of an Egyptian; the belly push-and-play of a Dumyatiyan; the rump-rocking of a Simanudiyah; the desireful out-crying of a Bulaqiyah; and the joy-snorting of a Sa'eediyah [2]).

And she in whom these qualities stand out will be the Mistress renowned of Women, destined for gaiety and belly-friction.

It is mentioned in the " Field of Gold ", of Mas'oudi [3])

---

likewise also the men, leaving the natural use of the women, burned in their lust one toward another; men with men working that which is unseemly.... God gave them over to a reprobate mind, to do those things which are not convenient. (*Vide Burton's article at end of book*).

[1]) It will by noticed how abruptly the subject is at times changed. I have preferred to translate literally from the Arabic to filling up with stuff from my own imagination, which, while it might make the text smoother, would cease to be a translation (*Trans.*)

[2]) Countries lying within the Arabian Peninsula, and more or less under Moslem rule.

[3]) A work otherwise known by its Arabic title: "*A Murouj El-Thahab.*" Mas'oudi enjoys the reputation of being one of the most brilliant historians of the palmiest days of Islam. Flourishing in the 10th century, when the fire of civilization was kept alight by the torch of Arabian learning, he fathomed the science, philosophy, history and literature of the times in which he lived. For his age, he was a marvel of erudition, with a broadness of mind and penetration of in-

that when the mother of Al-Hajjaj Thakafi [1]), who was Phara'ah, the bath-girl, gave birth to her phenomenal son, he had no orifice in his back-side, and a hole was pierced. He refused his mother's breast, and other things; and this matter caused them no small vexation. And it is said that Satan, transformed into the guise of the peasant Ibn Kindah, demanded: "What fresh news is there?" They replied: "A child has been born to Joseph Al-Thakafi, which is a son, and it has refused to take the breast of his mother."

"Then," counselled he, "sacrifice for him a black buck and catch him his blood, and smear it on his face for three days."

And they did this, and on the fourth day the child took his mother's breast; and when grown up, had no patience to rest from spilling blood, and the commission of things that others dared not do.

The Hajjaj, it is related, became separated one day from his soldiers, when he fell in with an Arab; and he said to him:

"O face of an Arab! How's the Hajjaj?"

The other said to him: "He's an unjust Tyrant, and a brutal Oppressor." "Have you not complained then against him to Abd-ul-Malik Ibn Marwan?"

---

telligence that marked him out from all his contemporaries. He is said to have died in the Egyptian capital about 956. Amongst his works only *"The golden Fields"* has ben done into an European language. It exists in French under the title of: *" Les Prairies d'Or."*

[1]) A celebrated and tyrannical despot, after whose death no less than 600,000 prisoners were found in his jails.

asked Al-Hajjaj. "He is a greater tyrant still, and more cruel," said the Bedawin. While they were thus talking, the soldiers overtook them, when the Arab perceived that it was Al-Hajjaj himself with whom he had been talking; and he exclaimed: "O Prince of the Faithful! The secret is between me and between thee. Do not let out upon it except Allah will." The Hajj smiled, and kindly giving him a present, went away, trying to persuade himself that the meeting was no more than a dream.

There was with him, on one of the days of the days, Khalid Ibn Araftah; to whom he said: "O Khalid! bring me a Story-teller from the Mosque." And when Khalid came to the Mosque he found a young man praying, so he sat himself down until he had finished reciting the prayer-blessing; then he said to him: "The Prince of the Faithful demandeth thee." The reciter asked: "Did he himself send for me expressly?" Answered he: "Yes." So he went off with him until they had come up to the door, when Khalid asked: "How art thou?" And the Prince's Story-teller responded: "Thou wilt find in me what thou desirest". And, when he had entered into where the Prince was seated, the Hajj said to him: "Hast thou read the Kuran?" He answered: "Yes, and can recite it from memory." He asked again: "Dost thou know anything from the Poets?" Said he: "There is no poetry but what I can repeat from."

Asked he again: "Dost thou know aught of the Arabs and the Happenings of their History?" He returned: "Nothing of that ever escapes me."

All-Hajjaj said: "O young man, inform me what

women be the best and the most enjoyable." [1])—
"One in winning ways excelling, and in comeliness
exceeding, and in speech killing: one whose brow
glanceth marvellous bright to whoso filleth his eyes
with her sight, and to whom she bequeatheth sorrow
and blight; one whose breasts are small, whilst her
lips are large and her cheeks are ruby red and her
eyes are deeply black and her lips are full-formed;
one who if she look upon the heavens even the rocks
will be robed in green, and if she look upon the
earth her lips [2]) unpierced pearls shall rain; one the
dews of whose mouth are the sweetest of waters; one
who in beauty hath no peer, nor is there any loveliness
can with hers compare: the pleasure of the eyes to
great and small; in fine, one whose praises certain of
the poets have sung in these harmonious couplets: [3])—

---

[1]) Of course the conversation drifts into matters sexual and
inter-sexual. In a similar story, "Tawaddud," the learned
slave-girl, "hangs down her head for shame and confusion"
(vol. V. 225); but the young Sayyid speaks out bravely as
becomes a man.

[2]) In the text: "Allatí lau nazarat ilà 'l-samá la-a'shab
(fourth form of 'ashab with the affirmative "la") al-Safá (pl.
of Safát), wa lau nazarat ilà 'l-arz la amtar taghru—há (read
thaghru—há) Lúluan lam yuskab wa riku—há min al-zulál
a'zab (for a'zab min al-zulal)," which I would translate: Who
if she look upon the heavens, the very rocks cover themselves
with verdure, and if she look upon the earth, her lips rain
unpierced pearls (words of virgin eloquence) and the dews of
whose mouth are sweeter than the purest water.

[3]) These lines have often occurred before; see index (vol.
X. 443) "Wa lau anunahá li 'l-Mushrikin," etc. I have therefore borrowed from Mr. Payne, vol. VIII 78, whose version is
admirable.

"A fair one to idolaters if she herself should show, They 'd
leave their idols and her face her only Lord would know.
If in the Eastward she appeared unto a monk, for once He'd
cease from turning to the West and to the East bend low;
And into the briny sea one day she chanced to spit, Assuredly
the salt sea's floods straight fresh and sweet would grow."

Hereupon quoth Al-Hajjaj, "Thou hast said well
and hast spoken fair, O young man; and now what
canst thou declare concerning a maiden of ten years
old?" Quoth the youth, "She is a joy to behold."
"And a damsel of twenty years old?"—"A joy to
eyes manifold." "And a woman thirty of age?"—
"One who the hearts of enjoyers can engage."
"And in her fortieth year?"—"Fat, fresh and fair
doth she appear." "And of the half century?"—
"The mother of men and maids in plenty." "And
a crone of three-score?"—"Men ask of her never
more." "And when three score and ten?"—"An
old trot, and remnant of men." "And one who
reacheth four score?"—"Unfit for the world and for
the faith forlore." "And one of ninety?"—"Ask
not of whose in Jahim be." [1]) "And a woman
who to an hundred hath owned?"—"I take refuge
with Allah from Satan the stoned." Then Al-Hajjaj
laughed aloud, and said, "O young man, I desire of
thee even as thou describedst womankind in prose so
thou show me their conditions in verse; "and the
Sayyid, having answered," Hearkening and obedience,
O Hajjaj," fell to improvising these couplets: [2])—

---

[1]) For the Jahim-hell, see vol. VIII, III.

[2]) For the Seven Ages of Womankind (on the Irish model)
see vol. IX. 175. Some form of these verses is known throughout

"When a maid owns to ten her new breasts arise, * And like
  diver's pearl with fair neck she hies:
The damsel of twenty defies compare, * 'Tis she whose disport
  we desire and prize:
She of thirty hath healing on cheeks of her; * She's a pleasure,
  a plant whose sap never dries:
If on her in the forties thou happily hap * She's best of her
  sex, hail to who with her lies!
She of fifty (pray Allah be copious to her!) * With wit, craft
  and wisdom her children supplies.
The dame of sixty hath lost some force, * Whose remnants
  are easy to ravenous eyes:
At three-score ten few shall seek her house; * Age—threadbare
  made till afresh she rise:
The fourscore dame hath a bunchy back * From mischievous
  eld whom perforce Love flies:
And the crone of ninety hath palsied head, * And lies wakeful
  o'nights and in watchful guise;
And with ten years added would Heaven she bide * Shrouded
  in sea with a shark for guide!"

And he ceased not to converse with him concerning
what he loved, until he gave permission for his with-
drawing, saying to Khalid: "O Khalid! Order the
young man to receive a mule, and a page, and a
female slave, and 4,000 dirhams." And the young
man said: "May Allah bestow benefits on the Prince;
there still remaineth of my recital the wonderfullest
part and the most agreeable."

Then the Hajjaj returned to his sitting, and said:

---

the Moslem East to prince and peasant. They usually begin:—
From the tenth to the twentieth year * To the gaze a charm
  doth appear;
and end with:—
From sixty to three score ten * On all befal Allah's malison.

"Recite it to me." He began, "May Allah prosper the Prince! My father perished while I was yet little, and I grew up on the knees of my Uncle, who had a daughter of my age.—And in youthful blood foams passion's flood.—But nothing of further wonder happened in my life until she attained the age of womanhood, when I obtained of her satisfaction of my love's ambition—And Allah knoweth the flame of desire, whenas in Youth-tide's veins it burneth like fire."—

It is related that an Arab entered in before the Hajjaj with a complaint of the hardness of his lot, and, while he was about his recital, he coughed and farted. Without the slightest shame or disconcertedness he said: "And that also is from the burden of my misery through the misfortunes of the Age." Then laughed the Hajjaj out-right, and ceased not to laugh; and it is related that the Bedawin again let off a trump, when, perceiving that everybody was reproaching him because of the same, he recited:

"It is true that I farted || But that is nothing new;
No evil have I wrought || 'Gainst the world that I rue;
And no forbidden thing || Has my backside done
That for it I should repent, || Or your presence shun.
Were all the world's arses || At one time to go off;
There would still therein be found || Little matter for your scoff;
And if, as I said, all men were to fart || At a foregiven signal, or sign,
There would still remain nothing || For your control, nor for fine."

It is related that Abou Nowas was once seated in the midst of company when a trump slipped from him, upon which he rose straight up and, unsheathing his sword on them, three times exclaimed: "I will not permit a single one of you to depart hence until he farteth a fart like unto mine." He said his say; and all present trumped, except a big man, who said: "O Abou Nowas, there is no power in me to break off with a bang. I have only the ability to let off just quietly, and without noise. Then take ten silent explosions for the one loud cracker you demand."

It hath been told that amongst the men of that day there was one who said:

"I fell into a great wrangle and quarrel, and a serious brangle and scandal, that was raised between me and the dearest of my comrades and the closest of my bosom-companions, through my supposed divulgation of a secret that, nevertheless, I had concealed in my heart. But I merited my treatment [1]); and I followed therefore the example of the Sayer, when he said:

In solitude, O my brethren! || Do I now find peace,
For all my past unhappiness, || Sprang from friends whom
   I prized;
And, if from the world's || Society had I not ceased,
My soul had been wrung out || Of me in tears and sighs.
Of my shame they made a mock, || And my fall they pointed
   out;
Though for no mere idle tongue-slip || Did our estrangement
   come about.
But now perfect quiet || At last I've found
And treat with scorn || Their shout and flout.

---

[1]) He meant, no doubt, for having *associated* with them; as he denies having disclosed the secret confided.

Related likewise is it of another of them that he said : " I desired breaking off connection from one of my friends [1]), and had almost determined upon "paying him back in his own coin" for what he had done to me, as I had the opportunity to do so.

But I pardoned him, entering into the spirit of the speaker who said:

Avoid and flee the world ‖ To the utmost of your power,
Taking Allah Almighty for guide; ‖ Since you may stir the world round,
However you decide, ‖ Nothing in it but scorpions you'll find,
And surely rue the hour, ‖ When in Man you began to confide.

The cause of love, it hath been stated, is composed of three [2]) things; and no one is void of their knowledge, or requireth a hint as to any one of them; though the conditions of mankind vary in their regard. In the Destiny of the poor man are verily united all the three peculiarities, and never doth he succeed in saving himself from them, unless the Time is generous towards him, and bestoweth upon him of her favours. It is he who is mentioned in the Poem of Youth— the poem wherein are celebrated the Kiss and Cuddle- force, the Intertwining of one leg with another, and the passionate Suction of refined lips.

---

[1]) In the Arabic:—'an ahad ashabi is understood.

[2]) In his *Hygiène de l'Amour*, Mantegazza says:—With the man in good health, the aurora of love should announce itself by the simultaneous appearance of three new facts; the secretion of the sperm, erection, the ardent desire to approach a woman for the first sexual embrace (French transn. Chap. I. *L'Aube de la Virilité.*)

Then be seated in a chamber-hall, where are found the elevated couch, the sparkling fountain, and a column of spouting water; and repasts of seven kinds take place, and the throwing of roses and sweet-scented jasmines; while, in the well-stocked wallet let there always be a thousand golden dinars. There stay with a chosen lady-love of the white women, tall of stature and black eyes, and smooth and oval cheek, and buttocks stout and thick, and chubby-faced, plump orifice, and a countenance beauty-lined, as the Poet, speaking on that subject, has with chosen words defined:

O thou the best of creatures || In the days of their prosperity
The rivals of my love with me || Of thee did remonstrate.
" Gladly e'en my life I'd give || In order possession to have of thee.
With torment and with bitter taunt, || They sought my heart's flame to abate.
What is it that troubles thee so ? " said they; || " Is it nectar-wine that floweth free " ?
" In the saliva of her lips is the wine ", quoth I, || " And the best of beings on earth is she ".
" Is it then ambrosia that troubles thy brain ?" || " For to know the truth ", said they, " are we fain ".
" In the beauty of her mouth is ambrosia ", said I, || " And tis not honeyed wine that is my bane ".
Said my tormentors then, " We had known " || Of all this, had you named her ".
" She is the most beautiful creature on earth ! " || Exclaimed I, " Glory to her Excellent Maker ! "
"By God!" returned they then, || "What may her name be called?"
" That is my secret, " said I, " which, || I'll not reveal for all the world ".
" But, of my mystery's meaning, || I now offer ye this part:
I complain to you of a passion || I'd fain keep from all concealed. "

Then, O my Comrades! when one of you pillareth-out for shagging a woman, let him kiss her on the mouth before clasping her by the neck; and pinch and squeeze her limbs before coupling with her; increasing his toying and touching and teasing her, and, then commence by frictioning before futtering; and know that the white women are the enjoyment of mankind as well its adornment, while black women are its sorrows and afflictions—as was said:

> Remember that the white pearl
> Can really boast no peer:
> While a bushel of black coal
> Is for a few pence bought;
> But Allah's first-preferred
> Are the white of skin-clear
> While' mongst Hell's folk, the Black
> Are surely pitchforked there.

THINGS WOMEN SHOULD HAVE

Quoth the Hafiz [1]) to some of his boon companions: —If we desire knowledge of the manner in which beauty-perfection consisteth, then remember that in the woman there should be four [2]) things black—four

---

[1]) *Hafiz* is an arabic word meaning a person who has learnt the whole of the sacred *Kuran* by heart—no uncommon feat among Musulman students. The study of the *Kuran* tends to keep up and fix the purity and standard of the Arabic language, of which it is deemed the matchless model.

[2]) Lane, in giving another analysis of a similar kind says "this is the most complete, I can offer."

Of course, he was *unable* to give a fuller list for fear of Mother Grundy.

An unnamed author quoted by El-Ishàkee, in his account

white—four veiled—four narrow—four red—four round
—four short—four long—four delicate—and four
perfumed.

Now, the four black ones are the hair of the head,
the eyebrows, and the eyelashes;—the four white—
the white of the eyes *very* white, the nails, teeth and
forehead;—the four red—the tongue, lips, cheeks, and
finger-ends;—the four round—the head, neck, fore-
arms and ancles;—the four narrow—the nostrils, hole
of the ears, the navel and the vulva; –the four large
—the forehead, eyes, bosom, and hips;—the four fine
—the mouth, palms of the hands, sides of the nostrils,
and the nose;—the four long—the back, ear, fingers,
and legs;—the four perfumed—the mouth, armpits,
pudenda, and nose.

Counselled Aboubin-Seena: *"take care that you do
not go beyond the mark in Coition, for on such practice there ensues diminution of health-condition."* And,
said Al-Ahtaf bin-Kees: *"To the prodigal of coition's
boon, Old age arriveth very soon; with weakening of
his strength, and the bending of his back, and the man
becometh stricken with the whiteness of age."*

It is necessary that one charge himself with three
things: –the first, that he abstain from moving over-

---

of the *'Abb'asee khaleefek El-Mutawekkil,* gives four other parts
of the woman which should be thick,—*the lower part of the
back, the thighs, the calves of the legs, and the knees.*

"Arabian Society etc."

In the *"Old Man Young Again"* is to be found a very
original classification of the same sort.

In *Les Dames Galantes,* of Brantome there is a similar list
derived from the Spanish.

much, nor altogether to leave off walking [1]). For know that as regardeth Man, he should see that his stomach remaineth free from superfluity of the slightest morsel, and if he omit to move in the appointed time great illness therefrom results. Therefore must he move with moderate movements, and digest what he hath taken, and the best time for movement is when the stomach is empty and void of food, such movement being termed promenades, which hath place when a man moveth with a light movement like unto the jog-trot of a mare or horse, or a saunter, or attendance on business affairs, or while reading, and other things of the same kind.

Secondly: it behoveth that man neglect not eating; for be it known that strength is derived from satisfaction in moderation, and the belly should not be filled to the brim.

On this subject our Prophet Mohammad — Lord of the Learned — upon whom be peace and prayer-blessing — hath stated: "A son of Adam can over-fill no other vessel which for him shall bring such evil consequence as the over-filling of the belly. Morsels of bread alone suffice to strengthen his back-bone. And if, for his guidance, it be imperative, then let him divide his interior into three parts:—a third for eating—another for drinking—and the last for respiration."

The third section appertaineth to that man should

---

[1]) Orientals rarely hasten over-much. This would, for one thing, be due to the enervating influence of the sun-scorched climate. Lord Beaconsfield's slow gait was attributed to his Eastern origin.

not neglect copulation. For the water of a well which is not drawn from cannot remain clear bright, neither will its source course freely.

O my dear son! know that the sages liken connection with a woman unto the strength of a burnt earthenware pitcher, which being filled with water and inclined to one side, some of it runneth down, while other remaineth: and if it be turned upside down the whole of the contents thereof runneth away.

Thus, likewise, is man, whenas he joineth himself with a woman, lying meanwhile, to accomplish it, upon his side; some of it runneth down, and other remaineth;—from which arrive infirmities of body; while whoever seeeth him in his outward condition reckoneth him to be in the perfection of health, little deeming that he be in reality on the burning verge of a gulf full of woes and ills. Because his bed is demolished in that he sleepeth upon his bed with a woman in the manner of a woman, and she asketh from him what he used to ask from her; but he is inwardly disquieted anent his state, and the thing, perhaps, increaseth upon him until she saith unto him: "By God! thou art busying thyself away from me with other women", while all the time he is suffering by reason of the despicableness of his malady, which he trieth to conceal under whatever possible pretext [1]).

---

[1]) Reference is here made to sexual impotence, which is dwelt upon, to a considerable extent, in the book called "The Old Man Young Again" or to give the genuine Arabic title "The Book of Age Rejuvenescence in the Science of Concupiscence" (2 vols, Paris, 1898).

He who goeth to excess for a long time in copulation, weakeneth his forces, and cracketh up his limbs.—Allah is All-Knowing.

Learned doctors have observed: He who can restrain himself from *four* things will steer clear of sundry detestable calamities [1]).

He who avoideth overmuch haste will get the better of the after-regret.—He who abstaineth from pride will escape detestation.—He who keepeth himself from importuning will not suffer privation.—He who refraineth from offence-giving will not fall into grief and humiliation.

It hath been further remarked by certain sages

---

[1]) There is no doubt that sexual power does prevent the alienation of female affection, as the following Turkish story testifies. "A Singular Motive of Affection": "Why are you so attached to your husband?" a lady one day asked her daughter.

"Once he returned suddenly from a journey," replied the young lady. "Still dressed in his travelling clothes, he opened the door, entered, and at once began the act of love. I was then suffering from a severe fever; I was burning hot, and my hair was in disorder. I had not even time to perfume myself before abandoning myself to his caresses. In spite of that I saw him advance with his dart as firm as a pike with the ardour of passion, insert it boldly into my slit, and thus take his pleasure. It is this proof of love that makes me so attached to him."

"What, my child," cried the mother, "is that why you are so fond of him. You quite frighten me, for on hearing you I feel my desires aroused to such a point that I believe I shall die."

Such was their conversation.

that the Bath possesseth *four* good qualities:—the putting-to-flight of care—the dissolution of the system's noxious humours—the refreshing of the body—and the cleansing away of dirtiness.

Again, there are *four* things which chase sleep from the eyes:—the abandonment of a friend, the fatigue-worry engendered by travel, the burden-care of debts, and the intention to commit a forbidden crime.

THE LASCIVIOUS SAVANT

Of a grammarian it is recounted that he desired to copulate with a certain woman, and calling out to her, cried:—" Aye, Young woman, over there! Come here to me, and bend thy back over on the ground, lift both thy legs up in the air, and put a little saliva for me on the affair. "

To this she responded: "If thou seeest me with my eyes sinking in, and rising stronger on me the thing, then give not over pushing until fullest satisfaction for me thou dost win therein. "

Whereupon he broke forth: " O Harlot! I have determined on a ride, so expose the crack, show thy backside, exhibit thy arse, turn round thy behind, agitate thy middle, and curve up thy knee " [1]).

She returned: " Mount, and mind thou dost not

---

[1]) Different words are employed in the original to express various shades of vulgarity in the designation of the posterior parts, and also, most likely, purposely to show the grammarian's richness of vocabulary.

soon get tired and outspun, slap on it a little with
thy hand, and pull off at least a two thousand run. "

STORY OF THE YOUTH WHO WOULD FUTTER HIS FATHER'S WIVES [1]).

It is related that there was a man who had a
grown-up son, but the youth was a ne'er-do-well [2])
and whatever wife his sire wedded, the son would
devise him a device to lie with her, and have his
wicked will of her, and he so managed the matter
that his father was forced to divorce her. Now the
man once married a bride beautiful exceedingly, and
charging her beware of his son, jealously guarded her
from him.—The father applied himself to safe-guarding
his wife, and gave her a charge, warning her with
threats against his son, and saying, "Whenas I wed
ever a woman, yonder youth by his cunning manageth
to have his wicked will of her." Quoth she, "O man,
what be these words thou speakest? This thy son is
a dog, nor hath he power to do with me aught, and
I am a lady amongst women." Quoth he, "Indeed I
but charge thee to have a care of thyself [3]). Haply
I may hie me forth to a journey, and he will lay some
deep plot for thee, and work with thee as he wrought
with others." She replied, "O man, hold thyself
secure therefrom, for an he bespeak me with a single

---

[1]) This violating of the Harem is very common in Egypt.

[2]) Arab. "Fadawi," here again = a blackguard, see Vol. IV,
281.

[3]) The Irishman says, sleep with both feet in one stocking.

word I will slipper him with my papoosh [1]); " and
he rejoined, " May safety be thine ! " He cohabited
with her for a month till one day of the days when
he was compelled to travel ; so he went into his wife,
and cautioned her, and was earnest with her, saying;
" Have a guard of thyself from my son the debauchee,
for he's a froward fellow, a thief, a *misérable*; lest he
come over thee with some wile and have his will of
thee." Said she, " What words are these? Thy son
is a dog, nor hath he any power over me in aught
whereof thou talkest, and if he bespeak me with
one injurious word, I will slipper him soundly with
my footgear." [2]) He rejoined, " If thou happen to
need aught [3]) never even mention it to him;" and she
replied, " Hearkening and obedience." So he said farewell unto her, and fared forth wholly intent upon his
journey. Now when he was far enough from the town,
the youth came to the grass-widow, but would not address
a single word to her, albeit fire was lighted in his
heart by reason of her being so beautiful. Accordingly he contrived a wile. It happened to be summer-

---

[1]) Arab., or rather Egypt., "Bápuj," from "Bábúg," from the
Pers. "Pay-púsh" = footclothing, vulg. "Papúsh." To beat
with shoe, slipper, or pipe-stick is most insulting; the idea,
I believe, being that these articles are not made, like the rod
and the whip, for corporal chastisement, and are therefore
used by way of slight. We find the phrase "he slippered the
merchant" in old diaries, *e.g.* Sir William Ridges, 1683,
Hakluyt's, Voyages.

[2]) Arab. "Sarmújah" = sandals, slippers, shoes, esp. those
worn by slaves.

[3]) Suggesting carnal need.

tide, so he went [1]) to the house and repaired to the
terrace-roof, and there he raised his clothes from his
sitting-place, and exposed his backside stark naked to
the cooling breeze; then he leant forwards, propped
on either elbow, and, spreading his hands upon the
ground, perked up [2]) his bottom. His stepmother
looked at him, and marvelling much, said in her mind,
" Would Heaven I knew of this froward youth what
may be his object ! " [3]) However, he never looked at
her nor ever turned towards her but he lay quiet in
the posture he had chosen. She stared hard at him,
and at last could no longer refrain from asking him,
" Wherefore dost thou on this wise?" He answered,
" And why not? I am doing that shall benefit me in
the future, but what that is I will never tell thee;
no never." She repeated her question again and again,
and at last he replied, "I do thus when it is summer-
tide and a something of caloric entereth my belly
through my backside, and when 'tis winter the same
cometh forth and warmeth my body; and in the cool
season I do the same, and the cold cometh forth
in the dog-days and keepeth me, in heats like these,
fresh and comfortable." [1]) She asked, " If I do what

---

[1]) The young man being grown up did not live in his
father's house.

[2]) Arab. "Tartara". The lexicons give only the sigs.
" chattering " and so forth. Prob. it is an emphatic reduplic-
ation of " Tarra "—sprouting, pushing forward.

[3]) The youth plays upon the bride's curiosity, a favourite
topic in Arab. and all Eastern folk-lore.

[4]) There is a confusion in the text easily rectified by the
sequel. The joke suggests the tale of the Schildburgers,

thou doest, will it be the same with me?" and he answered, "Aye." Therewith she came forward beside him, and raised her raiment from her behind till the half of her below the waist was stark naked; and she did even as her husband's son had done, and perked up her buttocks, leaning heavily upon her knees and elbows. Now when she acted in this wise, the youth addressed her, saying, "Thou canst not do it aright." "How so?" "Because the wind passing in through the postern passeth out through thy portal, thy solution of coutinuity." "Then how shall I do?" "Stop thy slit wherethrough the air passeth." "How shall I stop it?" "An thou stop it not thy toil will be in vain." "Dost thou know how to stop it?" "Indeed I do!" "Then rise up and stop it." Hearing these words he arose, because indeed he greeded for her, and came up behind her as she rested upon her elbows and knees, and taking in hand his prickle, nailed it into her coynte, and did manly devoir. And after having his will of her he said, "Thou hast now done thy best, and thy belly is filled full of the warm breeze." In this wise he continued every day, enjoying the wife of his father for some time during his journey, till the traveller returned home, and on his entering the house, the bride rose, and greeted him, and said, "Thou hast been absent overlong!" [1]) The

---

who on a fine summer's day carried the darkness out of the house in their caps and emptied it into the sunshine which they bore to the dark room.

[1]) A kindly phrase popularly addressed to the returning traveller, whether long absent or not.

man sat with her a while and presently asked of her
case, for that he was fearful of his son; so she
answered, "I am hale and hearty!" "Did my son
ask of thee aught?" "Nay, he asked me not, nor
did he ever address me: withal, O man, he hath
admirable and excellent expedients, and indeed he is
deeply versed in natural philosophy? He tucketh
up his dress, and exposeth his backside to the breeze,
which now passeth into his belly and benefiteth him
throughout the cold season, and in winter he doeth
exactly what he did in summer with effect as beneficial.
And I also have done as he did." Now when the
husband heard these her words, he knew that the
youth had practised upon her, and had enjoyed his
desire of her; so he asked her, "And what was it
thou diddest?" She answered, "I did even as he did.
However, the breeze would not at first enter into my
belly, for whatever passed through the back postern
passed out of the front portal, and the youth said to
me:—Stop up thy solution of continuity. I asked
him, Dost thou know how to stop it? and he
answered, Indeed I do! Then he arose and blocked
it with his prickle; and every day I continued to do
likewise and he to stop up the peccant part with
the wherewithal he hath." All this was said to the
husband, who listened with his head bowed down-
wards; but presently he raised it, and cried, "There
is no Majesty and there is no Might save in Allah,
the Glorious, the Great;" and suddenly, as they were
speaking on that subject, the youth came in to them,
and found his stepmother relating all they had
done whilst he was away, and the man said to him,

"Wherefore, O youth, hast thou acted in such wise?"
Said the son, "What harm have I done? I only
dammed the waterway, that the warm air might abide
in her belly and comfort her in the cold season." So
the father knew that his son had played this trick in order
to have his will of her. Hereat he flew into a fury, [1])
and forthright divorced her, giving her the contingent
dowry; and she went her way. Then the man said.
in his mind, "I shall never get the better of this boy
until I marry two wives and ever keep them each
with the other, so that he may not cozen the twain."
Now after a couple of weeks he espoused a fair
woman, fairer than the former, and during the next
month he wived with a second, and cohabited with
the two brides. Then quoth the youth in his mind,
"My papa hath wedded two perfect beauties, and here
am I abiding in single blessedness. By Allah, there
is no help but that I play a prank upon both of
them!" Then he fell to seeking a contrivance, but
he could not hit upon aught, for whenever he
entered the house he found his two step-mothers
sitting together, and thus he could not avail to address
either. But his father never fared forth from home
or returned to it without warning his wives, and
saying, "Have a care of yourselves against that son
of mine. He is a whoremonger, and he hath made my
life distraught, for whenever I take to myself a wife
he serveth some sleight upon her; then he laugheth
at her, and so manageth that I must divorce her."
At such times the two wives would cry, "Walláhi,

---

[1]) In the text "Hamákah."

an he come near us and ask of us amorous mercy we will slap him with our slippers." Still the man would insist, saying, "Be ye on your guard against him," and they would reply, "We are ever on our guard." Now one day the women said to him, "O man, our wheat is finished," and said he, "Be ye watchful while I fare to the Bazar in our market-town, which lieth hard by, and fetch you the corn." When the father had gone forth and was making for the market-town, his son happened to meet him, and the two wives went up to the terrace wishing to see if their husband be gone or not. Now, by the decree of the Decreed, the man had by some carelessness forgotten his papooshes, so he turned to the youth who was following him, and said, "O my son, go back and bring me my shoes." The women still stood looking, and the youth returned in mighty haste and hurry till he stood under the terrace, when he looked up and said, "My father hath just now charged me with a charge saying:—Do thou go sleep with my wives, the twain of them, and have each of them once." They replied, "What, O dog, O accursed! thy father bespake thee in this wise? By Allah, indeed thou liest, O hog, O ill-omened wight." "Walláhi," he rejoined, "I lie not!" So he walked back till he was near his father, when he shouted his loudest, so as to be heard by both parties, "O my papa, O my papa, one of them or the two of them? One of them or the two of them?" The father shouted in reply, "The two, the two! Allah disappoint thee: did I say one of them or the two of them?" So the youth returned to his father's wives, and cried, "Ye have heard what my papa

said. I asked him within your hearing:—One of them or
the two of them? and ye heard him say:—Both, both. "
Now the man was speaking of his slippers, to wit
the pair; but the women understood that his saying,
"the two of them" referred to his wives. So one
turned to her sister spouse, and said. "So it is [1]),
our ears heard it, and the youth hath in no wise
lied: let him lie with me once, and once with thee,
even as his father bade him." Both were satisfied
herewith: but meanwhile the son stole quietly into
the house and found his father's papooshes: then he
caught him up on the road and gave them to him,
and the man went his way. Presently the youth
returned to the house, and taking one of his father's
wives lay with her and enjoyed her and she also had
her joy of him; and when he had done all he wanted
with her, he fared forth from her to the second wife
in her chamber and stretched himself beside her and
toyed with her and futtered her. She saw in the son
a something she had not seen in the sire, so she
joyed in him and he joyed in her. Now when he
had won his will of the twain, and had left the house,
the women foregathered, and began talking and saying,
"By Allah, this youth hath given us both much
amorous pleasure, far more than his father ever did;
but when our husband shall return let us keep our
secret, even though he spake the words we heard:
haply he may not brook too much of this thing."
So as soon as the man came back with the wheat,
he asked the women, saying, "What befel you?"

---

[1]) Arab. "Adi" which has occurred before.

and they answered, " O Man, art thou not ashamed
to say to thy son:—Go sleep with both thy father's
wives? 'Tis lucky that thou hast escaped." Quoth
he, " Never said I aught of this;" and quoth they,
" But we heard thee cry;—The two of them:" He
rejoined, " Allah disappoint you: I forgot my papooshes
and said to him, Go fetch them. He cried out, One
of them or the two of them? and I replied, The
two of them, meaning my shoes, not you." " And
we," said they, " when he spake to us such words,
slippered him and turned him out, and now he never
cometh near us." " Right well have ye done," he
rejoined, " 'tis a fulsome fellow." This was their
case; but as regards the youth, he fell to watching
and dogging his father's path, and whenever the
man left the house and went afar from it, he would
go in to the women, who rejoiced in his coming.
Then he would lie with one, and when he had
won his will of her, he would go to the sister-wife
and tumble her. This lasted for some time, until
the women said each to other, " What need when
he cometh to us for each to receive him separately
in her room? Let us both be in one chamber, and
when he visiteth us, let us all three, we two and he,
have mutual joyance, and let him pass from one to
other." And they agreed to this condition, unknowing
the decree of Allah which was preparing to punish
the twain for their abandoned wantonness. The two
women agreed to partnership in iniquity with the youth
their stepson. Now on the next day the man went
forth, and left his house for some pressing occasion,
and his son followed him till he saw him far distant:

then the youth repaired to the two wives and found them both in one chamber. So he asked them, "Why doth not each of you go to her own apartment?" and they answered, "What use is there in that? Let us all be together and take our joy, we and thou." So he lay between them, and began to toy with them and tumble them; and roll over them and mount upon the bubbies of one, and thence change seat to the others's breasts, and while so doing all were plunged in the sea of enjoyment [1]). But they knew not what lurked for them in the hidden World of the Future. Presently, lo and behold! the father returned, and entered the house when none of them expected him or was ware of him; and he heard their play even before he went into the chamber. Here he leant against a side-wall, and privily viewed their proceedings and the lewd state they were in; and he allowed time to drag on and espied them at his ease, seeing his son mount the breasts of one woman and then shift seat to the bubbies of his other wife. After noting all this, he fared quietly forth the house, and sought the Wali, complaining of the case; so the Chief of Police took horse, and repaired with him to his home, where, when the two went in, they found the three at the foulest play. The Wali arrested them one and all, and carried them with elbows pinioned to his office. Here he made the youth over to the headsman who struck off his head, and as for the two women, he bade the executioner delay till night-

---

[1]) The "little orgie," as moderns would call it, strongly suggests the Egyptian origin of the tale.

D

fall and then take them and strangle them, and hide their corpses underground. And lastly he commanded the public Crier to go about all the city, and cry:— " Such is the reward of treason."

THE BATH-KEEPER WHO LENT HIS WIFE

It hath been told of a bath-keeper, whose baths used to be frequented by very good society and the noblest among them to boot, that, on a certain day of the days, there entered his baths a young man, one of the progeny of the vizir, and he was big and stout. And the bath-man remained standing [1]) and rubbing palm against palm in sign of sorrow [2]). Noticing this, the young man asked him: " What is thy trouble?" Said he to him: " I am sorry on thy account, seeing that thou art in a state of such natural opulence, and yet withal, possess nothing like other men, except a thing resembling a small nut, wherewith to enjoy and render thyself happy."

" Thou art right ", replied the young man: " thou hast remarked a matter of which I had become completely oblivious, and I therefore desire that thou takest this dinar and conduct hither a good-looking woman, and with her will I experience myself a little."

Forthright the bath-keeper takes the money, and

---

[1]) Arabic: *Waqif bein yadeihi*, meaning, continued to stand before him.

[2]) To rub one hand over against another, before a person in such circumstances, is an eastern custom, signifying regret for something that one does not like to say without permission.

hying away to his own house, says to his wife: " Rise up and sit with him an hour. " His wife took the dinar and rose up, decking and decorating herself out in her best.

This lady was endowed with beauty in due proportion; and she sallied forth with her husband, who presented her to the vizir's son in his private cabinet. And she beheld a young man like unto the moon, whereat she was fairly taken aback and amazed. And the young man also regarded her, and found her to be a sympathetic damsel, gifted with eyebrows soft, curved and flexible like an archer's bow, and pearly-white teeth, and sweet sugared lips, and breasts ivory white, and a belly beautified with five lovely folds and, lower down between them Something puffed-out, swollen up, long, awful, wondrous, like a generous morsel cut off a sheep's tail; and in his heart sprang up strong love for her.

So he bolted the door from within, whilst the bath-keeper was without on the other side, standing behind the door [1]) waiting to see what should happen between them; and the young man uncovered her coral treasure, and, introducing therein his stirrer-up, vigorously raked her on the door of her lips, pushing it up until he had emptied out his stream into her stream. Then saith he to her: " Go outside now to thy husband, for he is at the door calling thee. " But answered she: " Do not pay attention to what he saith, for he is crazy and mad. " And ceased not he

---

[1]) This tautology is a faithful reproduction of the Arabic, evidently intentional, to circumstantialise the husband's position.

before he had performed for her the trick more than ten times; and as often as her husband without (who had believed the man was almost prickless), overheard her love-sighing, and cooing, and amorous bewooing, he became as one ready to start out of his senses until the aggressor within had done and quite finished with her, and gone upon his way and about his business, when her lord received again his spouse, and departed once more with her to his house as though she were a young twig tender and graceful, or the slender branch of a bamboo-stick even as the love-seized poet in her regard hath sung:

'Twas for the earliest dawning, when, upon the desert stealing, || Rideth forth the Half-Moon in the sheen and brightness of her witching power, || That my dearest love for me had named a meeting, whilst my heart was split within me, || As drew nearer, slowly nearer, the wistful, watched for hour.

I tarried there alone and, feared she'd never come, who had robbed me of my life, and sped then, gazelle-like away; || When lo! A change comes o'er the scene. Am I awake, or imagining? || For from the bright moon rent in two, comes a fairy form in view, || And the loved one of my heart draws near again.

From the proud, quick flashes of her eyes Stole the moon his jewel crest of teeth, || And her body's balancing gave the cypress tree her wondrous grace, || While the grapes sucked all their sweetness from the saliva of her mouth || That Allah made so beautiful on her marvellous face.

I cannot tell her qualities, for she soars in all her loveliness || Far beyond the sorcery of poet's song in human words to say; || A golden tongue could not describe the witchery of the softness she shoots from 'neath her half-closed lashes, || Resembling heaven's houris, in the passion-light that dwells there, like the sun at mid-day.

With a sword-cut has she slain me of dark eyes' flash like lightning. || Proves it my blood that runs its course on her two rose-color'd cheeks.

But slowly she withdraws now, as for the Feast's adorning, She goeth to adorn herself, while the rays of the sun the horizon streaks [1]).

THE STRANGE TRANSFORMATIONS THAT BEFELL A CERTAIN BELIEVER'S PRICKLE.

A certain Believer, whose name has not been set down on record, desired intensely to witness and experience the blessed "Night of Power," [2]) and, on one of the days of the days, Allah, the All-Merciful had compassion on his state, and gratified the man's wish. It was revealed unto him during the night, and, turning towards his wife, who was sleeping the sleep of wifely innocence at his side, he awoke her and made known unto her the occurrence of the revelation that he had received from his Lord. Quoth then his partner to him, on hearing the news: "All

---

[1]) It was impossible to translate the form of the original literally, but I trust I have preserved the sense, and not gone too far in the freedom of my rendering. (TRANS).

[2]) Compare *Russian Folk-lore Stories* "The Enchanted Ring" and Burton's version of this tale in *The Thousand Nights and a Night*.

[3]) A mysterious night in the month of Ramazan, the precise date of which is said to have been known only to the Prophet and a few of the Companions.

"The Lailat 'ul Qadr excelleth a thousand months: Therein descend the angels and the spirit by permission

Of their Lord in every matter; and all is peace until the breaking of the dawn."

Kuran, Surat 'ul Qadr (97)

things in the World are vain, and idle, and useless
fleeting Vanities and Snares, but the Pleasure of Man
consisteth in his Tool's Utility and Strength, so
therefore, call thou on Allah that he may lengthen
thy Instrument."

The man obeyed the counsel of his wife, calling
on the Master of Destinies, the Creator of Things,
and Allah heard the prayer, and sending forth His
fiat, caused the man's prizzle to become elongated
until it became even as a straight column which
would neither display suppleness, nor show itself
capable of the power of elasticity and movement, nor
of rest. A grievous woe! When the woman perceived that of it, she said: "I will no longer settle
down with thee after such a happening." He replied:
"Every whit of what has come to pass hath come
about through the badness of thy advice in our respect." Responded she: "I had not certainly reckoned
that things would so transpire, and such a state acquire,
and if thy weapon so continueth you must pronounce
against me the words of the divorce, and let me go free."

Upon hearing this speech, and anxious not to lose
his dear wife, the man lifted up his hand towards
the heavens, and exclaimed: "Oh Allah! Take away
from me this condition!"

Forthright his unsupple monster began to lessen
its intensity and decrease its totality, until it had
become almost effaced, and well-nigh blotted out without trace; which, when the woman perceived that of
it, she said to him: "Divorce me! For there is no
longer left me any living with thee, since thou hast
thus ceased to count as a man among men."

Whereupon the man broke out against her: "O cursed one! All this hath fallen upon us and come to pass through the wickedness of thy wish." Said she then: "There yet remaineth unto thee the asking of one more prayer: entreat therefore Allah, the Compassionate, to return thee upon the way of thy former condition wherein thou wast at first." So the man thus lost his three petition-favours and opportunities through the misfortune of his wife's luckless wish, and the perversity of her judgment, and failed to profit by the blessing of the Night of Power that Allah had vouchsafed him.

THE WIDOW AND HER RICHLY-FURNISHED HUSBAND.

Tellers of stories relate that there lived, at no great distance from us, a woman who possessed a sufficiency of means, and she was a widow. And a man of equal rank and station to her own, proposed and offered her marriage, but she would in nowise accept him, nor look upon his suit with favour.

The woman who acted as intermediary between them, said to her: "What hast thou heard against him in his disfavour, that causeth such bitterness?"

The lady responded: "I have heard that he is the possessor of an enormous prizzle, like unto this my arm here, and there is no room nor capacity enough in me for the reception of such a monster."

On learning this, the man goeth off to her mother, and saith to her: "Marry her to me on the condition that I will not put into her aught except with her permission."

When therefore he had married the timorous dame, and had entered into the bridal-chamber to her, he sent to seek her mother, who taking his fierce upstander in her hand, introduced a quarter of it into the vulva of her daughter, asking: " Does that suffice for you my girl?" Her frightened child answered: " I can support a trifle more." So her mother slipped then the half of her son-in-law's tool into her daughter, saying: " Will that, my daughter, now content thee?" Her timorous child replied: " I can bear a wee little bit further of it. Thereupon the mother thrusteth into her daughter's belly the whole of the man's yard, again querying: " Is it now enough for thee, my dear one?" The daughter replied: " Again a little more of it."

Whereat the mother exclaimed: " By God! My girl! Nothing now remaineth of it all, except the balls."

" Then," said her daughter to her, " my grandmother is undoubtedly right in what she saith; said she to me: There is no good in whatever thy mother hath and holdeth, for the blessing thereof diminisheth and goeth away."

THE PIOUS WOMAN AND WHAT HAPPENED TO HER FROM BEHIND.

A certain woman had prostrated herself, and placed her forehead to the ground in the act of prayer, and was praying, when a man came up to her in the rear, and buried his organ of erection into her the while she was prostrate in adoration before her Lord.

And when her assailant had withdrawn and stood

up, she also stood up from the saying of her reverences, and turning towards him, said: " O Valiant and Brave! Didst thou imagine that this thy act and operation would be the means of disoccupying and keeping me from the worship of the only true One, and that I should nullify and render vain my prayer on such account for thee?" [1])

---

[1]) Brantôme, in *Vie des Dames Galantes*, has a similar story concerning a LADY AND HER VALET: " J'ai ouï conter à un honnête gentilhomme, mien ami, qu'une dame de son pays, ayant plusieurs fois montré de grandes familiarités et privautés à un sien valet de chambre, qui ne tendaient toutes qu'à venir à ce point, ledit valet, point fat et sat, un jour d'été trouvant sa maîtresse, par un matin, à demi endormie dans son lit toute nue, tournée de l'autre côté de la ruelle, tenté d'une si grande beauté, et d'une fort propre posture, et aisée pour l'investir et s'accommoder, étant elle sur le bord du lit, vint doucement et investit la dame, qui, se tournant, vit quel était son valet qu'elle desirait; et, toute investie qu'elle était, sans autrement se désinvestir, ni remuer, ni se défendre, ni dépêtrer de sa prise tant soit peu, ne fit que dire, tournant la tête, et se tenant ferme de peur de ne rien perdre.

— Monsieur le sot, qui est-ce qui vous a fait si hardi de le mettre-là?

Le valet lui répondit en toute révérence:

— Madame, l'ôterai-je?

— Ce n'est pas ce que je vous dis monsieur le sot, lui répondit la dame. Je vous dis: „Qui vous a fait si hardi de le mettre—là?"

L'autre retournait toujours à dire:

— Madame, l'ôterai-je? et si vous voulez, je l'ôterai.

Et elle à redire:

— Ce n'est pas ce que je vous dis encore, monsieur le sot.

Enfin, l'un et l'autre firent ces mêmes répliques et dupliques par trois ou quatre fois, sans se débaucher autrement de leur besogne jusques à ce qu'elle fut achevée; dont la dame s'en

47

THE WHORISH WIFE WHO VAUNTED HER VIRTUE

It is related that once upon a time there was a
man who was an astronomer, [1]) and he had a wife
who was singular in beauty and loveliness. Now she
was ever and aye boasting, and saying to him, " O
man, there is not amongst womankind my peer in
nobility [2]) and chastity;" and as often as she repeated
this saying to him, he would give credit to her words,
and cry, " Walláhi, no man hath a wife like unto the
lady my wife, for chastity and continence!" Now
he was ever singing her praises in every assembly;
but one day of the days, as he was sitting in a séance
of the great, who all were saying their says anent
womankind and feminine deeds and misdeeds, the man
rose up and exclaimed, " Amongst women there is
none like my wife, for that she is pure of blood and
behaviour;" hereat one of those present said to him,
" Thou liest, O certain person!" " Wherein do I lie?"
quoth he, and quoth the other " I will teach thee and
show thee manifestly whether thy wife be a lady or
a whore. Do thou rise up from amongst us and

---

trouva mieux que si elle eût commandé à son galant de l'ôter,
ainsi qu'il lui demandait.

Et bien servit à elle de persister en sa première demande
sans varier, et au galant en sa réplique et duplique: et par
ainsi continuèrent leurs coups et cette rubrique longtemps
après ensemble; car il n'y a que la première fournée ou la
première pinte chêre, dit-on.

[1]) "Sáhib al-Hayát:" this may also = a physiognonist, which,
however, is probably not meant here.

[2]) In text " Harárah " = heat, but here derived from "Hurr" =
freeborn, noble.

hie thee home and go thou in to her and say:—O Woman, I am intent upon travelling to a certain place, and being absent for a matter of four days, and after will return; so do thou arise, O Woman, and bring me some bread and a mould of cheese by way of viaticum. Then go thou forth from beside her, and disappear for a while; and presently returning home, hide thee in a private place without uttering a word." Cried those present, " By Allah, indeed these words may not be blamed." Accordingly the man went forth from them, and fared till he entered his house, where he said, " O Woman, bring me something of provision for a journey: my design is to travel and to be absent for a space of four days, or haply six." Cried the wife, " O my lord, Thou art about to desolate me, nor can I in any wise bear parting from thee; and if thou needs must journey do thou take me with thee." Now when the man heard these the words of his wife, he said to himself, " By Allah, there cannot be the fellow of my spouse amongst the sum of womankind," presently adding to her, " I shall be away from four to six days, but do thou keep watch and ward upon thyself, and open not my door to anyone at all." Quoth she, " O Man, how canst thou quit me? [1]) and indeed I cannot suffer such separation." Quoth he, " I shall not long be separated from thee;" and so saying he fared forth from her, and disappeared for the space of an hour, after which he returned home, softly walking, and hid himself in a place where none could see

---

[1]) In text "Azay má tafút-ní?"

him. Now after the space of two hours behold, a greengrocer ¹) came into the house and she met him and salam'd to him and said, "What hast thou brought for me?" "Two lengths of sugar-cane," said he, and said she, "Set them down in a corner of the room." Then he asked her, "Whither is thy husband gone?" and she answered, "On a journey: may Allah never bring him back, nor write his name among the saved, and our Lord deliver me from him as soon as possible!" After this she embraced him, and he embraced her, and she kissed him and he kissed her and enjoyed her favours till such time as he had his will of her; after which he went his way. When an hour had passed a Poulterer ²) came to the house, whereupon she arose and salam'd to him and said, "What hast thou brought me?" He answered, "A pair of pigeon-poults;" so she cried, "Place them under yon vessel. ³)" Then the man went up to the woman, and he embraced her and she embraced him,

---

¹) In the Arab. "Rajul Khuzari" = a green-meat man. [The reading "Khuzarí" belongs to Lane, M. E. ii. 16. and to Bocthor. In Schiaparelli's Vocabulista and the Muhít the form "Khuzrí" is also given with the same meaning.

²) In text "Farárijí," as if the pl. of "Farríy" = chicken were "Farárij" instead of "Faráry." In modern Egyptian these nouns of relation from irregular plurals to designate tradespeople not only drop the vowel of the penultimate but furthermore, shorten that of the preceding syllable, so that "Farárijí" becomes "Fararjí". Thus "Sanádikí," a maker of boxes, becomes "Sanadkí," and "Dakhákhiní, a seller of tobacco brands," "Dakhakhní." See Spitta Bey's Grammar, p. 118.

³) In the Arab. "Al-Májúr," for "Maajúr" = a vessel, an utensil.

and he tumbled [1]) her and she tumbled him; after which he had his will of her, and presently he went off about his own business. When two hours or so had gone by there came to her another man who was a Gardener [2]); so she arose and met him with a meeting still fairer than the first two, and asked him, "What hast thou brought with thee?" "A somewhat of pomegranates," answered he; so she took them from him, and led him to a secret place, where she left him and changed her dress, and adorned herself, and perfumed herself and kohl'd [3]) her eyes. After that she returned to the pomegranate man, and fell a-toying with him, and he toyed with her, and she hugged him and he hugged her, and at last he rogered and had his wicked will of her and went his way. Hereupon the woman doffed her sumptuous dress, and garbed herself in her everyday garment. At this all the husband was looking on through the chinks of the door behind which he was lurking, and listening to whatso befel, and, when all was ended, he went forth softly and waited a while, and anon returned home. Hereupon the wife arose, and her glance falling upon her husband she noted him and accosted him and salam'd to him and

---

[1]) In text, "shaklaba" here = "shakala" = he weighed out (money, whence the Heb. Shekel), he had to do with a woman.

[2]) The trade of the man is not mentioned here, p. 22 of the 5th vol. of the MS., probably through negligence of the copyist, but it only occurs as far lower down as p. 25.

[3]) A certain reviewer proposes "stained her eyes with Kohl," showing that he had never seen the Kohl-powder used by Asiatics.

said, "Hast thou not been absent at all?" Said he,
"O Woman, there befel me a tale on the way, which
may not be written in any wise, save with foul water
upon disks of dung ¹), and indeed I have endured sore
toil and travail, and had not Allah (be he praised
and exalted!) saved me therefrom, I had never returned."
Quoth his wife, "What hath befallen thee?"—And
he answered, "O Woman, when I went forth the
town and took the road, behold, a basilisk issued
from his den, and coming to the highway stretched
himself there along, so I was unable to step a single
footstep; and indeed, O Woman, his length was that
of yon sugar cane, brought by the Costermonger and
which thou hast placed in the corner. Also he had hair
upon his head like the feathers of the pigeon-poults
presented to thee by the Poulterer, and which
thou hast set under the vessel; and lastly, O Woman,
his head was like the pomegranates which thou tookest
from the Market Gardener ²) and carried within the
house." Whenas the wife heard these words, she
lost command of herself and her senses went

---

¹) [" Bi-Má al-fasíkh 'alá Akrás al-Jullah." "Má al-Fasíkh =
water of salt-fish, I would translate by " dirty-brine" and
"Akrás al-Jullah" by " dung-cakes," meaning the tale should
be written with a filthy fluid for ink upon a filthy solid for
paper, more expressive than elegant.]

²) " Al-Janínáti; or, as Egyptians would pronounce the word
" Al-Ganínátí." [Other Egyptian names for gardener are
" Janáini," pronounced " Ganáiní," " Bustánjí," pronounced
" Bustangi," with a Turkish termination to a Persian noun,
and " Bakhshawángi," for " Baghchawánjí," where the same
termination is pleonastically added to a Persian word, which
in Persian and Turkish already means " gardener."]

wrong and she became purblind and deaf, neither
seeing nor hearing, because she was certain that her
spouse had seen and heard what she had wrought
of waywardness and frowardness. Then the man
continued to her, " O Whore! O Fornicatress,
O Adulteress! How durst thou say to me, 'There is
not amongst womankind my better in nobility and
purity?' and this day I have beheld with my own
eyes what thy chastity may be. So do thou take
thy belongings and go forth from me and be off with
thee to thine own folk." And so saying, he divorced
her with the triple divorce, and thrust her forth from the
house. Now when the Emir heard the aforesaid tale
from his neighbour, he rejoiced thereat; this being such
a notable instance of the guiles of womankind which
they are wont to work with man, for " Verily great
is their craft." [1]) And presently he dismissed the
fourth lover, his neighbour, even as he had freed the
other three, and never again did such trouble befal
him and his wife, or from Kazi or from any other [2]).

THE LADY AND THE BARBER

A woman, they say, sent out a domestic to seek
and bring in a Barber, and when the man entered

---

[1]) A Koranic quotation from " Joseph," chap. XII, 28: Sale
has " for verily your cunning is great," said by Potiphar to
his wife.

[2]) I have inserted this sentence, the tale being absolutely
without termination. So in the Mediæval Lat. translations
the MSS. often omit " explicit capitulum (primum). Sequitur
capitulum secundum ", this explicit being a sine qua non.

in before her, she uncovered to his eyes the secret cleft between her thighs, saying to him: "Trim off the hairs from this;" and he trimmed them off for her straitghtway, even as the lady had requested, and when he had finished he asked her for his fee.

Upon which she said to him. "Demand thy recompense from the place of thy labours, and if it doth not pay thee, then futter and shag it." So the man asked therefrom his price and received for answer only a certain gaping of lips which twitched and opened, but uttered no sound. Then the Hair-dresser stood up to the speechless creature, doing verily as the lady had bade him, and gave not over until he had got clean through with his new business, when he said:

"As long as recompense such as this remaineth the recompense thou givest, send for me every time that a hair lengtheneth out on thy moss-bank, and I will not tarry to obey thy wishes and commands."

THE SLEEPING WOMAN WHO WAS MOUNTED BY A MAN

It is reported that a man once made stealthy, amorous onslaught upon a woman while she was fast asleep, and introduced into her loins the proof of his virile powers; and the activity and largeness of the instrument woke her up; whereupon he said: "Whatever thou commandest that will I do; If thou biddest me to fetch it out, or, if not, to let it remain in its place; that will I do and obey."

Quoth she, in reply (and verily doth not her answer

show sign of much wisdom?)—" Let him go and come;
working to and fro until I make up my mind what
will be the best thing and safest to do. "

THE JUDGE AND HIS COITION-COOING WIFE

A certain Kadi married a wife who, at the time of
copulation, was accustomed through the force of habit,
to make love-delighted noises; and when her husband
for the first time lay with her and went in unto her,
he heard her give forth noises and ejaculations of
pleasure such as never before had he heard come
from other ladies that he had treated in like manner
as his wife. Bewildered therefore, and troubled by
the strangeness of this discovery, he forbade her the
repetition, and enjoined her to keep quiet under him.

And when, afterwards, he returned again the second
time to get into her, and make an amorous attack
on the woman he had wedded, he heard no more
proceed from her those sounds which had greeted his
ears and shocked his dignity on the first occasion,
for she remained quiet and passive, no longer hastening
to give him a display of her fondness for him, nor
exhibiting that subtle art of love-sighing and cooing and
groaning she had before shown. Whereat he said:
" Go back to and resume again the *finesse* of that
fine art wherein thou excellest, for it behoveth that
the amorous coquetry of the wife should accompany
with nice beat and measure the vigorous shagging of the
partner of life, like unto the rise and fall of a choir
singing in time together, the singers whereof do not contrary each other by lagging back nor shooting unduly

forward; and harmony such as this increaseth the
joy and pleasure of the strife, as the poet has set it
down. "

" We passed the night together
    And such was my pertubation
From the movements that we made
    In the rowing and the rock of copulation,
That I lost my senses quite,
    And forgot my hearing's power,
In the passes that gave rise
    To our sensation.

She possesses love's fine trick
    Of sweetest bo ttom-modulation
When, upon her proud-faced vulva,
    I shag with vigorous excitation,
Like a well-matched choir that keeps
    Good time in singing's rise and fall,
'Tis this that gives such witching joy
    To conjoint agitation."

THINGS MEN MOST DETEST IN WOMEN

Offensiveness of smell of the Pudenda [1]); humidity
and consequent flabbiness; unsmoothness or roughness;

---

[1]) Shaykh Nafzáwih says: "The principal and best causes
of pleasure in cohabitation are the heat of the Vulva; the
narrowness, dryness, and sweet exhalation of same. If any
one of these conditions is absent, there is at the same time
something wanting in the voluptuous enjoyment. A moist
Vulva relaxes the nerves, a cold one robs a member of all its
vigour, and bad exhalations from the Vagina detract greatly
from the pleasure, as is also the case if the opening is very
wide."

" The Scented Garden Man's Heart to Gladden" (chap. XIII.)

largeness of the Passage; and smallness of the form
of the Vulva; and its engulphment in the entry of
the two thighs, whenas it becometh lost, swallowed
up and doth not project forth. Preferable to all
such are the contrary conditions, wherein such dis-
figurations are not found.

Detested also by men is the woman who is worn-
out and over-used; and she who is never satisfied in
the marital relation, and resteth seldom quiet from
seeking its commission until she hath been lien with
and given the connection to the extent of her necessity's amorous condition; and for neither the one nor
the other is there any separation except Death step
in and prevent continuation; even as the Poet hath
observed:

" Me upon her thin breast she pressed;
     A breast outline like the outline of a spider's web.
Came she to me and asked me her to kiss:
" I will lie with her and shag her well," cried I,
     Tho' Death snatch me clean away for this. "

ARS AMANDI

Despised likewise and hated by men is the braying
woman, who brayeth out like an ass, and she who,
raising high her voice, talketh twangingly through
the nose at coition's time and trial, as though it were
her natural manner, whereas it is no part of her real
character so to behave, but an artificiality and a
feigned mannerism beauty-void. From such a woman
as this the spouse maketh haste to obtain divorce-
freedom and complete disembarrassment as, in the

meaning of the line of poetry, hath already been intimated:

" Like a camel doth she bray in her love enticing arts,
And 'tis that which saves th'adulterer from punishment's darts."

Silence should reign at the moment of copulation. O what Seductiveness is there in it when accompanied by a manifestation of willingness to accept the amorous mount and the man's close embrace, giving him thereto from time to time co-assistance with the buttockry movement! Such wiles as these should, above all, be observed by the lovers and the loved.

But, if the woman be stupid and unintelligent she straineth herself to learn Love's ways, and arriveth only on the committal of something ugly and disgraceful. How many women are accustomed, in their moment of love-joy and ecstasy, to perpetrate villainous things, and are unable to break themselves of the practice, for so used are they to it that the discontinuance would prove hard for them, while going on in the same way is natural.

Some are there who hug the man up against them close with over-forceful squeeze, while others put their partner under them and ride violently atop [1] And other women still are there whose Coquetry consisteth of insults and name-flinging, and without that no pleasure do they find in the relation,.

It is incumbent on the woman that she be active

---

[1] The " St. George "—the delight of many generations of vigorous Anglo-Saxons,—is sternly forbidden by Qu'ranic injunction.

in her limbs at coition-time, and display gracefulness of movement, with the slightest hint and indication to the man of what he should do.

And, as to the Man well-informed and learned in the amorous conditions of woman, he knoweth how to educate her, and to draw her out as he will in copulation-time, unless her stupidity, perchance, be altogether past repair.

On her side also, the Woman who is wise, knoweth how to draw out the man, and to bend and polish up his character. But some of them are there who, inexperienced like unto beasts, either keep silence, or mutter barbarous things, unknowing how to beautify the seductiveness of love's act.

Imperative therefore, it is that the woman observe gentleness and humiliation, with lowering of the eyelids, and relaxation of her joints without stiffness nor undue movement, and refinement of speech in that conversation with the man which may be necessary. At one moment she encourageth him, and increaseth his desire, at another charmeth and attracteth by the bewitching delicacy of her voice, and the refining kindness of love-coquettishness, as saith the poet:

> "Enchanted am I at coition with thee
> O life of souls, and bashful of glance!
> Fairest of women to love and see, as we
> Rock to and fro in passion's love-trance."

Manners such as these strengthen the voluptuousness of the conjugal movement, and storm-lash the man up (especially the real lover) to the excitement of repetition.

More so still if, into the bargain, she do but fling

all shame away and employ that craft of utter dissolution's way reckoned among woman's peculiar qualities designed to lure and fast-bind for aye.

No omission either, ought there be of that delicate pleasure-snorting, with a caressful kiss following at once on a little bite; the bite, in its turn, succeeded by a fresh caress accompanied by a straight lance-thrust meeting and, in the same second, opposing the belly out-lunging and parry, and ensuring thereby closer connection. When later, the man decideth upon withdrawal she close-clingeth upon him until, enjoying the ecstatic moment, he verseth the life-bearing liquid and reposeth the surcharge of his voluptuous nature in her womb. Then is it beautiful, at this supreme moment that the fair one exhibit her amorous arts and love's joy-heavings, because that is it which magnetiseth the lifeladen water from the body's heights and the brain's depths and from the marrow of the bones, as hath been chaunted:

" To slay th'opposing foe is the best thing of the best,
As 'tis, mounted on swift courser's back, firm in the seat to rest,
In the morning-tide of every day the loved one's face to see,
Or with visit from long-absent friend without warning to be blest."

DEMOLITION OF THE BODY

Quoth Al-Harith-bin-Kindah : " There are four things that emaciate the body, these are :—To go into the bath when the stomach [1]) is in an empty state; and

---

[1]) Mohammad is reported to have said : " The stomach is the house of disease, and diet is the head of healing; for the origin of all sickness is indigestion, that is to say, corruption of the meat."

to visit it also, when one has taken his bellyful; To
eat old meat reserved; And to have carnal connection
with an old woman [1])."

It so befell that, when the before-mentioned Qu'ranist
was at death-grips, they asked him in the last
moments: "Command us a commandment and we will
hold on to it nor go away therefrom after thy departure."

Said he thereat to them: "Do not take to wife
any except a young demoiselle; neither partake ye of
fruits except in the days of their ripeness; let no
one of you be treated by medicine unless his body
be able to withstand the wear-and-tear of medicine-
taking; and upon ye be care and practice of stomach-
purging, for the stomach is the city of bile, which
wipeth man off from the earth and causeth him to
perish.

When any of you hath taken the mid-day meal
let him sleep thereupon a little, but, after the evening's
repast a gentle walk should be observed, if only of
forty steps. Do not draw nigh to a woman with
carnal intent unless thy stomach be light; touch then
often thy partner's breasts to ensure greater love-
delight, and when thou shalt have risen up from
coition's task, turn over on to thy right side for the
repose of the members and the circulation of the
blood in the body; do not commence copulating anew
without purification, because this rule's neglect bringeth

---

[1]) The Imam Ali added: "Avoid copulation on a plethora
of blood and lying with an ailing woman; for she will weaken
thy strength and infect thy frame with sickness; and an old
woman is deadly poison."

upon the transgressor *Elephantiasis* '), and madness;
nor do thou wash thy member with cold water until
it shall have cooled down somewhat, neither rub
it with thy hand, for this produceth inflamma-
tion." ²)

LENGTHENING OF LIFE

Recounted likewise is it of another Shaykh, Ali
ibn Abi Talib ³) (May Allah be gracious to him)—
that he said: "There are four things which give life-
time increase, and work thereby man's peace:—
Marriage with Virgins: washing with Warm water;
sleeping on the Left side; and apple-eating at the
night's close."

And said Julinus, the Philosopher ⁴), "There are
three Minor maladies that ward off three Greater;—a

---

¹) *Webster's Dict* gives this as: "A disease of the skin, in
which it becomes enormously thickened, and is rough, hard,
and fissured like an elephant's hide." See also *Ethnology of
the Sixth Sense* (Paris, 1899) by Dr. Jacobus, and "*Recherches
historiques sur les Maladies de Vénus dans l'Antiquité et le
Moyen Age*, (par P.-L. Jacob, bibliophile), for many other
interesting details.

²) Does he allude here also to Onanism, or self-masturbation?

³) A 'Companion' of the Prophet. He was despatched from
Al-Medinah to Meccah by Mahommad to promulgate the
Koranic chap of "*The Ant*," and meeting the assembly at
Al'Akabah he also acquainted them with four things: 1. No
Infidel may approach the Meccah temple; 2. naked men must
no longer circuit the Ka'abah; 3. only Moslems enter Paradise,
and; 4. public faith must be kept.

⁴) i. e. Galen, a physician of Asia Minor in the second
Christian century, much affected to the use of drugs.

cold beateth back the pleurisy;—boils guard against the pest; and opthalmia saves from total blindness."

While Aflatun [1]), another Philosopher, said: "Love is a natural force engendered by the suggestive promptings of Nature, and consisteth of magnified dissolvable phantoms which aggrandize the natural character according to the malady's gravity, making of the Courageous a coward, and the Coward courageous; clothing every man with a character contrary to his nature, until to the spiritual sickness there is added passionate folly, and these conduct their possessor to a graver malady for which exist no remedies."

And saith Aristalis [2]), when dwelling on philosophy: "Passion blindeth the Lover to the faultful drawbacks of the Beloved, which correspondeth with the pronouncement of the Prophet—whom Allah bless and advance in rank—Thy love of anything blindeth thee, and maketh thy ear deaf to its bad quality." The poet too, did but follow in the same strain when he sang:

"Of all thy love's defects thou dost not see a sign.
Nay! none at all! since all thy view thou dost thyself confine.
Whereas Displeasure's eye doth all faults manifest,
The gaze of blind Contentment can nothing there define."

---

[1]) For Plato. Because our Arab author quotes the 'broadshouldered' philosopher's name, it must not be imagined that he countenanced what is known as 'platonic love', i. e. love without any mixture of the physical.

[2]) i. e. Aristotle whose Ethics and Physics were early familiar, by means of translations, to the cultured scholars of Egypt and Damascus.

Ali Ibn Sin'a [1]) hath said that: " Passion is a fantastic, devil-suggesting malady, close akin to melancholy, wherein the Stricken draweth upon himself the domination of his own thought as to the preferableness of certain fancies and good qualities mindcreated."

And said Asma'i [2]) "I asked a Bedouin woman, 'What is love?' answered she, 'By God!' It hath more power in it than there seemeth, and from his observation surely is it hid who seeketh. In the breasts of men is it it buried as wood in the fire; rub, and up-springeth it brightening higher; neglect it only, and knowledge of its whereabouts 'twere vain to enquire."

Others have declared: " Of Madness there are various kinds, the Love-passion being but a sub-division of one of the categories into which madnesses are classed

---

[1]) The famous Avicenna, whom the Hebrews called Aben Sina. The early European Arabists, who seemed to have learned Arabic through Hebrew, borrowed their corruption, and it long kept its place in Southern Europe. For the life of this remarkable scholar see Louis Figuier's "*Vies des Savants illustres du moyen age,*" (Paris, 1867); Born 980 of Persian parents, he lived for 57 years a life of adventure, in which love of women strangely jostled the scholar's hunger after science.

[2]) Abú Sa'id Abd al-Malik bin Kurayb, surnamed Al-Asma'i from his grandfather, flor. A. H. 122— 306 (=739—830) and wrote amongst a host of compositions the well-known Romance of Antar. See in D'Herbelot the right royal directions given to him by Harun al-Rashid, commencing. "Ne m'enseignez jamais en public, et ne vous empressez pas trop de me donner des avis en particulier."

and fall ". Strongly dwelt he upon this point who sang:

> " Have you gone ", queried they, " stark
>   Mad through love's taunting ? "
> " Love's passion," said I, " is a far greater thing
>   Than lies within reach of madman's fling.
> For, while Life lasts, to the lover true
>   Can Time for his curing no love-relief bring ;
> But setteth Folly of mere madman
>   Never 'pon him lasting sting ".

'BIRDS OF A FEATHER'.

Abu-l-Leys [1]) gave it forth—may Allah the All-great show him compassion—"Who sitteth down with the Rich, God wil increase in his heart the rage of fashion and the restlessness of the Age, and the lust after them.

Who frequenteth the company of the Poor will attain unto contentment of life, and give thanks to his Lord for the part to him allotted out ;

Who walketh with the World in its rut-and-furrow usages, upon him will God lay hatred and haughtiness ;

Who companieth overmuch with Women, God will deepen his ignorance and intensify his desires ;

Who his stay prolongeth with the Young, in love of play and pleasantry will go on ;

Who dwelleth long with the Debauched, in crime-audacity advanceth, and deferreth the date of the repentance day ;

---

[1]) i. e., Father of the Lion.

Who seeketh the society of Scholars, shall be satiated with knowledge and sobriety.

CHARACTER OF THE CLANS

One day a man came to 'Amr Ibn al 'Aas [1]) and to him said:—"Describe to me the people of the various Cities;" replied he: "The Syrians are the most obedient to those created with power and authority, and towards their Creator most rebellious; the Egyptians, to those who overthrow and subdue them, are the most slavish; the folk of the Hijàz are, of all, the most ready for revolution; those of Iràk the most searching of men after knowledge and the farthest removed from attaining it [2]).

---

[1]) One of the greatest captains that the first Musulmans ever had, his conquests including Egypt, Nubia and a great part of the Libyan. Reputed as the cleverest and most adroit of the Arabs, he was chosen by the first Mu'awiyyah as arbitrator in his quarrel with Ali for the Khalifate. His intermediation succeeded and Mu'awiyyeh was proclaimed the First of the Ommiadian Khalifs. He died about 65 (A. H.) at Mecca. His son too, has made his own name for ever famous by the compilation of the *Ahadith*, or sayings of the Prophet from whom he first obtained permission to write them down as they fell from his lips. These "sayings" form a very important monument of Musulman Tradition. For further information see Al-Fakhri's History and D'Herbelot's *Bibliothèque Orientale*.

[2]) The trueness of these definitions is striking, especially as regards the Egyptians, who fought tenaciously against Napoléon, but slavishly *knuckled under* when once their overthrow was assured. The profession of Islam by the great diplomatist counted, of course, for much in this change of front.

Quoth [1]) Generosity:—"I shall fare me forth to Syria"; said the sharp-cutting Sabre, "and I will go with thee"; "As for me", spake Riches, "I wend my way to Egypt;" said Humility, "and I will be thy companion"; Sobriety declared, "my home lieth towards the Hijaz;" "and mine also," chimed in the soft voice of Patience.

Science, in proud tones proclaimed:—"My path lies across to Irak;" "and with thee there will I abide also," added Intelligence. "With none of you will I go," hurled in the rasping accents of Badness of Character, "but my own way make towards Morocco" [2]) "and thitherwards will I wend in thy company;" eager Avarice loud broke in.

THE WOMEN WORTHY OF COPULATION

When Harith, a renowned physician of the Arabs, was asked by Kisra Anushirwan [3]) which was the

---

[1]) This epigram (Arabic, "*nukta*") is given to rest the reader's attention and *change the subject*. Those who know Arabia will not fail to notice that the remarks are true, even at this distance of time.

[2]) Arabic "*Al-Gharb*", derivative "Maghrib" i. e. the Land of the Setting sun, from which we get the word Mauritania, Morocco, this transmogrification occurring through the letter "Ghayn", generally unpronounceable by Europeans as also by the modern Cairenes. For character of the Moroccans by a modern traveller, see Leared's (Arth. M. D.) "*Morocco and the Moors*" (pp. 222—224) Lond. 1876. Leared was Burton's friend.

[3]) This beautiful name stands for the Persian "*Anushin-rawan*"—Sweet of Soul; and the glorious title of this contemporary of Mohammad is "*Al Malik al Adil*"—the Just

best of womankind, he answered:—"She who possesses the moulded form of a Medinah girl, with height above the ordinary, a large forehead and firm nostrils, and skin of unique whiteness, with transparent-pure cheeks of perfect form, ornamented by eyelashes overarching and meeting together across a nose of pride like lovers stealing a kiss; underneath should gleam a well-formed range of pearl-white teeth flashing with smiles: her buttocks should be large and round, her shoulders broad and well-thrown back; the whole poised upon tiny feet which in suppleness and softness of allurement should betray, the grace the Garden-Houris show for ever and for aye ¹).

And as to the various kinds of women, those of the Greeks are the cleanest in that which appertaineth to their vulvas, and most of them possess broad bottoms well-adapted to the sitting posture, and favourable for coition; the women of Andalusia are the most beautiful of face, and their smell is the best; the women of India, and Scinde ²), and of

---

King. Kisra, *the* Chosroë per excellentiam, is also applied to the godly Guebre of whom every Eastern dictionary gives details. Burton, (*Nights* Vol. V. 87).

¹) Arabic:—" *Zat in'itaf wa-leen ka-innaha min al-Hur al-'Een*". Cf. Kuran, *Súratu-l-Waqi'ah* (lvi.), 12-39:—" and theirs shall be the Houris with large dark eyes, like pearls hidden in their shells, in recompense for their labours past... on lofty couches and of a rare creation have we made the Houris, and we have made them ever virgins, dear to their spouses and of equal age, for the people of the right hand. "

²) At that time the province of Sind was known as a separate kingdom. Sind, so-called from Sindhu, the Indus (in Pers.

Sicily are the most reprehensible in their conditions, the ugliest of feature, the dirtiest in what concerneth their vulvas and the most debased in intelligence; the daughters of Zanzibar [1]) and Abyssinia are by nature

---

Sindab), is the general name of the riverine valley: in early days it was a great station of the so-called Aryan race, as they were migrating eastward into India Proper, and it contains many Holy Places dating from the era of the Puranas. (See Burton's "*Sind Revisited*" vol. I. chap. VIII. Also Taylor's "*Origin of the Aryans*).

[1]) Arab. "Zanj" of Persian zang-bar—(Black-land), our Zanzibar. See Burton's "Zanzibar".

I have not been able to control the statement as to the "obedience" and "sweet-smellingness" of the Zanzibar "*belles*"; but, I think the following notelet from Burton's "*Nights*" (vol. I. p. 6) cannot fail to be interesting in this connection.

"Debauched women", he says, "prefer negroes on account of the size of their parts. I measured one man in Somali-land who, when quiescent, numbered nearly six inches. This is a characteristic of the negro race and of African animals; *e. g.* the horse; whereas the pure Arab, man and beast, is below the average of Europe; one of the best proofs by the by, that the Egyptian is not an Asiatic, but a negro partially white-washed. Moreover, these imposing parts do not increase proportionally during erection; consequently, the "deed of kind" takes a much longer time and adds greatly to the woman's enjoyment. In my time no honest Hindi Moslem would take his women-folk to Zanzibar on account of the huge attractions and enormous temptations there and thereby offered to them."

With regard to "*Imsak*, or retention of semen, and prolongation of pleasure", this is a point that Burton has touched upon further in "*Nights*", (vol. V. pp. 76-77), in a footnote where he says it is a practice much cultivated by Moslems. Yet Eastern books on medicine consist mostly of two parts; the first of general prescriptions, and the second of aphrodisiacs

more sweet-smelling than the rest and the most obedient; the women of Baghdad and Babylonia are the greatest drawers-down [1]) of men's voluptuousness in

---

especially those *qui prolongent le plaisir* as did the Gaul by thinking of *sa pauvre mère*.

The *Ananga-Ranga* by the Reverend Koka Pandit gives a host of recipes which are used either externally or internally, to hasten the paroxysm of the woman and delay the orgasm of the man. Some of these are curious in the extreme. I heard of a Hindi who made a candle of frogs' fat and fibre warranted to retain the seed till it burned out; it failed notably because, relying upon it, he worked too vigorously. The essence of the "retaining art" is to avoid over-tension of the muscles and to pre-occupy the brain, hence in coition Hindus will drink sherbet, chew betel-nut and even smoke. Europeans ignoring the science and practice, are contemptuously compared with village-cocks by Hindu women, who cannot be satisfied, such is their natural coldness, increased doubtless by vegetable diet and unuse of stimulants, with less than twenty minutes. Hence too, while thousands of Europeans have cohabited for years with and have had families by "native women;" they are never loved by them:—at least I never heard of a case."

[1]) Arab. " *Ajlab shahwatan lir-rijal* ", " alluding to a peculiarity highly-prized", says Burton, by the Egyptians (" *Nights* ", vol. IV, p. 227). where he refers to the power possessed by some women of " clasping the member " by which all the semen is drawn or sucked out of it; i. e. " The use of the constrictor vaginal muscles, the sphincter for which Abyssinian women are famous. The " *Kabbazah* "—(holder, from *kabaz*, to arrest) as she is called, can sit astraddle upon a man and can provoke the venereal orgasm, not by wriggling and moving, but by tightening and loosing the male member with the muscles of her privities; milking it as it were. Consequently the *casse-noisette* costs treble the money of other concubines " (Ananga-Ranga, p. 127).

the love-act above any other women in the world, while the Syrian women are towards men the unkindest. The women of the Bedouins, and of Persia, are the most charming in respect of their secret conditions, and their children the most intelligent; for eloquence they are unrivalled, and in Sociability outshine all the rest; their faithfulness is known.

The Kenniyan [1]) and Nubian women are the hottest of slit, the largest-buttocked, the softest of body, and the most passionate for copulation, of any known. And for Turkish women, they are the uncleanest in their private parts, the most rapid in child-producing, the worst of tempers, the most rancorous in disposition, and the least gifted with brains.

The women of Busra [2]) are, in the love that women bear to men, the most intense; the ladies of Aleppo very powerful in body, and between the legs the most solidly-constructed; the daughters of Egypt [3]) are in

---

[1]) Kenneh, the modern capital of Thebaid about thirty miles below the site of ancient Thebes. Used to buy dates and coffee from Mecca.

Vide Pickering's " *Races of Man* ", p. 211-212. (Bohn's edit.) The data here given would probably be founded on the *practical* experience of Traders.

[2]) Or Bassorah.

[3]) More especially the Cairene woman whose wiliness and perfect abandonment when once "set agoing" is common tradition. See Artin Pasha's little book of " *Contes populaires de la vallée du Nil* ". (Paris, Maisonneuve, 1895.)

In the " *Tale of the Jewish Doctor* ", (*Nights*, vol. 1, 298-299), it is stated that a woman "had learnt wantonness and un-graciousness from the people of Cairo. " Burton (*in loco*) says: " This is no unmerited scandal. The Cairenes, especially the

71

E

speech seductive, in character refined, and as to the craft of dissoluteness they exceed in it; this many histories show; while in Upper Egypt, their sisters are the most pleasureable to lie with and to mount. Of all the women in the world, it is reported that the beautiful daughters of Lower Egypt possess the greatest coyntes; and the peasant women that adorn the borders of the Nile are the strongest in the desire for a large-sized prizzle.

THE JEWISH KAZI AND HIS WIFE [1])

Among the children of Israel, one of the Kazis had a wife of surpassing beauty, constant in fasting and

---

feminine half (for reasons elsewhere given, see Excursus I, on "Fierceness of woman's desire") have always been held exceedingly debauched. Even the modest Lane gives a "shocking" story of a woman enjoying her lover under the nose of her husband, and confining the latter in a madhouse (See "*Modern Egyptians*). With civilization, which objects to the good old remedy, the sword, they become worse: and the Kazi's court is crowded with would-be divorcees. Under English rule the evil has reached its acme because it goes unpunished: in the avenues of the new Isma'iliah Quarter, inhabited by Europeans, women, even young women, will threaten to expose their persons unless they receive "bakhsheesh." It was the same in Sind when husbands were assured that they would be hanged for cutting down adulterous wives: at once after its conquest the women broke loose; and in 1843-50, if a young officer sent to the bazar for a girl, half-a-dozen would troop to his quarters. Indeed, more than once the professional prostitutes threatened to memorialise Sir Charles Napier, because the "modest women," the "ladies," were taking the bread out of their mouths.

[1]) This story and the following one occur in the "*Nights*"

abounding in patience and long-suffering; and he being minden to make the pilgrimage to Jerusalem, appointed his own brother Kazi in his stead during his absence, and commmended his wife to his charge.

Now this brother had heard of her beauty and loveliness, and had taken a fancy to her. So no sooner was his brother gone, than he went to her and sought her love favours; but she denied him and held fast to her chastity. The more she repelled him, the more he pressed his suit upon her; till despairing of her, and fearing lest she should acquaint his brother with his misconduct whenas he should return, he suborned false witnesses to testify against her of adultery; and cited her and carried her before the king of the time, who judged her to be stoned. So they dug a pit, and seating her therein stoned her, till she was covered with stones, and the man said: " Be this hole her grave? "

But when it was dark a passer-by, making for a neighbouring hamlet, pulling her out of the pit, carried her home to his wife, whom he bade dress her wounds. The peasant woman tended her till she recovered and presently gave her her child to nurse; and she used to lodge with the child in another house by night. Now a certain thief saw her, and lusted

---

of the MacNaghten Arabic edition. It was Englished therefore by Burton, who enjoyed the advantage, moreover, of recourse to M S.S. more various than those at my command. Doubtful of my own powers to excel. or even match, work that this master of the art of Arabic translation had executed already, I consider I owe no apologies to the reader for giving him Burton's version instead of my own. (" *Bohemian.*")

after her. So he sent to her seeking her love-favour, but she denied herself to him; wherefore he resolved to slay her, and making his way into her lodging by night (and she sleeping), thought to strike her with a knife; but it smote the little one and killed it [1]).

---

[1]) The amorous exploits of brigands and highwaymen with ladies is no novelty. In Europe, as in the East, instances used to be quite frequent, and still are, if we may believe certain half-stifled reports. In a lane in lone Sussex, not long ago, an English officer was driving with his wife, when a party of London "rowdies" coming in the opposite direction, having made some insolent remark, an altercation ensued, with the result that the military man was "lugged out" of his trap, bound to a tree, and his dame violated by these sporting "gentlemen" before his eyes. The matter we are told was hushed up for imperative family reasons. Sometimes the ardent mount of strange men comes as a welcome surprise to the wife, as witness the following Turkish story.

An adventure with thieves. One night, some thieves in search of booty, broke noiselessly into a house. They rummaged in every direction and found nothing but a woman, her husband, and a sheep. The house contained nothing else;—all the rooms were empty. Disappointed in their hopes of booty, they were very dissatisfied with the result of their expedition, and held a consultation.

"If you will take my advice," said one of them, "we may get some good out of our adventure. To begin with we will kill the man, then cut the throat of the sheep, roast it, and of the skin we will make a leather bottle to hold our drink. We will remain till the morning, and eat and drink, and we can all amuse ourselves in turn with the woman. Thus we shall enjoy all the pleasures at once.

All applauded this proposal. The husband and wife, who,—suspecting nothing—had been sleeping peaceably, awoke during this conversation.

"Did you hear what was said?" the husband asked the wife.

Now when he knew his misdeed, fear overtook him and he went forth the house, and Allah preserved from him her chastity. But as she awoke in the morning, she found her child by her side with throat cut; and presently the mother came and seeing her boy dead, said to the nurse: "Twas thou didst murther him." Therewith she beat her grievous, and purposed to put her to death; but her husband interposed and delivered the woman, saying: "By Allah, thou shalt not do this in this wise." So the woman, who had somewhat of money with her, fled forth for her life, knowing not whither she should wend.

Presently she came to a village, where she saw a crowd of people about a man crucified to a tree-stump, but still in the chains of life: "What hath he done?" she asked, and they answered: "He hath committed a crime, which nothing can expiate but death or the payment of such a fine by way of alms. So she said to them: "Take the money and let him go;" and they did so. He repented at her hands and vowed to serve her, for the love of Almighty Allah, till death should release him.

"Yes," she replied, "but all we can do is to patiently abide events."

"That is all very well for you," said the husband, "but patience is not quite so easy for me and the sheep."

The thieves, who had heard the conversation, burst out laughing and went away.

The conduct of the woman shows clearly, that however many years she may have been married, when danger comes, to save herself she will consent to the death of her husband. Place no confidence therefore in the sex. Hence comes the proverb; "Trust not in woman; lean not on the water."

Then he built her a cell and lodged her therein: after which he betook himself to wood-cutting and brought her daily her bread.

As for her, she was constant in worship, so that there came no sick man or demoniac to her, but she prayed for him and he was straightway healed; and it befell by decree of the Almighty that he sent down upon her husband's brother (the same that had caused her to be stoned), a cancer in the face, and smote the villager's wife (the same who had beaten her) with leprosy, and afflicted the thief (the same who had murdered the child) with palsy. Now when the Kazi returned from his pilgrimage, he asked his brother of his wife, and he told him that she was dead, whereat he mourned sore and accounted her with her Maker. After awhile, very many folk heard of the pious recluse and flocked to her cell from all parts of the length and breadth of the earth, whereupon said the Kazi to his brother: "O my brother wilt thou not seek out yonder pious woman? Haply Allah shall decree thee healing at her hands!" and he replied: "O my brother carry me to her." Moreover, the husband of the leprous woman heard of the pious devotee, and carried his wife to her, as did also the people of the paralytic thief; and they all met at the door of the hermitage. Now she had a place wherefrom she could look out upon those who came to her without their seeing her; and they waited till her servant came, when they begged admittance and obtained permission.

Presently she saw them all and recognized them; so she veiled and cloaked face and body, and went out and stood in the door, looking at her husband

and his brother and the thief and the peasant woman; but they could not recognize her.

Then said she to them, " Oh folk, ye shall not be relieved of what is with you till you confess your sins; for when the creature confesseth his sins the Creator relenteth toward him and granteth him that wherefore he resorteth to Him." Quoth the Kazi to his brother, " O my brother, repent to Allah and persist not in thy frowardness, for it will be more helpful to thy relief. " And the tongue of the case spake this speech:

This day oppressor and oppressed meet,
And Allah sheweth secrets we secrete:
This is a place where sinners low are brought;
And Allah raiseth saint to highest seat.
Our Lord and Master shows the truth right clear,
Though sinner froward be or own defeat:
Alas [1]) for those who rouse the Lord,
As though of Allah's wrath they nothing weet.
O whoso seekest honours, know they are
From Allah, and His fear with love entreat.

Then quoth the brother, " Now I will tell the truth: I did thus and thus with thy wife;" and he confessed the whole matter, adding, " And this is my offence. "

Quoth the leprous woman, " As for me, I had a woman with me, and imputed to her that of which I knew her to be guiltless, and beat her grievously; and this is my offence." And quoth the paralytic,

---

[1]) Arab. " *Wayha* ", not so strong as " Woe to ", etc... Al-Hariri often uses it as a formula of affectionate remonstrance.

"And I went into a woman to kill her, after I had tempted her to commit adultery and she refused; and I slew a child that lay on her side; and this is my offence." Then said the pious woman, "O my God, even as thou hast made them feel the misery of revolt, so show them now the excellence of submission, for Thou over all things art Omnipotent!"

And Allah (to whom belong Majesty and Might!) made them whole. Then the Kazi fell to looking on her and considering her straightly, till she asked him why he looked so hard, and he said. "I had a wife and were she not dead, I had said thou art she?"

Hereupon, she made herself known to him and both began praising Allah (to whom belong Majesty and Might) for that which he had vouchsafed them of the reunion of their loves; but the brother and the thief and the villager's wife joined in imploring her forgiveness.

So she forgave them one and all, and they worshipped Allah in that place and rendered her due service, till Death parted them. And one of them, Sayyids [1]), hath, related this tale of [2]).

---

[1]) As a rule (much disputed) the Sayyid is a descendant from Mohammed through his grand-child Hasan, and is a man of the pen; whereas Sharif derives from Husayn and is a man of the sword. The Najib-Altaraf is the son of a common Moslemah by a Sayyid, as opposed to the "Najib-Altarafayn", when both parents are of Apostolic blood. The distinction is not noticed in Lane's Modern Egyptians. The sharif is a fanatic and often a dangerous one, as I have instanced in Pilgrimage III, 132.

[2]) In the "Nights" there are two other Stories sandwiched in between the above and the one here following, but, as these

THE TAILOR AND THE LADY AND THE CAPTAIN [1]).

It is related that a Tailor was sitting in his shop facing a tall house tenanted by a Yúzbáshi, and this man had a wife who was unique for beauty and loveliness. Now one of the days as she looked out at the latticed window, the Snip espied her, and was distraught by her comeliness and seemlihead. So he became engrossed by love of her, and remained all day a-gazing at the casement, disturbed and perturbed, and as often as she approached the window and peered out therefrom, he would stare at her, and say to her, "O my lady, and O core of my heart, good morning to thee, and do thou have mercy upon one sore affected by his affection to thee; one whose eyes sleep not by night for thy fair sake." "This pimp be Jinn-mad!" quoth the Captain's wife "and as often as I look out at the window he dareth bespeak me: haply the folk shall say:—Indeed she must needs be his mistress." But the tailor persevered in this proceeding for a while of days, until the lady was offended thereby, and said in her mind, "Wallahi, there is no help but that I devise for him a device which shall make unlawful to him this his staring and casting sheep's eyes at my casement; nay more, I will work for ousting him from his shop." So one day of the

are not given in any M.S.S. I have seen of " *The Book of Exposition* ", I naturally refrain from swelling out the present work beyond its limits by unwarrantably quoting them. *Bohemian*.

[1]) Scott (VI. 386) " The Cauzee's story : " Gauttier (VI. 406) does not translate it.

days when the Yuzbashi went from home, his wife
arose and adorned and beautified herself, and donning
the best of what dresses and decorations she had,
despatched one of her slave-girls to the Tailor, instructing her to say to him:—"My lady salameth to thee
and biddeth thee come and drink coffee with her."
The handmaiden went to his shop and delivered the
message; and he, when hearing these words, [1]) waxed
bewildered of wits and rose up quivering in his
clothes;—But indeed he recked not aught of the wiles
of woman-kind. So after padlocking his shop he
went with her to the house and walked upstairs,
where he was met by the lady, with a face like the
rondure of the moon, and she greeted him right mer-
rily, and taking him by the hand led him to a well-
mattressed Divan, and bade her slave-girl serve him
with coffee, and as he drank it she sat facing him.
Presently the twain fell to conversing, she and he;
and she soothed him with sweet speech, whilst he
went clean out of his mind for the excess of her
beauty and loveliness. This lasted until near midday,
when she bade serve the dinner-trays, and took seat
in front of him, and he began picking up morsels [2])
designed for his lips and teeth, but in lieu thereof
thrust them into his eye. She laughed at him, but
hardly had he swallowed the second mouthful and
the third when behold, the door was knocked, where-

---

[1]) In the text the message is delivered verbatim: this
iteration is well fitted for oral work, with its changes of tone
and play of face, and varied "gag.," but it is most annoying
for the more critical reader.

[2]) Arab. "Lukmah "—a balled mouthful: vols. I. 261, VII. 367.

upon, she looked out from the casement and cried, "Oh my honour! this is my husband." Hereat the man's hands and knees began to quake, and he said to her, "Whither shall I wend?" Said she, "Go into this closet," and forthright she thrust him into a cabinet, and shot the bolt upon him, and taking the key she tore out one of its teeth [1]) and put in her pocket. After this she went down and opened the door to her husband, who walked upstairs, and finding the dinner trays bespread, asked her, " What it this?" She answered, "I and my lover have been dining together." "And what may be thy lover?" "Here he is [2].") "Where may he be?" to which she replied, "He is inside this closet". Now as soon as the Tailor heard her say this he piddled in his bag-breeches and befouled himself, and he was in a filthy state with shite and piss [3]).

---

[1]) The "Miftah" (prop. "Miftah") or key used throughout the Moslem East is a bit of wood, 7—14 inches long, and provided with 4—10 small iron pins which correspond with an equal number of holes in the "Dabbah" or wooden bolt. If one of these teeth be withdrawn the lock will not open. Lane (M.E. Introduction) has a sketch of the "miftah" and "Dabbah."

[2]) In text "Ayoh" which is here, I hold, a corruption of "I (or Ayy) hú—"yes indeed he." I take "aywah" (as I would read the word) to be a different spelling for "aywa" = eyes indeed, which according to Spitta Bey, Gr. p. 168 is a contraction of "Ay ﹙I﹚ wa'llahi," yes by Allah, "What? thy lover?" asks the husband, and she emphatically affirms the fact, to frighten the concealed tailor.

[3]) In the Arab. "Al-Ashkhakh," plur. of "Shakhkh" and literally "the stales," meaning either dejection. (I read: "bi-'l-Shakhakh," the usual modern word for urine. "'Allaya Shakhakh" is: I want to make water. See Dozy. Suppl. s. v.

Hereupon the Captain asked, "And where's the key?" and she answeréd, "Here it is with me." [1] "Bring it out", said he, so she pulled it from her pocket and handed it to him. The Captain took the key from his spouse and applying it to the wooden bolt of the cabinet rattled it to and fro [2] but it would not open, so the wife came up to him and cried, "Allah upon thee, O my lord, what wilt thou do with my playmate?" Said he, "I will slay him;" and said she, "No, 'tis my opinion that thou hadst better pinion him, and bind him as if crucified to the pillar in the court floor, and then smite him with thy sword upon the neck, and cut off his head, for I, during my born days, never saw a criminal put to death, and now 'tis my desire to see one done to die." "Sooth is thy speech, "quoth he: so he took the key and fitting it into the wooden bolt, would have drawn it back, but it could not move because a tooth had been drawn therefrom, and the while he was rattling at the bolt, his wife said to him, "O my lord, 'tis my desire that thou lop off his feet until he shall become marked by his maims [3]), and after do thou smite his neck." "A sensible speech," cried the husband, and during the whole time her mate was striving to pull the bolt, she kept saying to him, "Do this and do that with the fellow," and he ceased

---

[1]) In text "Ahu ma'i "-pure Fellah speech.

[2]) In the Arab. "laklaka-ha "-an onomatopœia.

[3]) In text "Ilà an yasír Karmu-hu." The Karm originally means cutting a slip of skin from the camel's nose by way of mark, in lieu of the normal branding.

not saying to her, " 'Tis well." All this and the
Tailor sat hearkening to their words and melting in
his skin, but at last the wife burst out laughing
until she fell upon her back, and her husband asked
her, " Whereat this merriment?" Answered she, " I
make mock of thee for that thou art wanting in wit
and wisdom." Quoth he, " Wherefore?" and quoth
she, " O my lord, had I a lover and had he been
with me should I have told aught of him to thee?
Nay, I said in my mind:—Do such with the Captain,
and let's see whether he will believe or disbelieve.
Now when I spake thou didst credit me, and it became
apparent to me that art wanting in wit." Cried he
to her, " Allah disappoint thee. Dost thou make jibe
and jape of me? I also said in my thoughts:—How
can a man be with her and she speak of him in the
face of me?" So he arose and took seat with her,
the twain close together, at the dinner tray and she
fell to morselling him and he to morselling her, and
they laughed and ate until they had their sufficiency
aud were filled; then they washed their hands and drank
coffee. After this they were cheered and they toyed
together and played the two-backed beast until their
pleasure was fulfilled and this was about mid-afternoon—
the Yuzbashi fell to toying with his wife, and thrusting
and foining at her cleft [1], her solution of continuity,
and she wriggled to and fro to him, and bucked up
and down, after which he tumbled her and both were

---

[1] In text " Yazghas-há," the verb being probably a clerical
error for " Yazaghzagh," from " Zaghzagha "—he opened a
skin bag.

in gloria [2]).   This lasted until near mid-afternoon when he arose and went forth to the Hammam.   But as soon as he left the house she opened the cabinet and brought out the Tailor, saying, " Hast thou seen what

---

[2]) This is the far-famed balcony-scene in " Fanny " (of Ernest Feydeau translated into English and printed by Vizetelly and Co.) that phenomenal specimen of morbid and unmasculine French (or rather Parisian) sentiment, which contrasts so powerfully with the healthy and manly tone of The Nights. Here also the story conveys a moral lesson and, contrary to custom, the husband has the best of the affair.   To prove that my judgment is not too severe, let me quote the following passages from a well-known and popular French novelist, translated by an English littérateur, and published by a respectable London firm.

1n " A Ladies' Man : " by Guy de Maupassant, we read:—.

Page 62.   " And the conversation, descending from elevated theories concerning love, strayed into the flowery garden of polished black-guardism.   It was the moment of clever double meanings, veils raised by words, as petticoats are lifted by the wind; tricks of language, cleverly disguised audacities; sentences which reveal nude images in covered phrases, which cause the vision of all that may not be said to flit rapidly before the eyes of the mind, and allow well-bred people the enjoyment of a kind of subtle and mysterious love, a species of impure mental contact, due to the simultaneous evocations of secret, shameful, and longed-for pleasures.

Page 166.   Georges and Madeleine amused themselves with watching all these couples, the woman in summer toilette and the man darkly outlined beside her.   It was a huge flood of lovers flowing towards the Bois, beneath the starry and heated sky.   No sound was heard save the dull rumble of wheels. They kept passing by, two by two in each vehicle, leaning back on the seat, clasped one against the other, lost in dreams of desire, quivering with the anticipation of coming caresses. The warm shadow seemed full of kisses.   A sense of spreading

awaiteth thee, O pander, O impure? Now, by Allah, an thou continue staring at the windows, or durst bespeak me with one single word, it shall be the death of thee. This time I have set thee free, but a second time I will work to the wasting of thy heart's blood." Cried he, " I will do so no more, no, never." Thereupon said she to her slave girl, " O handmaid, open to him the door," and she did so, and he fared forth (and he foully bewrayed as to his nether garments) until he had returned to his shop. Now when the Emir heard the tale of the Kazi, he

---

lust rendered the air heavier and more suffocating. All the couples intoxicated with the same idea, the same ardour, shed a fever about them.

Page 187. As soon as she was alone with George, she clasped him in her arms, exclaiming: " Oh, my darling pretty boy, I love you more every day." The cab conveying them rocked like a ship.

" It is not so nice as our own room," said she.

He answered: " Oh, no." But he was thinking of Madame Waller.

Page 198. He kissed her neck, her eyes, her lips with eagerness, without her being able to avoid his furious caresses and whilst repulsing him, whilst shrinking from his mouth, she, despite herself, returned his kisses. All at once she ceased to struggle, and vanquished, resigned, allowed him to undress her. One by one he neatly and rapidly stripped off the different articles of clothing with the light fingers of a lady's maid. She had snatched her bodice from his hands to hide her face in it, and remained standing amidst the garments fallen at her feet. He seized her in his arms and bore her towards the couch. Then she murmured in his ear in a broken voice, " I swear to you, I swear to you, that I have never had a lover."

And he thought " That is all the same to me."

rejoiced thereat and said to him, " Up and gang thy gait;" so the Judge went off garbed in his gaberdine and bonnet. Then said the house-master to his wife, " This be one of the four, where's Number Two?" Hereat she arose and opened the closet in which was the Gentleman, and led him out by the hand till he stood before her husband, who looked hard at him and was certified of him and recognised him as the Shâhbandar, so he said to him, " O Khawajah, when didst thou make thee a droll?" [1]) but the other returned to him neither answer nor address and only bowed his brow groundwards.

THE LADY WITH TWO COYNTES.

It is told of a woman who was a fornicatress and adulteress, and a companion of catastrophes and calamities, that she was married to a Káim-makám [2]) who had none of the will of mankind to womankind at all. Now the wife was possessed of beauty and loveliness, and she misliked him for that he had no desire to carnal copulation, and there was in the house a Syce-man who was dying for his love of her. But her husband would never quit his quarters, and albeit her longing was that the horse-keeper might possess her person and that she and he might lie together, this was impossible to her. She abode perplexed for some sleight wherewith she might serve her

---

[1]) In text " Ant' amilta maskharà (for maskharah) matah (for matà)," idiomatical Fellah-tongue.

[2]) i.e. a deputy (governor, etc.); in old days the governor of Constantinople; in these times a lieutenant-colonel, etc.

mate, and presently she devised a device and said to him, "O my lord, verily my mother is dead and 'tis my wish to hie me and be present at her burial and receive visits of condolence for her; and, if she have left aught by way of heritage, to take it and then fare back to thee." "Thou mayest go," said he, and said she, "I dread to fare abroad alone and unattended; nor am I able to walk, my parent's house being far. Do thou cry out to the Syce that he fetch me hither an ass, and accompany me to the house of my mother, wherein I shall lie some three nights after the fashion of folk." Hereupon he called to the horse-keeper, and when he came before him, ordered the man to bring an ass [1]) and mount his mistress and hie with her; and the fellow, hearing these words, was hugely delighted. So he did as he was bidden, but instead of going to the house, they twain, he and she, repaired to a garden, carrying with them a flask of wine, and disappeared for the whole day, and made merry and took their pleasure [2]) until set of sun. Then the man brought up the ass, and mounting her thereon, went to his own home, where the twain passed the entire night sleeping in mutual embrace on each other's bosoms, and took their joyance and enjoyment until it was morning tide. Hereupon he arose and did with her as before, leading her to the garden, and the two, Syce and dame, ceased not to be after this fashion for three days, solacing themselves and

---

[1]) Which. as has been said, is the cab of Modern Egypt, like the gondola and the caïque. The heroine of the tale is a Nilotic version of "Aurora Floyd."

[2]) In text "Rafaka" and infrà (p. 11.) "Zafaka."

making merry and tasting of love's ease. On the fourth day he said to her, "Do thou return with us to the house of the Kaim-makam," and said she, "No; not till we shall have spent together three days more enjoying ourselves, I and thou, and making merry till such time as I have had my full will of thee and thou thy full will of me; and leave we yon preposterous pimp to lie streched out, as do the dogs [1]), enfolding his head between his two legs." So the twain ceased not amusing themselves, and taking their joyance and enjoyment, until they had ended the six days, and on the seventh they wended their way home. They found the Kaim-makam sitting beside a slave who was an old negress; and quoth he, "You have disappeared for a long while!" and quoth she, "Yes, until we had ended with the visits of condolence, for that my mother was known to many of the folk. But, O my lord, my parent (Allah have ruth upon her!) hath left and bequeathed to me an exceeding nice gift." "What may that be?" asked he, and answered she, "I will not tell thee aught thereof at this time, nor indeed until we remain, I and thou, in privacy of night, when I will describe it unto thee."

" 'Tis well," said he; after which he continued to address himself, " Would Heaven I knew what hath been left by the mother of our Harím!" [2]) Now when

---

[1]) In text "Misla 'l-Kalám," which I venture to suggest is another clerical blunder for: "misla 'l-Kiláb" = as the dogs do.

[2]) i. e. my wife. I would observe that " Harím " (women) is the broken plur. of " Hurmah ;" from Haram, the honour of the house, *forbidden* to all save her spouse. But it is also

darkness came on, and he and she had taken seats together, he asked her, " What may be the legacy thy mother left?" and she answered, " O my lord, my mother hath bequeathed to me her Coynte, being loath that it be given to other save myself, and therefore I have brought it along with me." Quoth he of his stupidity (for he was like unto a cosset) [2]), " Oh thou, solace me with the sight of thy mother's Coynte." Hereupon she arose, and doffing all she had on her of dress until she was mother-naked, said to him; " O my lord, I have stuck on my mother's Coynte hard by and in continuation of mine own cleft, and so the twain of them have remained each adjoining other between my hips." He continued, " Let me see it;" so she stood up before him and pointing to her parts, said, " This which faceth thee is my coynte whereof thou art owner;" after which she raised her backside, and bowing her head groundwards showed the nether end of her slit between the two swelling cheeks of her sit-upon, her seat of honour, crying, " Look thou! this be the coynte of my mother; but, O my lord, 'tis my wish that we will it unto some good man and pleasant, who is faithful and true and not likely treason to do, for that the coynte of my mother must abide by me, and whoso shall intermarry

---

an infinitive (whose plur. is Harîmá = the women of a family; and in places it is still used for the women's apartment, the gynæceum. The latter by way of distinction I have mostly denoted by the good old English corruption, " Harem."

[1]) In text " Misla 'l-khárúf) a common phrase for an " innocent," a half idiot; so our poets sing of " silly (harmless, Germ. *Selig*) sheep."

therewith I also must bow down to him whilst he
shall have his will thereof." Quoth the Kaim-makam,
" O sensible words! but we must seek and find for
ourselves a man who shall be agreeable and trustworthy;" presently adding, " O woman, we will not
give the coynte of thy mother in marriage to some
stranger, lest he trouble thee and trouble me also;
so let us bestow this boon upon our own syce."
Replied the wife of her craft and cursedness, " Haply,
O my lord, the horsekeeper will befit us not;" yet
the while she had set her heart upon him. Rejoined
the Kaim-makam, her husband, " If so it be that he
have shown thee want of respect we will surely
relieve him his lot." But after so speaking he said
a second time, " 'Tis better, that we give the coynte
of thy mother to the syce;" and she retorted, " Well
and good! but do thou oblige him that he keep strait
watch upon himself." Hereat the man summoned his
servant before him, and said to him, " Hear me, O
syce; verily the mother of my wife to her hath
bequeathed her coynte, and 'tis our intent to bestow
it upon thee in lawful wedlock; yet beware lest thou
draw near that which is our own property." The
horsekeeper answered, " No, O my lord, I never will."
Now after they arrived at that agreement concerning
the matter in question, whenever the wife waxed hot
with heat of lust, she would send for the syce and
take him and repair with him, he and she, to a place
of privacy within the Harem, whilst her mate remained
sitting thoroughly satisfied; and they would enjoy
themselves to the uttermost, after which the twain
would come forth together. And the Kaim-makam

never ceased saying on such occasions, " Beware, O
Syce, lest thou poach upon that which is my property ; "
and at such times the wife would exclaim, " By Allah ;
O my lord, he is a true man and a trusty." So they
continued for a while ¹) in the enjoyment of their
lust and this was equally pleasurable to the husband and wife and the lover. Now when the Emir
heard this tale from the Butcher, he began laughing
until he fell upon his back and anon he said to him,
" Wend thy ways about thine own work;" so the
Flesher went forth from him not knowing what he
should do in his garb of gaberdine and bonnet. Hereupon the woman arose, and going to the fourth closet,
threw it open, and summoned and led the Trader-man
by the hand, and set him before her husband, who
looked hard at him in his droll's dress, and recognized
him, and was convinced that he was his neighbour.
So he said, " Oh, Such-an-one! Thou art our neighbour,
and never did we suspect that thou wouldst strive to
seduce our Harim ²) ; nay rather did we expect thee

---

¹) In text this ends the tale.

²) In text " Wa lá huwa 'ashamná min-ka talkash'ata
Harimi-ná." " Ashama ", lit = he greeded for; and Lakasha " =
he conversed with. There is no need to change the " talkas "
of the text into " talkash." " Lakasa " is one of the words
called " zidd," *i.e.* with opposite meanings; it can signify " to
incline passionately towards, " or " to loath with abhorrence."
As the noun " Laks " means " itch " the sentence might perhaps
be translated: " that thou hadst an itching after our Harím."
What would lead me to prefer the reading of the M.S. is that
the verb is construed with the preposition " ata " = upon,
towards, for; while " lokash," to converse, is followed by
" ma' " = with.

to keep watch and ward over us and fend off from us all evil [1]). Now, by Allah, those whom we have dismissed wrought us no foul wrong, even as thou wroughtest us in this affair; for thou at all events art our neighbour. Thou deservest in this matter that I slay thee out of hand, but Default cometh not save from the Defaulter; therefore I will do thee no harm at all, as did I with thy fellows.

THE DEVOUT TRAY-MAKER AND HIS WIFE

There was once among the children of Israel, a man of the worthiest, who was strenuous in the service of his Lord, and abstained from things worldly, and drove them away from his heart. He had a wife who was a helpmate meet for him, and who was at all times obedient to him.

They earned their living by making trays [2]) and fans, whereat they wrought all through the light hours; and, at nightfall the man went out into the streets and highways seeking a buyer for what they made. They were wont to fast continually by day [3]),

---

[1]) Such was the bounden duty of a good neighbour.

[2]) Arab. "Abtak"; these trays are made of rushes, and the fans of palm-leaves or tail-feathers.

[3]) Except on the two great festivals when fasting is forbidden. The only religion which has shown common sense in this matter is that of Guebres or Parsis: they consider fasting neither meritorious nor lawful; and they honour Hormuzd by good living "because it keeps the soul stronger." Yet even they have their food superstition e.g. in Gate IV°. xxiv; "Beware of sin, specially on the day thou eatest flesh, for flesh is the diet of Ahrimàn." And in India the Guebres have copied the Hindus in not slaughtering horned cattle for the table.

and one morning they arose fasting, and worked at
their craft till the light failed them, when the man
went forth, according to custom, to find purchasers
for his wares, and fared on until he came to the
house of a certain man of wealth, one of the sons
of this world, high in rank and dignity. Now the
traymaker was fair of face and comely of form, and
the wife of the master of the house saw him and
fell in love with him, and her heart inclined to him
with exceeding inclination; so, her husband being
absent, she called her handmaid and said to her,
" Contrive to bring yonder man to us ". Accordingly
the maid went out to him, and called him and stopped
him as though she would buy what he held in hand,
and asked him : " Come in ; my lady hath a mind to
buy some of thy wares, after she has tried and looked
at them. " The man thought she spoke truly, and
seeing no harm in this, entered and sat down as she
bade him ; and she shut the door upon him.

Whereupon her mistress came out of her room, and
taking him by the gaberdine ¹), drew him within, and
said, " How long shall I seek union of thee ? Verily
my patience is at end on thy account. See now
the place is perfumed and provisions prepared, and
the Householder is absent this night, and I give to
thee my person without reserve. I, whose favours
kings and captains and men of fortune have sought
this long while, but I have regarded none of them. "
And she went on talking thus to him, whilst he

----

¹) Arab. *"Jalldbiyah"*. a large-sleeved Robe of coarse stuff
worn by the poor.

raised not his eyes from the ground, for shame before Allah Almighty, and fear of the pains and penalties of His punishment; even as saith the poet:

Twixt me and riding many a noble dame,
Was nought but shame which kept me chaste and pure.
My shame was cure to her; but haply were,
Shame to depart, she ne'er had known a cure.

The man strove to free himself from her, but could not; so he said to her, "I want one thing of thee." She asked, "What is that?" and he answered, "I wish for pure water, and that I may carry it to the highest place of thy house, and do somewhat therewith, and cleanse myself of an impurity which I may not disclose to thee". Quoth she, "The house is large, and hath closets and corners and privies at command."

But he replied; "I want nothing but to be at a height." So she said to her slave girl, "Carry him up to the belvedere on the house terrace;" accordingly the maid took him up to the very top, and, giving him a vessel of water, went down and left him. Then he made the ablution and prayed a two-bow prayer; after which he looked at the ground, thinking to throw himself down, but seeing it afar off, feared to be dashed to pieces by the fall [1]). Then he bethought him of his disobedience to Allah, and the consequences of his sin; so it became a light matter to him to offer his life up, and shed his

---

[1]) His fear was that his body might be mutilated by the fall.

blood; and he said, " O my God and my Lord, Thou seest that which is fallen to me; neither is my case hidden from Thee. Thou indeed over all things art Omnipotent, and the tongue of my case reciteth and saith:

> I show my heart and thoughts to Thee, and Thou
>   Alone my secret's secrecy canst know.
> If I address Thee, fain I cry aloud;
> Or if I'm mute, my signs for speech I show.
> O Thou to whom no second be conjoined!
> A wretched lover seeks Thee in his woe.
> I have a hope my thoughts as true confirm;
> And heart that fainteth as right well canst trow.
>   To lavish life is hardest thing that be,
>   Yet easy as Thou bid me life forego;
> But, as it be Thy will to save me from stour,
> Thou, O my Hope, to work this work hast power!

Then the man cast himself down from the belvedere. But Allah sent an angel, who bore him upon his wings, and brought him down to the ground, whole and without hurt or harm. Now when he found himself safe on the ground, he thanked and praised Allah (to whom belong Majesty and Might)! for his merciful protection of his person and his chastity; and he went straight to his wife who had long expected him, and he came empty-handed. Then seeing him, she asked him why he had tarried, and what was come of that he had taken with him, and why he returned empty-handed; whereupon he told her of the temptation which had befallen him, and she said, " Alhamdolillah! praised be God for delivering thee from seduction, and intervening between thee and such calamity! " Then

she added, " O man, the neighbours use to see us
light our oven every night; and if they see us fireless
this night, they will know that we are destitute.
Now it behoveth, in gratitude to Allah, that we hide
our destitution, and conjoin the fast of this evening
to that of the past, and continue it for the sake of
Allah Almighty. " So she rose, and, filling the oven
with wood, lighted it, to baffle the curiosity of her
women-neighbours, reciting these couplets:

Now I indeed will hide desire and all repine;
And light up this fire that neighbours see no sign;
Accept I what befals by order of my Lord;
Haply He too accepts this humble act of mine.

After the good wife had lit the fire to baffle the
curiosity of her women-neighbours, she and her husband
made the Wuzu-ablution and stood up to pray, when,
behold, one of the neighbour's wives came and asked
leave to take a firebrand from the oven. "Do what
thou wilt with the oven, " answered they; but when
she came to the fire, she cried out, saying, "Ho, such
an one (to the traymaker's wife) take up thy bread
ere it burn!" Quoth the wife to her husband, "Hearest
thou what she saith?" Quoth he, " Go and look. "
So she went up to the oven, and behold, it was full
of fine bread and white. She took up the scones and
carried them to her husband, thanking Allah (to whom
belong Majesty and Might) for his abounding good
and great bounty; and they ate of the bread and
water and praised the Almighty. Then said the
woman to her husband, " Come let us pray to Allah
the most Highest, so haply he may vouchsafe us

what shall enable us to dispense with the weariness
of working for daily bread, and devote ourselves wholly
to worshipping and obeying Him." The man rose
in assent and prayed, whilst his wife said, " Amen,"
to his prayer, when the roof clove in sunder and
down fell a ruby, which lit the house with light.

Hereat they redoubled in praise and thanksgiving
to Allah, praying what the Almighty willed [1]), and
rejoiced at the ruby with great joy. And the night
being far spent, they lay down to sleep, and the
woman dreamed that she entered Paradise, and saw
therein many chairs ranged and stools set in rows.
She asked what the seats were, and it was answered
her, " These are the chairs of the prophets ; and those
are the stools of the righteous and pious."

Quoth she, " Which is the stool of my husband,
such an one? " and it was said to her, " It is this."
So she looked, and seeing a hole in its side, asked "What
may be this hole?" and the reply came, " It is the
place of the ruby that dropped upon you from your
house-roof." Thereupon she awoke, weeping and
bemoaning the defect in her husband's stool among
the seats of the Righteous; so she told him the
dream, and said to him, "Pray Allah, O man, that
this Ruby return to its place ; for endurance of hunger
and poverty during our few days here were easier
than a hole in thy chair among the just in Paradise " [2]).

---

[1]) This phrase means "Offering up many and many a prayer".

[2]) A Saying of Mohammed is recorded "Alfakru fakhri
(poverty is my pride!) intelligible in a man who never wanted
for any thing.

Here he is diametrically opposed to Ali who honestly abused

Accordingly, he prayed to his Lord, and lo! the ruby flew up to the roof and away whilst they looked at it. And they ceased not from their poverty and their piety till they went to the presence of Allah, to whom be Honour and Glory!

---

poverty; and the Prophet seems to have borrowed from Christendom, whose "Lazarus and Dives" shows a man sent to Hell because he enjoyed a very modified Heaven in this life, and which suggested that one of man's greatest miseries is an ecclesiastical virtue—"Holy Poverty"—represented in the Church as a bride young and lovely. If a "rich man can hardly enter the kingdom", what must it be with a poor man whose conditions are far more unfavourable? Going to the extreme, we may say that Poverty is the root of all evil, and the more so as it curtails man's power of benefiting others. Practically I can observe that those who preach and praise it the most, practise it the least willingly; the ecclesiastic has always some special reasons, a church or a school is wanted; but not the less he wishes for more money. In Syria, this Holy Poverty leads to strange abuses. At Bayrut, I recognised in most impudent beggars well-to-do peasants from the Kasrawàn district, and presently found out that whilst their fields were under snow they came down to the coast, enjoyed a genial climate, and lived on alms. When I asked them if they were not ashamed to beg, they asked me if I was ashamed of following in the footsteps of the Saviour and Apostles. How much wiser was Zoroaster who found in the Supreme Paradise (Minuwàn-Minu) "many persons, rich in gold and silver who had worshipped the Lord and had been grateful to him."

Dabistan, I 265).

THE MOTHER'S MARRIAGE-ADVICE

It is related—and Allah is All-knowing, All-wise [1])—
that a mother was about to marry her daughter, a
girl famous amongst all the tribes of the Arabs for
her surpassing beauty—her face was oval-shaped!
her form upright and perfect; her buttocks swung
from side to side, as she walked, like the balancing
of a poplar-tree trembling in the evening-breeze; her
eyes were coal-black, and the light of a Virgin's desire
shone from beneath her half-closed lids; firm as a rock
on a billowy sea-shore her breasts stood out bold
and prominent above her navel—may Allah have
mercy on her, the fairest of his creatures, fashioned
in the likeness of the peerless Houris, reserved for
true Believers [2])—and underneath it, down below,
nestling between two ivory-columned thighs, hid
Something wonderful and of astonishing stoutness,
puffed-up proudly, looking out from behind her flowing
skirts like the head of a patient calf awaiting pas-
turage—And the mother spake to her daughter coun-
selling [3]) her this counsel—quoth she to her:—" O

---

[1]) A formula employed when the Story-teller is not quite
sure of his facts, as though he should say, " and God alone
knows whether it be true or not."

[2]) See note as to the Kuranic doctrine of the Houris, page 72.
It must in fairness be stated that many Moslems maintain
that these references to sensual joys should be read in a
spiritual light, as, for instance, Christian divines interpret the
lusty realism of " *Solomon's Song.*"

[3]) This is a point to be noted. In Europe, mothers are, as
a rule, very chary about giving their marriageable daughters
advice as to the functions of the marriage state, and what

daughter mine! ward off from thyself all affliction of misfortune and hearken to my saying, and in thus wise act with the men who shall lie with thee and love thee. For I counsel thee, O my dear Daughter! a counsel; in thy heart therefore treasure it up, and to remember it well be careful, and, on every night that thou liest with man, of its diligent practice be wareful. Surpassing shall it make thee above all other women of similar rank and station, and spread abroad 'mong men, like a sweet perfume, the glory of thy reputation." Thereupon, the girl exclaimed to her mother, her curiosity roused to the highest pitch:—" By God! out and tell me what this counsel is that thou speakest of." Said she then to her:—" O daughter mine, listen to what I say. When thy husband shall draw near to thee, and be stretched out along by thy side, then move with gracefulness, changing and turning about with decency and becomingness, and to him manifest only innocent unguardedness, and fatigue-weariness, and sweet lovesighing of abandoned languidness. So will his heart be inclined towards thee and his love flame forth. When thou seest this, increase thy playfulness with him before his lance doth enter thee or give over its upswelling, until strong-swollen, stiff and warm 'tween

---

they may have to confront in fulfilling their mission of maternity; such squeamishness too often gives rise to a rude disillusioning, the reverse, to many natures, of pleasant, and is the frequent fore-runner of disgust, life-long disappointment, and divorce. Eastern matrons envisage the subject from a standpoint at once practical and natural. From whom should such instruction come if not from the mother?

him and thee breaks forth in might the fierceness of
the storm." [1])   Then she recited, saying:

O Daughter mine! thy Wooers long to leave thee never durst
So that thou manifest them nor repulsion and disgust,
And when thy lover comes to thee fired mad with passion's
[thirst,
Soften him thy heart for fear he may depart or tire to thrust;
Discover him thy bosom and twin high-swelling breasts,
Until thy Bower of bliss be seen, and thy buttocks are undrest [2]),
Then sigh thy full and give forth cries of love-joyed tenderness
So shall men seek no other fire than that of thy recess;
And when they hear the happy cries of thy love-gentleness
Upon Allah will they call that she who bore thee may be
[blessed.

Abù-Bilàl has related to us of the Partner of the
son of the Happy-one, who had it from Long Cross-
grained heir of the Flamer, who received it from
Good-for-Nothing the offspring of Horny-Head son
of Mournful Face [3]) that he laid it down in his work
on Definitions and Technical terms, ' that the real
lover never can be satisfied by mere Kissing and
Cuddling unless it leadeth to Clipping and Climbing
and Coynting.'   On the basis of this rule therefore,
ceased not the mother to counsel her daughter saying:
" When thy Lord shall have come between thy legs

---

[1]) Arab. *hatta yahsul beinak wa beinahi al-heiyaj* = until the
storm rage between thee and between him.

[2]) Arab. *hatta yubeiyin al-kuss w-al-òwraki* i. e. until slit (the
rudest word) and backsides are manifest mother-nude.

[3]) These names are given in a spirit of pleasantry to prepare
the mind for what follows.   In Arabic they run into rhymed
prose.

then prevent him not from passing through the rosy
portals of thy vulva, and redouble for his delight thy
amorous groaning and happy crying and soft caressing.
For know, my Dear! that man's dormant prizzle puts
on tougher gristle, and starts up excitedly at woman's
half-refusal. So show him thy teeth and make pretence
to bite him, then tighten thy close-hold upon him,
and wind arms and legs more securely about him,
thus wilt thou find that his yard will rise stronger
and stronger against thee; and 'tis here thou must
exclaim, " Oh dear! Oh dear! what is this!", doing
with him in the same wise that he shall do with thee,
and failing not to let him see thy gentle love-panting
and delicious heaving and lost condition, whilst with
regular rub and repetition thou workest underneath
him the come-and-go swift motion of soft-limbed
oscillation. Thou must not omit either to lift up
towards him thy middle portion, and direct his hand
upon thy slit, and when thou feelest approach the
time of enjoyment [1]) and thou perceivest that he is
played out, then seize hold of him afresh with both
thy hands, and press him close against thee, and,
giving him a fiery kiss, lay hold upon his weapon
and stroke and slip it up and down, then wipe it,
and stir up anew mutual passion-desire, lest his yard
fall asleep or diminish its fire, and thus shall pleasure's
storm wage high and yet higher as the Sayer hath said:

The veins of Lord Prickle outswell for up-standing,
His proud head erected, like game-cock for cock-fighting;

---

[1]) Arab. *bi-inzâlihi* literally = on his descent (of the sperm)
i. e. the ecstatic moment or "spending."

When out he comes 'tis ever with agility and grace,
But once across the threshold, like a madman storms the
[place;
Leading at first the attack with prudence, but growing
In madness fast the longer lasts the chase,
And with giant-head uplifted, batters hard at love's recess [1]).

In these admonitions concerning Prizzles, the prizzle had in mind and intended by the Author is the prizzle of Egypt the Upper; and of the Coyntes described, the coynte in question is the coynte possessed by the Beauties of Rosetta [2]).

ESOTERIC PHYSIOGNOMY.

Said the Physician, "If the Mouth be large of the woman then must her slit be standing wide-open; but, if only of narrow dimensions, of her notch's tightness 'tis a sure indication [3]).

If the Mouth however be of almond-shape and swollen, the privy parts will surely bear the same proud puffed-up oval conformation [3]).

---

[1]) Arab. *yat'an ras hasháshati*, literally attacks the head of the intestines, or, as it may also be put, the spark or throb of life, i. e. the womb.

[2]) Arab. *Rasheed;* a City of about 16,000 inhabitants not far from Alexandria. It was here the famous Stone was discovered which permitted European scholars to open the mouth of the Egyptian Sphinx, closed for a hundred centuries. Taken by the English and placed in the Brit. Museum

[3]) The Size and Conformation of the facial features as offering points of analogy with the genital organs merits attention. So few things have been written on this delightful and most curious subject that we feel bound to call attention to Belot's

F

If the woman's two Lips be full-fleshed, and form of her sweet mouth the principal proportion, then will the twin shutters of love's chamber-hall be stout and well filled-out and of most voluptuous formation.

If too the colour of her Tongue by nature be strong crimson, then will her reception-room be dry and bereft of that dampness desirable in coition.

If the Nose be curved and of hunch-backed condition; this is a sign that a woman's desire for amorous rollicking with her lord is mixed with moderation.

If the Mouth be long, it is an indication of the development of the coynte, and the smallness of growth thereon of hair.

As to the Hands and Feet these are witnesses that do not lie; let them be full-formed and covered with much flesh, we know from such abundance that the woman's private parts must be of biggish dimensions; nay, exceeding in greatness.

If too, the woman's Visage be bold and severe-looking, besides abounding in flesh, rest assured that in clipping and coynting this one will show a want of patience, and be ravenous for the conflict.

La Bouche de Madame X, a provoking bit of realism. There is no doubt that Sexual emotion plays a large part in moulding the face, witness the massive lips of a Mirabeau and the thin, pinched "mousetrap" of Robespierre. The Latin student should consult old Sinibaldus' *Geneanthropoeia*, (Roma, 1642), where he will find a fascinating chap. (page 198 Lib. II, Tract II) on *Praefervidae, salacisque naturae Physiog. monici caracteres;* a model of clear exposition and acumen. Doctor Schurigius is likewise very outspoken and quaint, and despite the lapse of time, well worthy of heed, in these days of bombastic sciolism.

As to the Eyes, let them be piercing, penetrating, with the Gums and the two Lips always crimson, verily this doth prove that their proprietress lusteth strongly after man's mount, and even searcheth out opportunities of coynting.

When the Colour of the Face is red and the Eyes blue, it is a sign that the woman is the mistress of active-limbed solidity in sexual strife, capable of withstanding the shocks of rude chargers. "

AND ALLAH BE MOST PRAISED
The High-uplifted, the Exalted; it is
He only who is Most-knowing
As to the Right and True;
HE, THE BEGINNING AND THE END
From whom all things Proceed—
To whom all Return—
EVERLASTING SOURCE AND HOME
May His blessing rest upon our Lord Mohammad
And upon his Family and Companion-train.
SO, THUS FAREWELL
AND PEACE!

here end the Stories of Exposition
in the Science of Coition
with Completeness
and Perfection

NOTES
EXPLANATORY AND ILLUSTRATIVE
AND
EXCURSUS

" All these things here collected are not mine,
But divers grapes make but one kind of wine;
So I from many learned authors took
The various matters written in this book;
What's not mine own shall not by me be fathered,
The most part I in many years have gathered."
                                        Pisanus Fraxi.

EXCURSUS

HOLES IN WALLS

est it should seem *invraisemblable* that ladies would permit, or have the idea of permitting, men to have connection with them through *holes* made in walls, and other similar contrivances, we subjoin the following story in further corroboration of the note on page 4. We take it from the "SCENTED GARDEN" of the Shaykh Nafzàwi.

THE STORY OF THE USELESS PRECAUTIONS

It is related that a man had a wife who was endowed with all beauties and perfections; she was like the full moon. He was very jealous, for he knew all the deceits and ways of women. He therefore never left the house without carefully locking the street door and the door of the terrace.

One day his wife asked him, "Why do you do this?" "Because I know your ruses and fashions," said he. "It is not by acting in this way that you will be safe," she said; "for certainly, if a woman has set her heart upon a thing, all precautions are useless." "Well, well!" replied he; "it is always wise to keep the doors locked." She said: "Not at all; the fastenings of the door are of no avail, if a woman once thinks of doing what you mean."

"Well, then," said he, "if you can do it you may!"

As soon as her husband had gone out, the woman mounted to the top of the house, and, through a small hole, which she made in the wall, she looked to see what was going on outside. At that moment a young man was passing by, who, looking up, saw her, and desired to possess her. He said to her: "How can I come to you?" She told him that it could not be done, and that the doors were locked. "How could we get together?" he asked. She answered him: "I shall make a hole in the house door. Be on the watch for my husband when he returns to night, and after he shall have passed in, put your member through the hole, and it shall then meet my vulva, and you can thereupon do my business; in any other way it is impossible."

The young man watched until he had seen the husband return from evening prayer; and, after he had entered the house and locked the door, he went to find the hole made in it, through which, when found, he quickly passed his expectant member. The wife also was on the look out. Her husband had barely got into the house, and was still in the court-yard, when she went to the door, and, appearing to satisfy herself that the door was fast, she rapidly placed, her throbbing vulva to the member, which was dancing attendance through the hole, and seizing it in her hand, introduced it with a thrust into her vagina.

This done, she extinguished the lamp, and, calling to her husband, asked him to bring a light. Quoth he: "Why?" "Because," said she, "I have dropped a trinket and cannot find it." He then came with a lamp. The member of the young man was still in her vulva and at that moment ejaculating. "Where did you drop your trinket?" asked the husband. "It is here!" she exclaimed, drawing back quickly, and leaving the surprised verge of her lover there, naked and covered with sperm.

At this sight the husband fell to the ground with rage. When he was up again, the wife said to him; "Well! and those precautions?" "God grant me repentance!" he replied.

After this, appreciate the Deceits of Women, and what they are capable of.

Women have such a number of ruses at their disposal that they cannot be counted. They would succeed in making an elephant mount upon the back of an ant, and do work there. How detestable in their doings God has made them!

---

¹) For curious information as to the size and shape of the membrum virile we refer the reader to *The Old Man Young Again* (Vol. I, pages 102 to 114 inclusive, and 157 to 176, the latter treating of the "Lengthening and Thickening of the Yard"); and to *The Ethnology* of *the Sixth Sense;* and *Untrodden Fields of Anthropology*. In these three works the subject *inter alia* is practically exhausted, the enormous research and industry of the authors having laid all books, countries, and languages under contribution.

THE INCOMPLETE MEMORANDUM BOOK [1]).

After wasting his youth-time in debauchery, a certain merchant took a wife, and soon his jealousy became proverbial. The remembrance of his own former intrigues did not tend to reassure him as to the fate of husbands, and this reflection was constantly brought to his mind by the perusal of a memorandum-book, in which he had jotted down as they occurred, all the tricks which women whom he had seduced had, he knew, practised on their fathers, brothers, and husbands. Whenever his wife asked permission to go out for any purpose, he would answer that he must first consult his memoranda. Then he would search through the book, and invariably arrived at the conclusion that he had better accompany her to see if she told the truth. So in the end he followed her everywhere, and never lost sight of her when she was out of doors.

Such suspicions were not at all to his wife's taste, besides which she once had a chance of reading the book on the quiet, and learned there what excesses her old husband had committed in his youth. As may be imagined, she devoured with avidity these pages full of love adventures, and the perusal raised in her mind ideas which were not likely to calm down her newly-born desire for pleasure.

After having studied the matter in her own mind, she resolved to find out a plan by which she might,

---

[1]) We have translated this analogous and charming story from a Turkish M.S. in our possession.

at least once, enjoy the caresses of a young gallant who had wanted to marry her, but who had been regarded by her parents as an unsuitable match. She therefore carefully laid her plans, with the assistance of a servant who was devoted to her.

One day then,—the young man having been duly apprised of her plan.—she went to the bath, followed by her husband, who carried the towels and linen required for her ablutions. Suddenly, and precisely in the street where her lover lived. and close to his house, her foot tripped, as though by accident, against a stone, and she fell at full length in the mud. She got up with her clothes all soiled, and noticed that the door of her lover's house was open, and that there was no one to be seen in the vestibule.

"Let me go in here for a minute," she said to her husband, and wipe myself clean."

"Very good," he replied, "take these towels and get off the worst of the mud; but when you push to the door I will hold your cloak."

This was done: the lady entered, pushed to the door, but without closing it, and left outside the tail of her cloak, which her husband grasped; but he could not perceive that the lover, who was of a spare build, was hidden behind the door. The young man lost no time, but placed his mistress against the wall, pulled up her clothes, lugged out "lord Pharaoh," and covered his head with the hairy crown proper for a monarch, and to make him clean and of a good colour, rubbed it in and out briskly. The shaking of the cloak appeared to the husband the natural effects of the movements made by his chaste spouse in cleaning herself. When the business was over, the lady made haste to rub off some of the stains on her garments, then she re-opened the door, and thus hid her lover from her husband's sight, and followed her good man to the bath, which she now needed more than ever, and to which she owed such a fortunate chance.

In the evening, after they had returned home, she took advantage of the moment when her husband was absorbed as usual in reading the details of his experiences to say:

"My dear friend, I am not ignorant of the contents of that volume, for I have read it without your knowledge, but it is incomplete. To add the finishing touch to a work which may one day make you celebrated, you should add this. 'When going to the bath, and whilst her husband held her cloak, a woman was rogered by her lover, who was concealed behind a door'. *It is the more necessary that the story should be included as it happens to be true.*"

THE CRAFT OF WOMEN

Is further so well displayed in the following story as not inappropriately to be told in conjunction with the preceding. We extract it from the *fourth* volume of R. F. Burton's "*Supplemental Nights*" (page 368) who took it from the Turkish text given in a privately-printed book (M. E. J. W. Gibb's "Forty Viziers.")

THE MAN WITH THE TWO YARDS

" There was of old time a tailor, and he had a fair
wife. One day this woman sent her slave-girl to the
carder's to get some cotton teased. The slave-girl
went to the carder's shop and gave him cotton for
a gown to get teased. The carder while teasing the
cotton displayed his *yard* to the slave girl. She
blushed and passed to his other side. As she thus
turned round the carder displayed his yard on that
side also. Thus the slave girl saw it on that side
too. And she went and said to her mistress, " Yon
carder to whom I went has two yards." The lady
said to her: " Go and say to yon carder, 'my Mistress
wishes thee; come at night.' " So the slave-girl went
and said this to the carder. As soon as it was night,
the carder went to that place and waited. The woman
went out and met the carder, and said, " Come and
have to do with me while I am lying by my husband."
When it was midnight, the carder came and woke
the woman. The woman lay conveniently, and the
carder fell to work. She felt that the yard which
entered her was but one, and said, " Ah my soul,
carder, at it with both of them." While she was
softly speaking her husband awaked and asked, " What
means thy saying, '*At it with both of them*'?" He
stretched out his hand to his wife's kaze and the
carder's yard came into it. The carder drew himself
back and his yard slipped out of the fellow's hand,
and he made shift to get away. The fellow said:
" Out on thee, wife, what meant that saying of thine,
'*At it with both of them*'?" The woman said: " O

husband, I saw in my dream that thou wast fallen into the sea and wast swimming with one hand and crying out, "Help! I am drowning!" I shouted to thee from the shore, 'At it with both of them,' and thou begannest to swim with both thy hands." Then the husband said: "Wife, I too know that I was in the sea from this that a wet fish came into my hand and then slipped out and escaped; thou speakest truly." And he loved his wife more than before [1]).

THE FIERCENESS OF WOMEN'S DESIRE

This subject has been much debated at various times, and still forms the topic of conversation of many an after-dinner smoke. We do not remember to have seen any serious work upon the matter, although in his " *Tableau de l'Amour Conjugal* " [2]), Nicolas Venette has devoted a chapter to the discussion of the question. " *Qui est le plus amoureux de*

---

[1]) Compare rollicking old Brantôme *Vie des Dames Galantes* (Lives of Fair and Pleasant Ladies) for a passage which marvellously resembles the Arab tale:

Quelle humeur de femme! si bien qu'on dit qu'ayant une fois vu par la fenêtre de son château, qui disait sur la rue, un grand cordonnier, étrangement proportionné, pisser contre la muraille dudit château, elle eut envie d'une si belle et grande proportion, et, de peur de gâter son fruit pour son envie, elle lui manda par un page de la venir trouver en une allée secrète de son parc, où elle s'était retirée, et là elle se prostitutia à lui en telle façon qu'elle engrossa.

[2]) Two volumes, (Paris, 1812), published in English under the title: *Pleasures of the Marriage Bed*, and limited to 250 copies (numbered), Paris, 1898.

l'homme ou de la femme?" wherein he arrives at the
conclusion that women are *by nature* more lascivious
than men. He proves his thesis by a show of argument fairly well-sustained. He lays great stress on
the livelier imagination of woman, and the leisure
that her position in the social economy affords her,
as conducing to ideas and desires little short of
ungovernable. Certain it is that in Europe, as in
the Orient, the checks upon any outbreak of sexual
passion are too stringent to be lightly disregarded,
and any manifestation of lasciviousness would be
followed by serious consequences to the woman herself. Venette makes a point here:—"Personne ne
nie qu'elles ne soient plus humides que nous; leur
beauté et leurs règles en sont des remarques évidentes.
C'est leur tempérament qui leur fournit plus de semence
qu'à nous, et qui les expose souvent aux vapeurs et
à la fureur; car si leur semence se corrompt, ces
maladies en sont cause, ainsi qu'il arriva il n'y a pas
longtemps aux vierges de Loudun, selon la pensée de
Sennert et de Duncan."

In foot-note [1]) we give a longer extract from this

---

[1]) The matrix and the testicles are those parts situated
within the bodies of women, which are not, as are ours,
exposed to the injuries of cold air which extinguishes our
flame; we also observe that in animals the genital parts that
are hidden are more lascivious than the others. It is in order
to procure room for the matrix, that Nature has formed women
with the sides wide apart and high hips, that it has given
to them big buttocks and fleshy thighs; whereas men have
the upper parts of their bodies larger and thicker than the
lower parts, heat having dilated the one and fortified the others.
After all, if I might be allowed to join experience to reason,

curious and interesting writer, who proceeds soberly with the question on a physiological as well as a historical basis. We may remark that *History* can

---

1 would say that we have but too many examples in the pagan writers, and even in the Holy Scriptures, which it is unneccessary to reproduce here. Nectimena and Valeria both of them sought for the caresses of their own father; Agrippina prostituted herself to her son; Julia received amorous pleasures from the emperor Caracalla, her son-in-law, who afterwards married her; Semiramis abandoned herself to an infinite number of men. During the time of Pope Pius V, a Tuscan girl got herself covered by a dog, and at the present day most of the girls in Egypt couple with he-goats, and I doubt much whether the satyr that was brought before Sylla, when he was passing through Macedonia, was not rather the mark of lasciviousness of a woman than that of a man. I do not speak here of the two Faustinas nor of the two Joans of Naples: it is known that these females were impure and lascivious from their infancy, and that afterwards they spared nothing thoroughly to divert themselves with men; and never would the Councils of Eliberia and of Neocesarea have issued decrees against women, if they had not been found to be lascivious. The first of these decrees orders married ecclesiastics to repudiate their wives when the conduct of the latter is loose, otherwise it debars them from communion *in articulo mortis;* the second forbids the conferring of holy orders on the candidate whose wife is an adulteress, unless he repudiates her.

All other women were of a different temperament from that of Berenice, who, according to Josephus, separated from her husband because he used to caress her over much. As a fact, an amorous person is so in every sort of condition; be she girl or woman, married or a widow, barren or fruitful, empty or full, all that does not prevent her from being more lascivious than man.

Finally, we may add to that the authority of the theologians and of the jurisconsults. The first ingenuously admit that the

be made to prove almost *any* point, and should be eyed with caution askance.

More modern Davenport appears to entertain Venette's opinion. He says towards the end of his article on " Generation ":

---

passion of love is more excusable in women than in men because, they add, they are more liable to it, and the second for the same reason, punish with death the adulterer, but do not allow that a woman should be deprived of live for having fallen into the same disorder; they are satisfied with causing her to be whipped, to have her hair cut off, and herself shut up in a convent.

We must therefore conclude from all this, that women are far more lascivious and amorous than men. And if it were not that fear and the sentiment of honour restrain them more often from the violence of their passions, there are but very few that would not succumb; or to stop us or to engage, they would do for us what we are accustomed to do for them. As for myself, I every day admire the force of those handsome young girls who resist bravely, their combats astonish me, but their victories fill me with delight; everywhere they defend themselves valiantly, and are far more successful in love than were Alexander or Cæsar in victories. They often achieve conquest before having even fought. But, at last, one day this natural passion will assert its sway; so true is the idea set forth in the lines of Alciat:—

Qu'aisément l'amoureux poison
S'introduit dans le cœur d'une jeune pucelle,
Et qu'une mère avec raison
Fait, pour l'en garantir, une garde fidelle.
D'un ennemi qui plaît, l'abord est dangereux;
Un sage surveillant a peu de deux bons yeux
Pour être toujours en défense;
Argus en avait cent, et il découvrait tout;
Cependant, de sa vigilance,
Cupidon sut venir à bout.

"The Rabbis, so deeply interested in the preservation of *God's chosen people*, enacted a kind of *sumptuary law* to prevent the waste of semen. Thus, a peasant was restricted to enjoying his wife *once* a week; a tradesman or carrier to once a month; a sailor to twice a year; a man of letters to once in two years. "It is pretty evident," remarks our author, "that the *ladies* had no finger in this pie, for, if such had been the case, the allotment would certainly have been much more liberal."

It is impossible to regulate coition by decrees however wise; Human Passion is not to be controlled by Acts of Parliament. Nothing can be more personal. The *fit* will know how to govern their desires; the *unfit* must destroy themselves. Excess of passion is non-producing.

Davenport continues: "The amorous desires of women are not under such control as those of our sex, otherwise there would have been no necessity for the Lithuanian noble of bygone days to employ a coadjutor. The truth is, women very rarely feel exhausted by this amorous sport, even when they have suffered for a long time the vigorous assaults of many men in succession. Witness the libidinous Messalina, and the lecherous Cleopatra. The former, having taken the name of Lysisca, a noted Roman prostitute, when she frequented the brothels of the eternal city for the purpose of indulging her lust, surpassed by twenty-five *ictus* in less than twenty hours, the above-named celebrated courtezan:

> Ausa Palatino tegetem præ ferre cubili
> Sumere nocturnos meretrix Augusta cucullos

Linquebat comite ancillâ non amplius unâ
Et nigrum flavo crinem abscondente galero
Intravit calidum veteri centone lupanar
Et cellam vacuam atque suam; tunc nuda papillis
Constitit auratis, titulom, mentita et Lyciscae. [1])
(*Juvenal, Satire* VI).

While Cleopatra, if we can credit the letter of Marc Antony, one of her lovers, sustained the amorous efforts, during one night, of one hundred and six men, without evincing the slightest fatigue."

In another part of the same essay Davenport sensibly observes: "Seneca has remarked that man is never so great a boaster as in love matters, or when, for the purpose of being admired, he brags of exploits which he has never achieved. Most men appear as heroes when *speaking* of love, but show the white feather when *called up to the scratch*. It is not enough to kiss and toy with a woman, much more is required to prove his manhood, and that he is able to beget one of his own kind.

There have been men of so hot a temperament as to have enjoyed several women, many nights in succession, but the result has been that of having weakened themselves to such a degree that their semen lost all its fecundating virtue, and that their sexual parts refused to obey their orders. The Emperor Nero, according to Petronius Arbiter, was not the only one who wanted vigour and courage when locked in the arms of the lovely Poppœa. It must, however,

---

[1]) See Vol. II, *Untrodden Fields of Anthropology* concerning " White Messalinas."

be remarked that such accounts as those given by Crucius and Clemens, of Alexandria, are absurd. The former relates as a fact, that a serving man got ten servant girls with child in one night, and the latter tells us that Hercules, during twelve or fourteen hours that he lay with fifty Athenian girls, got them all with child, so that at the end of nine months each gave birth to a bouncing boy. But such accounts as these are evidently mere fables. In fact, after the fifth or sixth round of an amorous conflict, nothing more is discharged but a crude aqueous humour, and sometimes blood, instead of a rich and natural semen" [1]).

THE PROSTITUTE AND SOLDIERS

Debay mentions that Colonel Pol... recorded the incident of a prostitute kidnapped by the soldiers, and, carried off to the guard-room, she put on their mettle the thirty men there stationed on duty, without in the least appearing to suffer fatigue. Bertrand Rival cites the case of a beautiful and virtuous girl of Maëstricht, who, during the Revolutionary times of the last century, was forced to submit her person to the rude assaults of twenty-eight hussars. The after-effects of this riotous orgy was an irritation of the vagina, and several scratches which became cured in a few days. Our doctor sagely concludes that, from facts such as these, it results that the woman is capable of resisting

[1]) *Curiositates Eroticæ Physiologiæ; or Tabooed Subjects freely treated.*   Lond. 1875 (Privately printed).

for a longer time than the man the wear and tear of these erotic combats, and that it can never be anything but downright foolery and imprudence for the latter to attempt physically to demonstrate the contrary [1]).

With all this, we are in danger of losing sight of the passionateness of the *Orientale*, with whom, above all, our excursus is chiefly concerned. We will therefore conclude with a note from Burton, one of the best authorities on the subject, due to the insight gained from his immense experience of, and contact with, the inner life of various eastern peoples.

In the *Tale of Kamar al-Zaman* he translates:

"Answer me, O my beloved, and tell me thy name, for indeed thou hast ravished my wit! And during all this time he abode drowned in sleep, and answered her not a word, and Princess Budur sighed and said, "Alas! Alas! why art thou so proud and self-satisfied?" Then she shook him, and turning his hand over, saw her seal ring on his little finger, whereat she cried a loud cry, and followed it with a sigh of passion and said, "Alack! Alack! By Allah, thou art my beloved and thou lovest me! Yet thou seemest to turn thee away from me out of coquetry, for all, O my darling, thou camest to me whilst I was asleep and knew not what thou didst with me, and tookest my seal ring; and yet I will not pull it off thy finger.

So saying, she opened the bosom of his shirt, and bent over him and kissed him, and put forth her hand to him, seeking somewhat that she might take as a

---

[1]) *Hygiène et Physiologie du Mariage.* Paris, 1856.

token, but found nothing. Then she thrust her hand into his breast and, because of the smoothness of his body it slipped down to his waist, and thence to his navel and thence to his yard, whereupon her heart ached and her vitals quivered, and lust was sore upon her, *for that the desire of woman is fiercer than the desire of man*, and she was ashamed of her own shamelessness."

This extract we have given rather fully because it is not easy to grasp the situation when a quotation is over-abridged. Following are the remarks that the Author of the *"Pilgrimage to Mecca"* makes upon the action of the Arabian *belle*.

"This tenet of the universal East is at once fact and unfact. As a generalism asserting that women's passion is ten times greater than man's (Pilgrimage, II. 282), it is unfact. The world shows that while women have more philoprogenitiveness, men have more amativeness; otherwise the latter would not propose, and would nurse the doll and baby. Fact, however, in lowlying lands, like Persian Mazanderan versus the Plateau; Indian Malabar compared with Marathaland; California as opposed to Utah, and especially Egypt contrasted with Arabia. In these hot damp climates, the venereal requirements and reproductive powers of the female greatly exceed those of the male; and hence the dissoluteness of morals would be phenomenal were it not obviated by seclusion, the sabre, and the revolver. In cold-dry or hot-dry mountainous lands the reverse is the case; hence polygamy there prevails, whilst the low countries require polyandry in either form, legal or illegal (*i. e.* prostitution). I have discussed this curious point of "geographical morality" (for all morality is, like conscience, both geographical and chronological), a subject so interesting to the law-giver, the student of ethics and the anthropologist, in the "City of the Saints." But strange and unpleasant truths progress slowly, especially in England." [1])

EXTRACT FROM THE SCENTED GARDEN
Of the Shaykh Nafzàwih (XVI century)

The following two stories, much abridged, and borrowed from the "Scented Garden Man's Heart to Gladden", (by the Shaykh Nafzàwih), otherwise called in Arabic: "*Raudhát al-'Atir fi-Nuzat il-Khatir*", show the *other* side of the story recounted on page 112.

THE COURT JESTER'S GOLDEN ROBE

The man who deserves favours is, in the eyes of women, the one who is anxious to please them. He

---

[1]) Buckle in his very able "*History of Civilization in England*" gives incidentally large support to Burton's position by his doctrine of the influence of Climate on the condition of the human race, maintaining that the civilization of Europe is *governed* by climate. The student, however, will nowhere find the subject more exhaustively discussed than in Herbert Spencer's "*The Induction of Ethics*"; an author who will be better appreciated in fifty years than he is by the present money-grubbing generation.

G. P. Marsh also treats very ably this fascinating study in "The Earth as Modified by Human Action."

must be of good presence, excel in beauty those around him, be of good shape and well-formed proportions, true and sincere in his speech with women; he must likewise be generous and brave, not vainglorious, and pleasant in conversation.

A slave to his promise, he must always keep his word, ever speak the truth, and do what he has said.

The man who boasts of his relations with women, of their acquaintance and good will to him, is a dastard. He will be spoken of in the next chapter.

There is a story that once there lived a king named All-Mamoun [1]) who had a court fool of the name of Bahloul [2]), who amused the princes and Vizirs.

One day this buffoon appeared before the King, who was amusing himself. The King bade him sit down, and then asked him, turning away. "Why hast thou come, O son of a bad woman?"

Bahloul answered "I have come to see what has come to our Lord, whom may God make victorious."

"And what has come to thee?" replied the King, "and how art thou getting on with thy new and with

---

[1]) Abdallah ben Mamoun, one of the sons of Haroun al-Rashid. Having for a long time made war upon his brother al-Amin for the empire, and the latter having been vanquished and killed in a battle near Baghdad, Al Mamoun was unanimously proclaimed Khalifah in the year 178 of the Hegira. He was one of the most distinguished Abyssinian rulers with respect to science, wisdom, and goodness.

[2]) The word Bahloul, of Persian origin, signifies a man that laughs, derides; a knave, or sort of Court-fool. They were, more often than not, men of considerable learning, wit, and penetration, and, by a long way, not so foolish as their title.

thy old wife?" For Bahloul, not content with one wife, had married a second one.

"I am not too happy," he answered, "neither with the old one, nor with the new one; and moreover poverty overpowers me."

The King said, "Can you recite any verses on this subject?"

The buffoon having answered in the affirmative, Mamoun commanded him to recite those he knew, and Bahloul began as follows:

"While Misery torments, and Poverty grips me in chains,
Ill-luck me in Trouble's perilous sea hath cast;
And verily am I scourged with all misfortune's pains:
Man's gross contempt this having on me drawn
For to poverty such as mine Allah no favour deigns.
In the world's eyes base things, like these, opprobrious are;
And for long the miseries of misfortune have clutched on me
                                                    sore;
But the end draws near, and I fear without doubt,
That the dwelling-house of mine will soon know me no more."

Mamoun then said to him, "Where are you going?"

He replied: "To God and his Prophet, O Prince of the Believers."

"That is well!" said the King; "those who take refuge in God and his Prophet, and then in us, will be made welcome. But can you now tell me some more verses about your two wives, and about what comes to pass with them?"

"Certainly," said Bahloul.

"Then let us hear what you have to say!"

Bahloul then, with poetical words, thus began:

In the darkness of my ignorance I took two girls to wife:
With the silly promise that like a lamb between them would
[pass my life
But, like a ram 'tween two female jackals wedged, am I ta'en
[tight;
Stead of bouncing on sheep's bosoms, with husband's amorous
[strife
Nights succeed to days, and days give birth to night
And time sees me borne down in strangest of sad plight;
If kindness to one I show, the other gets cross-grained;
And from two such mad furies how can escape, poor wight.

When Al-Mamoun heard these words he began to laugh, till he nearly tumbled over. Then, as a proof of his kindness, he gave to Bahloul his golden robe, a most beautiful and gorgeous vestment worthy to adorn the back of an emperor.

Bahloul in high spirits, directed his steps towards the dwelling of the Grand Vizir. Just then Hamdouna [1]) looked from the height of her palace in that direction, and saw him. She said to her negress: "By the God of the temple of Mecca! There is Bahloul dressed in a fine gold-worked robe! How can I manage to get possession of the same?"

The negress said: "Oh my mistress, you would not know how to get hold of that robe."

Hamdouna answered: "I have thought of a trick to do it, and I shall get the robe from him."

"Bahloul is a sly man," replied the negress, "People think generally that they can make fun of him; but,

---

[1]) *Hamdouna*, from the Arabic root *hamad*, which means to praise; hence *Ahmed*, the most praiseworthy. From the same root comes the name of *Mohammad*, corrupted into *Mahomet*.

128

by Allah, it is he who makes fun of them. Give the idea up, mistress mine, and take care that you do not yourself fall into the snare which you are intending to set for him."

But Hamdouna said again; "It must be done!" She then sent her negress to Bahloul, to tell him that he should come to her. He said: "By the blessing of God, to him who calls you, you shall make answer." [1])

Hamdouna welcomed him, and said; "Oh, Bahloul, I believe you come to hear me sing." He replied: "Most certainly, Oh! my Mistress! She has a marvellous gift for singing," he continued.

"I also think that after having listened to my songs, you will be pleased to take some refreshments;" she observed. "Yes," said he.

Then she began to sing admirably, so as to make people who listened die with love.

After Bahloul had heard her sing, refreshments were served: he ate and he drank. Then she said to him: "I do not know why, but I fancy you would gladly take off your robe to make me a present of it." And Bahloul answered: "Oh, my Mistress! I have sworn to give it to her to whom I have done as a man does to woman."

"What! you know what that is, Bahloul?" said she.

"Whether I know it!" replied he. "I who am

---

[1]) "*To him who calls you, make answer.*" This sentence is taken from the *Ahadith*, or Traditions of Mohammed. Sometimes it is used in conversation in the same sense as above, but its true meaning is obscure. The words "By the blessing of God" in the same sentence is a form of acceptance or consent.

instructing God's creatures in that science? It is I who make them copulate in love, who initiate them in the delights a female can give, show them how you must caress a woman, and what satisfies her. Oh, my Mistress, who should know the art of coition if it is not I?"

Hamdouna was the daughter of Mamoun, and the wife of the Grand Vizir. She was endowed with the most perfect beauty; of a superb figure and harmonious form. No one in her time surpassed her in grace and perfection. Heroes on seeing her became humble and submissive, and looked down to the ground for fear of temptation; so many charms and perfections had God lavished on her. Those who looked steadily at her were troubled in their mind, and O! how many of the Valiant imperilled themselves for her sake. For this very reason Bahloul had always avoided meeting her for fear of succumbing to the temptation, and, apprehensive of his peace of mind, he had never, until that moment, ventured into her presence.

Bahloul began to converse with her. Now he looked at her and anon bent his eyes to the ground, dazzled by the radiancy of her beauty, and fearful of not being able to command his passion. Hamdouna burned with desire to have the robe, and he would not give it up without being paid for it.

"What price do you demand?" she asked. To which he replied, "Coition, O apple of my eye!"

"You know what that is, O Bahloul?" said she.

"By God," he cried, "no man knows women better than I; they are the occupation of my life. No one has studied all their concerns more than I. I know what they are fond of; for, learn, O Lady mine! that men choose different occupations according to their genius and their bent. The one takes, the other gives; this one sells, the other buys. My only thought is of love and of the possession of beautiful women. I heal those that are love-sick, and carry a solace to their thirsting vaginas."

Hamdouna was surprised at his words and the sweetness of his language. "Could you recite me some verses on this subject?" she asked.

"Certainly," he answered.

" Very well, O Bahloul! let me hear what you have to say."

Bahloul recited as follows:—

Entirely indifferent, alone in the world, am I.
Nor a snap I care for Persian, Turk, or Araby
For my heart's whole desire—Of that have no doubt,
Is with women, in bed, fast love-locked to lie.

Without vulva at hand to calm his fierce yearning
My member erected, is devoured with hot burning
By thy beauty excited, starts he up, when thou'rt present.
Admire his fine head lance-straightness, to pierce thy soft
[crescent!

By his quick movements in and out, between thy lovely thighs,
Would he quench, O lady-love of mine! the fire where pas-
sion lies.
Satisfaction full, I guarantee, again and again, thee to afford—
Thy hottest heat to put right out, O apple of my eyes!

Do not drive me from thee, let me come to thee,
As one who bringeth drink to the parched and love-thirsty!

My soul is eager for passion's joys, O do not bashful be!
Deign my hungry eyes in thy bosom to look, and its secret
[beauties see.

Shall then the panting of our love be thus restrained?
For all time must I hold it mute and muzzle-tied?
Only comes to pass that the will of Allah hath ordained;
And nothing happeneth He doth not decide.
By thy love am I sorely constrained.

While Handouna was listening she nearly swooned,
and set herself to examine the member of Bahloul,
which stood erect like a column between his thighs.
Now, she said to herself:

"I shall give myself up to him;" and now, "No, I
will not." During this uncertainty she felt a yearning for pleasure between her thighs, and Eblis made
flow to her natural parts a moisture, the fore-runner
of pleasure [1]). She then no longer combated her desire
to cohabit with him, and reassured herself by the
thought: "If this Bahloul, after having had his pleasure
with me, should divulge it, no one will believe his
words."

She requested him to divest himself of his robe,
and to come into her room, but Bahloul replied: "I
shall not undress till I have sated my desire, O apple
of my eye."

Then Hamdouna rose, trembling with excitement

---

[1]) The words "*Eblis made flow a moisture*" is an Arabic
idiom, expressing that on a woman getting lustful the sexual
parts get moist. Eblis is a rebellious angel who refused to
bow down before Adam when God ordered him to do so. Sometimes Eblis is also used as a general name for the devil, Satan,
or demon.

for what was to follow; she undid her girdle and left the room, Bahloul following her and thinking: "Am I really awake or is this a dream?" He walked after her till she had entered her *boudoir*. Then she threw herself on a couch of silk, which was rounded on the top like a vault, lifted her clothes up over her thighs, trembling all over, and all the beauty which God had given her was in Bahloul's arms.

Bahloul examined the belly of Hamdouna, round like an elegant cupola, his eyes dwelt upon a navel which was like a pearl in a golden cup; and descending lower down there was a beautiful piece of nature's workmanship, and the whiteness and shape of her thighs surprised him.

Then he pressed Hamdouna in a passionate embrace, and soon saw the animation leave her face; she seemed to be almost unconscious. She had lost clean her head; and, holding Bahloul's member in her hands, excited and fired him more and more.

Bahloul said to her: "Why do I see you so troubled and beside yourself?" And she answered: "Leave me, O son, of the debauched woman! By God I am like a mare in heat, and you continue to excite me still more with your words, and what words! They would set any woman on fire, even though she were the purest creature in the world. You will insist in making me succumb by your talk and your verses."

Bahloul answered: "Am I then not like your husband?" "Yes," she said, "but a woman gets in heat on account of the man, as a mare on account of the horse, whether the man be the husband or not; with this difference, however, that the mare gets

133

lustful only at certain periods of the year, and then receives the stallion, while a woman can always be made rampant by words of love [1]. Both these dispositions have met within me, and, as my husband is absent, make haste, for he will soon be back."

Bahloul replied: "Oh, my Mistress, my loins hurt me and prevent me mounting upon you. You take the man's position, and then take my robe and let me depart." [2]

PARALLEL ITALIAN STORY

To show the striking similarity of tricks and devices used by men to gain their nefarious ends over the supposed weaker sex, we quote the following from Poggio's "*Jocose Tales*" [3], not to prove that the present tale is derived from the preceding, or *vice versâ*, that we leave for "Storiologists" like Mr. W. Clouston [4]), but, to demonstrate how closely gentlemen living

---

[1] Rabelais says on the subject of women who, against the laws of nature, go on receiving the embraces of men after having conceived: "And if anybody should blame them for allowing men to explore them when full, considering that beasts in the like case never endure the male to enter, they will say that those are beasts: but they are women making use of their right of superfetation." See page 154 for complete passage).

[2] The continuation of this rather long but fascinating and most beautiful story may be read by the curious student in the "Scented Garden". In the whole range of erotic literature, we know of nothing more moving and voluptuous, or written with equal charm and effect.

[3] Latin and English edit. (Paris, Liseux, 1879). Poggio was one of the first to publish anything in this style, and his imitators have frequently borrowed unblushingly without acknowledgment.

[4] "*Popular Tales and Fictions*" by W. A. Clouston, (2 vols,

in times and countries widely apart, and dissociated in most other respects besides, yet employ pretty much the same methods to procure a little sexual *soulagement*.

In Latin, the title runs: " *De Rustico qui anserem venalem deferebat.*" We head it:

THE PEASANT WHO SOLD BOTH HIS GOOSE AND THE WOMAN!

A young peasant was trudging to Florence to sell a goose there, when a lady, who fancied herself witty, asked him, out of fun, what he charged for it:—" What you can very easily pay," said he.— " What is that?" she enquired.—" Only one bout with you," quoth he.—" You are joking," she replied: " Never mind let us go indoors, and we will agree upon the price." When inside, he would not abate one jot, and the lady assented. But, as she had acted the superior part, when she claimed the goose he flatly refused to give it up, arguing that it was not he that had had to do with her, but she who had borne him down.

The encounter had therefore to be renewed, and the youth went through the performances of a consummate rider. According to the bargain, the woman again claimed the goose; but the swain denied her a second time, asserting they were only quits; for he had not now received the price agreed upon, but merely avenged the insult offered him by the female, when she first lorded it over him.

Lond. 1887). These ably documented volumes are dedicated to Sir Richard F. Burton, and are a *thorough* piece of work, well worthy of both dedicator and dedicated.

The contention was still going on, when the husband came in and enquired what it was all about:—" I was anxious," said the wife, " to give you a good meal, had it not been for that lout; we were agreed upon twenty pence; now that he has entered the house, he has altered his mind and insists upon having two more."

" By Jove," exclaimed the husband," such a trifle shall not stand in the way of our supper! Come, lad, take your money, here it is." And the peasant went away with the cash, and the carnal acquaintance of the wife's virtue into the bargain.

AVOIDANCE OF SATIETY

From very early times the art of coition has formed the subject of many books. The Greek and Roman Poets and Dramatists teem with allusions, which, in the translations made of their works, are either inelegantly veiled, clumsily half-explained, or mystified out of all recognition as to their true import. The intelligent reader should consult Forberg's *Manual of Classical Erotology*, Latin and English text, Paris, 2 vols. 1899, and Blondeau's " *Dictionnaire de la Langue Érotique* " for the key to unlock the classics. These books are mines of knowledge; from them the student will learn more in a week than the painful thumbing of hated " *Cæsars* " and " *Horaces* " has taught him in five years.

Turning to the philosophic Orient, we find that amongst the Easterns the modes of congress have formed the subject of intelligent study on a very systematic scale, and their erotic works contain detailed explanation of every possible (and, to a European, impossible) position in which the act of venery can be performed. The *Ananga Ranga* gives thirty-two divisions; the *Scented Garden* forty divisions (together with six different movements during the coitus), and, in addition, describes the most suitable methods for hump-backs, corpulent men, pregnant women, etc.; whilst the *Old Man Young Again* and *The Secrets of Women* placing the act into six divisions, viz.;— 1. In the ordinary posture, 2. in the sitting posture, 3. side or reclining postures. 4. the prone postures, 5. the stooping postures, and, 6. the standing postures—subdivides each of these into ten varieties, thus arriving at the grand total of sixty! [1])

Before drawing aside the curtain concealing the " art and mystery of man's highest enjoyment," we venture to offer a few remarks as to the importance of the " Science and practice of Dalliance and Love-delight."

Says Kallyana Malla:—" It is true that no joy in the world of mortals can compare with that derived from the knowledge of the Creator. Second, however, and subordinate only to this, are the satisfaction and pleasure arising from the possession of a beautiful woman. Men, it is true, marry for the sake of undisturbed congress, as well as for love and comfort,

---

[1]) See notice of an English version of this book,—the only translation of it that has appeared in any European language, which has been prepared and is published by the Editor of the present work—at Commencement and end of the present book.

and often they obtain handsome and attractive wives.
But they do not give them plenary contentment, nor
do they themselves thoroughly enjoy their charms.
The reason of which is that they are purely ignorant
of the Scripture of Cupid, the Kama Shastra, and,
despising the difference between the several kinds of
women they regard them only in an animal point of
view. Such men must be looked upon as foolish and
unintelligent; and this book is composed with the
object of preventing lives and loves being wasted in
similar manner.

.... Thus all you who read this book shall know
how delicious an instrument is woman, when artfully
played upon, how capable she is of producing the
most exquisite harmony; of executing the most com-
plicated variations and of giving the divinest pleasures."

" No one, (he states in another part,) yet has written
a book to prevent the separation of the married pair,
and to show them how they may pass through life
in union .... The chief reason for the separation
between the married couple, and the cause which drives
the husband to the embraces of strange women, and
the wife to the arms of strange men, is the want of
varied pleasures, and the monotony which follows
possession. There is no doubt about it. Monotony
begets satiety, and satiety distaste for congress, especially in one or the other; malicious feelings are
engendered, the husband or the wife yield to temptation, and the other follows, being driven by jealousy.
For it seldoms happens that the two love each other
equally, and in exact proportion, therefore is the one
more easily seduced by passion than the other. From

such separations result polygamy, adulteries, abortions, and every manner of vice, and the erring husband and wife fall into the pit...."

"Fully understanding the way in which such quarrels arise, I have in this book shown how the husband, by varying the enjoyment of his wife, may live with her as with thirty-two different women, ever varying the enjoyment of her, and rendering satiety impossible. I have also taught all manner of useful arts and mysteries by which she may render herself pure, beautiful, and pleasing in his eyes."

No wiser words than these of Kallyana Malla, can, we opine, be framed to justify the purpose of our attempt, or serve as better introduction to that which is to follow in the next chapter.

THE MANNER OF COITION

The student is recommended to study the Article in the "Foreword," by Paul Mantegazza on "Copulation and its Ethnical Variations" in connection with this chapter.

The conjunction with the man bending over the woman on her back, is the most usual, and the one best adapted to nature. *Luisa Sigea* [1]) says:—

---

[1]) A storehouse of Realism in Refined language *The Dialogues of Luisa Sigea*, (Aloisiæ Sigeæ Satiar Sotadica de Arcanis Amoris et Veneris). Literally translated from the Latin of Nicolas Chorier. Dialogue I. The Skirmish. — II. Tribadicon. — III. Fabrice. — IV. The Duel. — V. Pleasures. — VI. Frolics and Sports. Three volumes (small 8vo). — Price.... £ 2.2s. This work, so well known under the name of *Aloisia* or *Meursius*, is the most famous production of the Neo-Latin private literature. In six "Dialogues", or more properly speaking, dissertations

"As for me, I like best the usual custom and the ordinary method: let the man lie upon the woman, who is on her back, bosom to bosom, stomach to stomach, pubes to pubes, his stiff spear opening her delicate cleft. What can in fact be sweeter than to imagine the woman extended on her back, supporting the welcome weight of an adored body, exciting by unceasing voluptuous lascivity to tender transports? What more pleasant than to take delight in the face of her lover, in his kisses, sighs, in the varying fire of his eyes? What better than to press her lover in her arms, or, wakening new fires, to participate in sensations, which neither age nor anything else can blunt? What more favourable to the voluptuous pleasures of both at lascivious movements given and received? What more opportune at the moment, when one expires voluptuously, than to *revive* under the vivifying balm of hot kisses?

The copulation face to face with the woman sitting obliquely, is described by Luisa Sigea with her usual elegance and vivacity: —

---

of gradually increasing interest, where perfection of vocabulary vies with the seductive charm of the subject, the Mysteries of Love and the Secret Refinements of Pleasure are set forth in methodical order. Two young women, lying side by side in the same bed, mutually initiate each other in the Science of Life in a series of indiscreet confidences, passionate scenes, and voluptuous descriptions, the language chosen, like a transparent veil, only serving to heighten the lascivious nudity of the pictures drawn; and the gracious tittle-tattle of the two women imparting a delicacy and fascination generally absent from this style of work. The edition was issued by our late friend, Isidore Liseux, and may fitly be termed the libertine's text-book.

"Caviceo comes on, blithe and joyous (Olympia's recital). He despoils me of my chemise, and his libertine hand touches my parts. He tells me to sit down again as I was seated before, and replaces the chairs under me in such a manner that my legs are in the air, the entrance to my garden was wide open to the assaults I was expecting. He then slides his right hand under my buttocks and draws me a little closer to him. His left hand holds his javelin; then he stretches himself down upon me with his rammer before my door, and introduces its head with one push in the cleft, opening his lips. There he rested awhile steady and not pushing further in. "My dear Octavia," he says, " clasp me tightly, raise your right thigh and rest it on my side." "I do not know what you want," I said. Hearing this he lifted with his own hand the thigh, and guided it round his loin, as he wished; finally he forced his arrow into the target of Venus. In the beginning he is pushing in bit by bit, then quicker, and at last at such a pace, that I could not doubt, that I was in great danger. His member was hard as horn, and he forced it in so cruelly, that I cried out, "You will tear me in pieces!" He stopped for a moment his work. "I implore you to be quiet, my dear," he said, " it can only be done in this way; endure it without flinching."

Nothing is more frequent than the conjunction whilst standing, the woman with her back to the man; it is indeed very easy to do it that way in any place, as you have only to lift up the clothes of your beloved, and exhibit your weapon; it is, therefore, the best manner for those who have to make instantaneous use of an opportunity when you take your pleasure in secret. Thus Priapus complains of the wives and daughters of his neighbours who came incessantly to him burning with ticklish desires.

" Cut off my genital member which the neighbouring women wear out. Every night they are always in rut, more lascivious than sparrows, Oh! I am bursting!...."

(*Priapeia* XXV)

I remember a medical man of our time, one of the most celebrated professors (I had nearly uttered his name) who to emphasize this, called his daughter, and pointing to the blushing girl, while his hearers could not help smiling, said: "I have fabricated her standing." A representation of this position is to be found in the "*Monuments de la vie privée des douze Césars*. Pl. XLVI, and another in the *Monuments du Culte Secret des Dames Romaines*, Pl. XIII.

Finally, one can get into a woman turning her back to the man, after the manner of the quadrupeds, who can have no connection with their females, than by mounting upon them from behind [1]). There are people, who believe that a woman conceives more easier while on all fours. Lucretius, says:—

Women are said to conceive
Easier when down after the manner of beasts,
On their hands and knees, because the organ absorbs
Better the seed, with the body prone and the hips elevated. [2])

---

[1]) Plinius has treated this extensively in his *Natural History*, Book X, Ch. 63.

[2]) (*Of the Nature of Things* IV, v. 1259)—And *Luisa Sigea*.

A singular reason for the necessity of encountering a woman that way is given by *Luisa Sigea* with her usual sagacity.

" For pleasure, one likes a vulva which is not placed too far back, so as to be entirely hidden by the thighs; it should not be more than nine or ten inches from the navel. With the greater number of young girls the pubes goes so far down, that it may easily be taken as the other way of pleasure. With such the coitus is difficult. Theodora Aspilqueta could not be deflowered till she placed herself prone on her stomach, with her knees drawn up to her sides. Vainly had her husband tried to manage her while lying on her back, he only lost his toil?

(*Dialogue VII.*)

FORTY-EIGHT
Erotic Postures.

We may here mention that in Forberg's famous "Manual of Classical Erotology", no less than Ninety modes of sexual union are enumerated by the learned German. It is only just to state that of these no more than Forty-Eight fall under the designation of legitimate intercourse between the sexes, the rest being composed of what are called *spinthriae*, or " bracelets " a species of coition where several men and women are simultaneously united in unnatural connection. For further information regarding these " positions ", we must beg the reader to consult for himself the extraordinary work of Dr. Carl F. Forberg.

THE MAN ON HIS BACK

This position vulgarly called " St. George ", and
" le Postillon " or " à Cheval ", in which the man lies
supinely upon his back, whilst the woman mounts on
him, and procures the orgasmic rapture by her own
activity, merits perhaps a little more space than bare
enumeration. In Boccaccio, the Abbot appears to have
disported himself with the trapped girl in this way [1]);
and if we may judge from the numerous references
to it in their writings, this posture must have been
a favourite one amongst the Romans.

Our book being from the Arabic, we must not lose
sight of the fact that, although probably practised by
certain masters of the voluptuous arts, the mode of
copulation here treated is sternly discountenanced by
Moslems. In tact we have introduced this subject
only to make our discussion complete.

The Quran says (chap. II):

" Your wives are your tillage; go in therefore unto
your tillage in what manner soever ye will." Usually
this is understood as meaning in any posture, standing
or sitting, lying, backwards or forwards. Yet there

---

[1]) " The girl, who was neither iron nor adamant, readily
enough lent herself to the pleasure of the abbot, who, after
he had clipped and kissed her again and again, mounted upon
the monk's pallet and having regard belike to the grave
burden of his dignity and the girl's tender age, and fearful
of irking her for overmuch heaviness, bestrode not her breast,
but set her upon his own, and so a great while disported
himself with her."

Decameron Day I. Novel 4 (Payne I. 69).

is a popular saying, which proves that the practice is held in horror, about the man whom the woman rides; "Cursed be he who maketh woman Heaven and himself Earth!"

(*The Book of the Thousand Nights and a Night*, vol. III, p. 304, note 2.)

PASSION GONE MAD

We cannot here resist quoting the following from " *The Scented Garden;*" it forms part of an impassioned story given in the chapter treating of the " *Names given to the Sexual Organs of Women.*"

———

"I was in love with a woman who was all grace and perfection, beautiful of shape and gifted with all imaginable charms. Her cheeks were like roses, her forehead lily white, her lips like coral; she had teeth like pearls and breasts like pomegranates. Her mouth opened round like a ring; her tongue seemed to be incrusted with precious gems; her eyes, black and finely slit had the languor of slumber, and her voice the sweetness of sugar. With her form pleasantly filled out, her flesh was mellow like fresh butter, and pure as the diamond.

As to her vulva, it was white, prominent, round as an arch: the centre of it was red, and breathed fire, and without a trace of humidity; for, sweet to the touch, it was quite dry. When she walked it showed in relief like a dome or an inverted cup. In reclining it was visible between her thighs, looking like a kid couched on a hillock.

This woman was my neighbour. All the others

played and laughed with me, jested with me, and met my suggestions with great pleasure. I revelled in their kisses, their close embracings and nibblings, and in sucking their lips, breasts and necks. I had coition with all of them, except my neighbour, and it was exactly her I wanted to possess in preference to all the rest; but instead of being kind to me, she avoided me rather. When I contrived to take her aside to trifle with her and spoke to her of my desires, she recited to me the following verses, the sense of which was a mystery to me:

" Among the mountain tops I saw a tent placed firmly,
Apparent to all eyes high up in mid-air.
But, oh! the pole that held it up was gone.
And like a vase without a handle it remained,
With all its cords undone, its centre sinking in,
Forming a hollow like that of a kettle " [1]).

.... When she had finished speaking these things I began to recite to her the verses which Abou Nowas [1]), had taught me.

As I proceeded I saw her more and more moved. I observed her giving way, to yawn, to stretch herself, to sigh. I knew now I should arrive at the desired result. When I had finished, my member was

---

[1]) For the ingenious explanation given of these lines we must refer to " The *Scented Garden*"; Space forbids our quoting here the story in full.

[1]) The real name of Abu Nowas was Abu Ali Hasoun. He also bore the surname of El Hakim. Born of obscure parentage about the year 135 of the "Flight" (Hegira), he acquired a great reputations as poet and philosopher. A number of very rollicking stories have been fathered on him.

in such a state of erection that it became like a pillar, still lengthening.

When Fadihat el-Jemal saw it in that condition she precipitated herself upon it, took it into her hands, and drew it towards her thighs. I then said, "O apple of my eyes, this may not be done here, let us go into your chamber."

She replied, "Leave me alone, O son of a debauched woman! Before God! I am losing my senses in seeing your member getting longer and longer, and lifting your robe. Oh, what a member! I never saw a finer one! Let it penetrate into this delicious, plump vulva, which maddens all who heard it described; for the sake of which so many died of love; and of which your superiors and masters themselves could not get possession."

I repeated, "I shall not do it anywhere else than in your chamber." She answered, "If you do not this minute enter this tender vulva, I shall die."

As I still insisted upon repairing to her room, she cried, "No, it is quite impossible; I cannot wait so long!"

I saw, in fact, her lips tremble, her eyes filling with tears. A general tremour ran over her, she changed colour, and laid herself down upon her back, baring her thighs, the whiteness of which made her flesh appear like crystal tinged with commine.

Then I examined her vulva—a white cupola with a purple centre, soft and charming. It opened like that of a mare on the approach of a stallion.

At that moment she seized my member and kissed it, saying: "By the religion of my father! It must penetrate into my vulva!" And, drawing nearer to me, she pulled it towards her vagina.

I now hesitated no longer to assist her with my member, and placed it against the entrance to her vulva.

As soon as the head of my member touched the lips, the whole body of Fadihat el Djemal trembled with excitement. Sighing and sobbing, she held me pressed to her bosom.

Again I profited by this moment to admire the beauties of her vulva. It was magnificent, its purple centre setting off its whiteness all the more. It was round, without any imperfection; projecting like a splendidly curved dome over her belly. In one word, it was a master-piece of creation as fine as could be seen. The blessing of God, the best Creator, upon it.

And the woman who possessed this wonder had in her time no superior.

I counted that during that day and night, I accomplished twenty-seven times the act of coition, and I became afraid that I should never more be able to leave the house of that woman.

THE WOMAN RIDING [1]

In the work called *Ananga Ranga*, or Stage of the Bodiless One [2] this *façon* is termed Purushayitabandha

---

[1] Mulier equitans; see the *Satyricon* of Petronius (Ch. CXL); also Horace (Satire II. 7, 47-50).

i.e. "When keen nature inflames me, any lascivious slut, who naked under the light of the lanthorn, takes the strokes of my swollen tail, or wriggles with her buttocks on her supine horse..." Vide also "*Priapeia*" pages 133 and 152.

[2] A treatise in Sanskrit more vulgarly known as Koka

which is thus described:—"It is the reverse of what men usually practise. In this case the man lies upon his back, draws his wife upon him and enjoys her. It is especially useful when he, being exhausted, is no longer capable of muscular exertion, and when she is ungratified, being still full of the water of love. The wife must, therefore, place her husband supine upon the bed or carpet, mount upon his person, and satisfy her desires. Of this form of congress there

Pandit from the supposed author, a Wazir of the great Rajah Bhoj, or, according to others, of the Maharajah of Kanoj. Under the title Lizzat al-Nisa (The Pleasures, or enjoying-of Women) it has been translated into all the languages of the Moslem East, from Hindustani to Arabic. It divides postures into five great divisions: [1] the woman lying supine, of which there are eleven subdivisions; [2] lying on her side, right or left, with three varieties; [3] sitting, which has ten; [4] standing, with three subdivisions, and [5] lying prone, with two. This total of twenty-nine, with three forms of "Purushayit", when the man lies supine (see the Abbot in *Boccaccio* i. 4), becomes thirty-two, approaching the French *quarante façons*. The Upavishta, majlis, or sitting postures, when one or both " *sit at squat* " somewhat like birds, appear utterly impossible to Europeans who lack the pliability of the Eastern's limbs. Their object in congress is to avoid tension of the muscles which would shorten the period ef enjoyment. In the text the woman lies supine and the man sits at squat between her legs: it is a favourite from Marocco to China. A literal translation of the Ananga-ranga appeared in 1873 under the name of Kàma-Shàstra, or the Hindoo Art of Love (Ars Amoris Indica); but of this only six copies were printed. It was re-issued (printed but not published) in 1885. The curious in such matters will consult the *Index Librorum Prohibitorum* (London, privately printed, 1879) by Pisanus Fraxi (H. S. Ashbee).

are three subdivisions:"—Kalyana Malla here proceeds
to explain these. We refer the curious reader to the
work itself. The chapter treating of it is most
interesting.

Juvenal (VI, 321-322) in speaking of the debauchery of women, says of Saufeia:—

> *Provocat, et tollit pendentis præmia coxæ.*
> *Ipsæ Medullinæ fluctum crissantis adorat.*

"She challenges them, and bears off the prize of
her hanging thigh; but she herself adores the undulating wriggling of Medullina's haunches."

The "hanging thigh" says "Neaniskos," the learned
commentator of "*Priapeia*," means Saufeia's thigh,
which hung over the girl who lay underneath her, the
reference being to tribadism.—

> *Tam tremulum crissat, tam blandum prurit ut ipsum,*
> *Masturbatorem fecerit Hyppolytum.*

"She wriggles herself so tremulously, and excites
such lubricous passions, that she would have made
Hyppolytus himself a masturbator."

Arnobius calls this posture *inequitatio*, "a riding
upon."

Lucretius (lib. IV, 5, 1265-1272) says:—"For the
woman prevents and resists conception if wantonly
she continues coition with a man with her buttocks
heaving, and fluctuates her whole bosom as if it were
boneless." (That is, whilst the woman bends over
the man and continually curves herself as if she had
no spine or bone in her back.) "For she thrusts out
the plough-share from the right direction and path of

her furrow, and turns aside the stroke of the semen from her parts. And the harlots think to move in this manner for their own sake, lest they should be in continual pregnancy, and at the same time that the coition might be the more pleasing for their men."

Apuleius has several passages bearing upon this posture. In his *Metamorphoses*, lib. II, we read:— "As she spoke thus, having leapt on my bed, she repeatedly sank down upon me and sprang upwards, bending inwards; and wriggling her flexible spine with lubricous movements, glutted me with enjoyment of a pendant coition, until fatigued, with our passions enervated and our limbs languid, together we sank panting in a mutual entwinement."

This subject is treated exhaustively in *Priapeia*, where a host of citations (with translation), are given that should satisfy the most exacting.

In an Arabic amatory work, entitled "The Old Man Young Again" an English version of which the present translator has issued since the first edition of the "Book of Exposition" was printed, some eight variations of the "sitting posture" are detailed, the woman being uppermost. The man and the woman sit in a swinging hammock on New Year's Day, the woman placing herself on the man's lap, over his yard, which is standing. They then take hold of one another, she placing her two legs against his two sides, and set the swinging hammock in motion. And thus when the hammock goes on one side the yard comes out of her, and when it goes to the other side it goes into her, and so they go on swinging without inconvenience or fatigue, but with endearment and tender playing, till depletion comes to both of them.—This is called " Congress of the New Year's hammock."

That our own English voluptuaries are no strangers to the vigorous practice of " St. George," the following happily conceived poem by an olden-time Earl is evidence:

With this we must conclude the chapter.   Our brief outline may be abundantly filled in by consultation of the various works we have quoted.

THE SQUIRE [1]

Last night, when to your bed I came,
You were a novice at the game,
I've taught you now a little skill
But I have more to teach you still,
Lie thus, dear Sir, I'll get above,
And teach you a new seat of love;
When I have got you once below me,
Kick as you will, you shall not throw me;
For tho! I ne'er a hunting rid,
I'll sit as fast as if I did,
Nor do I stirrup need,
To help me up upon my steed.
   This said, her legs she open'd wide,
And on her lover got astride
And being in her saddle plac'd
Most lovingly the squire embrac'd
Who viewed the wanton fair with wonder,
And smil'd, to see her keep him under,
While she, to shew she would not tire,
Spur'd like a fury on the squire,
And tho' she ne'er had rid in France,
She made him caper, curvet, dance,
Till both of them fell in a trance.
   'Twas long e'er either did recover

[1] *The Earl of Harrington's Poems* (p.p. 88-90).   Lond. 1824.

At last she kissed her panting lover,
And, sweetly smiling in his face,
Ask'd him, "How he liked the chase?"
He scarce could speak, his breath was short,
But sobbing, answer'd "Noble sport;
"I'd give the best horse in my stable,
That either I or you were able
To ride another, for I own
There never was such pastime known;"
   This answer pleased the frolic maid,
She sucked his breast, and, laughing, said,
"If you, good Sir, resolve to try
Another gallop here am I,
Ready to answer your desire,
Nor will you find me apt to tire
In such a chase: I'll lay a crown,
Start you the game, I'll run it down."
   The squire o'erjoyed at what she said,
Hugg'd to his breast the sprightly maid;
For he was young and full of vigour,
And Cherry was a lovely figure,
Was ever cheerful, brisk and gay,
And had a most enticing way.
She kiss'd his eyes, she bit his breast,
Nor did her nimble fingers rest,
Till he had all his toil forgot,
And found his blood was boiling hot,
While Cherry (who was in her prime
Still knew, and always nick'd her time)
Bestrid the amorous squire once more,
And gallop'd faster than before,
Fearing the knight might interrupt her,
She toss'd and twirl'd upon her crupper;
Nor did she let her tongue lay idle,
But thrust it in by way of bridle,
And giving him a close embrace,
Did finish the delightful chase.

ON THE LEGITIMACY OF WIDOW-MOUNTING

*(From the third chapter
of Master Francois Rabelais' " Gargantua"). [1])*

Grangousier was a good fellow in his time, and notable jester; he loved to drink neat as much as any man that then was in the world, and would willingly eat salt meat. To this intent he was ordinarily well furnished with gammons of bacon, both of Westphalia, Mayence and Bayonne, with store of dried neat's tongues, plenty of links, chitterlings and puddings in their season; together with salt beef and mustard; a good deal of hard roes of powdered mullet called botargos, great provision of sausages, not of Bolonia (for he feared the Lombard Boccone), but of Bigorre, Longaulnay, Brene, and Rouargue. In the vigour of his age he married Gargamelle, daughter to the King of the Parpaillons, a jolly pug and well-mouthed wench. These two did oftentimes do the two-backed beast together, joyfully rubbing and frotting their bacon gainst one another, in so far, that, at last she became great with child of a fair son, and went with him unto the eleventh month; for, so long, yea longer, may a woman carry her great belly, especially when it is some masterpiece of nature, and a person predestinated to the performance, in his due time, of great exploits.

As Homer says that the child which Neptune

---

[1]) Translated by Sir Thomas Urquhart, of Cromarty, and Peter A. Motteux.

begot upon the nymph, was born a whole year after the conception, that is in the twelfth month. For, as *Aulus Gellius* saith, *lib* 3, this long time was suitable to the majesty of Neptune, that in it the child might receive his perfect form. For the like reason Jupiter made the night, wherein he lay with Alcmena, last forty-eight hours, a shorter time not being sufficient for the forging of Hercules, who cleansed the world of the monsters and tyrants wherewith it was suppresed. My masters, the ancient Pantagruelists, have confirmed that which I say, and withal declared it to be not only possible, but also maintained the lawful birth and legitimation of the infant born of a woman in the eleventh month after the decease of her husband. (*Here follows a list we omit from this citation.   Editor.*)

By the means of laws such as these, the honest widows may without danger play at the close buttock game with might and main, and as hard as they can, for the space of the first two months after the decease of their husbands. I pray you, my good lusty springal lads, if you find any of these females, that are worth the pains of untying the cod-piece-point, get up, ride upon them, and bring them to me; for, if they happen within the third month to conceive, the child shall be heir to the deceased, if, before he died, he had no other children, and the mother shall pass for an honest woman.   When she is known to have conceived, thrust forward boldly, spare her not whatever betide you, seeing the paunch is full. As Julia, the daughter of the Emperor Octavian, never prostituted herself to her belly-bumpers, but when she found herself with child, after the manner of ships, that receive not their steersman till they have their ballast and lading. And if you blame them for this their rataconniculation, and reiterated lechery upon their pregnancy and big-belliedness, seeing beasts, in the like exigent of their fulness, will never suffer the male-masculant to encroach them, their answer will be, that those are beasts, but they are women, very well skilled in the pretty vales and small fees of the pleasant trade and mysteries of superfetation; as Populia heretofore answered, according to the relation of Macrobius, *lib.* 2, *Saturnal.*

If the devil will not have them to bag, he must wring hard the spigot, and stop the bunghole [1]).

Shocking as it may be to say, it has often been observed that women suddenly deprived by death of their husbands are often, when once the first terrible mortification at their loss has passed off, very eager for sexual intercourse for the apaisement of their natural desires — according as their late partner may have accustomed them to more or less rich and regular diet. Whether a saucy-eyed English matron (God bless them), Egyptian or Turkish dame, all are alike in their subjection to these laws of coynte-hunger to which nature has made them amenable. The following translation from a Turkish MS. illustrates our point.

---

[1]) We give the quotation in full as no Author is more easy of misconstruction than *Master* Rabelais when served up in "*bits and snatches*".

THE HOT-BELLIED WIDOW.

A certain peasant of Anatolia was one day at Constantinople. Nature had amply provided him with those gifts which please ladies, and he had a secret presentiment that perhaps his tool might make his fortune. Had he not seen many of his countrymen succeed in the same manner, and why should not he, who was one of the best furnished men in the country, meet with equal good-luck?

Full of these ideas he entered the city. He soon saw one of his fellow countrymen, seated in a shop and surrounded by vegetables and fruits, for he sold to the citizens the produce of market gardens in the suburbs which were cultivated by some of his country people.

The two Anatolians entered into conversation, and the new comer told the other of his intentions.

"Matters could not fall out better for you," cried the shop-keeper. "Exactly opposite here, lives a widow, well off, and still young, and who has never found a foot big enough to fill her slipper. There is the very chance for you."

The young fellow to whom this was addressed, did not lose a word of what was said. He reflected a minute and then hit on a plan.

"Give me one of your gourds," he said to his new friend.

"Choose one," replied the other.

He chose a straight and tolerably big one. It was as long as the distance from the wrist to the elbow, and as thick as his wrist. He peeled it, and let the white flesh of the vegetable show, then cut off one end, hollowed the gourd all through, and made a small hole at the rounded end.

That being done, he opened his chulwar, used the gourd as a sheath for the noble dagger which ladies delight to polish, and then went and pissed against the wall under the windows of the widow's house.

A negress slave. who through the casement had seen him talking to the fruiterer, noticed with what a gigantic instrument he was armed. She at once ran to inform her mistress. The latter approached the window, saw it with her own eyes, and was filled with joy.

" Go down," she said to her servant, " and bring that man to me."

The servant promptly obeyed her mistress, went out, and spoke to the fruiterer, who called his fellow countryman.

" The *hanum* [1]) wishes to speak to you," he said, and accompanied the words with a significant wink.

The man followed the negress and was ushered into the presence of the widow, who was enveloped in a veil, and who asked him to sit next her on a divan. After the exchange of the usual compliments, the widow asked him who he was, whence he came, and what he was doing in Constantinople. He told her his name, and the village from whence he came, and added that he had come to the capital to get married, being encouraged by the success which many of his comrades who had come to Constantinople with the same purpose, had met with.

---

[1]) *i.e.* lady.

The lady reflected for a few moments, and then she asked him to prove his capabilities, and give her a specimen of his powers, before sbe gave him a definite answer.

" Oh, no," he replied, " I am a good Mussulman, and would not for worlds commit a sin which is against the tenets of our holy religion."

The lady pressed him, and to tempt him the more, she laid hold, through his *chalwar*, [1]) of a handsome tool which made her mouth water, but he was resolute in his determination. Then the lady, finding that he would not play, resolved to treat the affair seriously, and offered him her hand. He accepted the offer, and the following day the marriage was celebrated at her house.

Night being come the bridegroom came to his newly married wife, took off her veil, laid her on the bed, and took his place by the side of her. She being very hot and randy, asked him to satisfy her longings; so, with the instrument with which nature had so liberally endowed him he began to work in the proper place.

" Why, how is this?" said the lady as she took it in her hand to put it in properly. "I thought you were better furnished."

" Ah, but I have two."

" You have two!" she cried, beside herself with pleasure. " Well, let me see what you can do with this one."

With that he continued the operation, and his wife was delighted with his magnificent dagger.

---

[1]) *i.e.*, drawers.

"Put them both in!" she cried in the excitement of her pleasure. "Put them both in. On good land you ought to sow with a double dibble!"

CREPITUS VENTRIS

Referring to the action which gives rise to the story on page 27, known to the Romans as crepitus ventris, and to English-Speaking peoples as *"breaking of wind"*, it will be of interest to the curious reader to note a few authors who have dealt with this subject. To the too fastidious and would-be respectable, I commend the lines found on an old tombstone:

"Let your wind go free, wherever you be,
For it was the wind that killed me."

Of classical writers we have Catullus (Carmen xxiii), Martil (x, 14), Juvenal, Suetonius (in Claud., xxxii), Lampridius (in Commod.), Hesiod, Diogenes Laertes on Pythagoras, Diodorus Siculus, Pliny (L. xxviii, c. 19), Plutarch, Aristophanes (Clouds), Herodotus, etc. *The Thousand Nights and a Night* (ii, 88; iv, 160, note 2; v. 99, 35; xii, 56) contains several rollicking anecdotes on the subject; Rabelais has a chapter upon the various kinds of wipe-breeches; Balzac has three tales (*The Merry jest of King Louis the Eleventh; The Clerks of St. Nicholas;* and *The Merry Tattle of the Nuns of Poissy*) in his inimitable *Droll Stories;* and Zola devotes a chapter in his much talked-of novel *La Terre* (The Soil) to the exploits of an old soldier who was greatly gifted that way. In fact, in French there is quite a literature on the subject, some of the works going so far as to describe the various sounds which can be produced. Such is the *Descriptions de six espèces de pets.*

Amongst other volumes, I may mention *L'art de peter,* — *L'Éloge du pet,* — *La Chezonomie, ou l'Art de ch....,* — *Le nouveau Merdiana* (which contains a translation of Swift's article, entitled *L'art de méditer sur la garde-robe).* — *Les Francs-Pet...,* — *L'art de désopiler la rate, l'Histoire de Pet-en-l'air et de la Reine des Amazones,—Physiologie inodore, illustrée et propre à plus d'un usage,* — *Sirop-au-cul, ou l'Heureuse Délivrance,* — *Gras et Maigres, ou Nouveau Merdiana-pissa-foirillyala, véritable code et art des chieurs, pisseurs et foireux,* — *Peteriana,* — *Le Directeur des Estomacs,* etc., etc. Piron, M. de Malesherbes, Père Kircher the Jesuit, Rabelais, Béroalde de Verville (*Le Moyen de parvenir*), and the *Cent Nouvelles Nouvelles,* all treat the matter; which is further expounded in the *Mémoires de l'Academie de Troyes.* Of English writers I will merely mention the names of Swift, Smollett (*Humphrey Clinker;* and *The Adventures of an Atom*), Sterne (*Sentimental Journey*), and Somerville (*The Officious Messenger* [1])

DEPILATION

Lest any person, on reading the note [1]) given at page 11 anent the clipping and burning off the hair

---

[1]) This bibliographic note we have borrowed from *Priapeia* page 105. Printed MDCCCXC, this book contains the Latin and English, accompanied by learned Commentaries, of the *Sportive Epigrams of Divers Poets on Priapus.*

from the privy parts, suppose that this practice is exclusively oriental, we think it proper to produce proof from the ancient writers of Greece and Rome to show that in those countries also, the habit, at least chiefly among the pædicatores and sybarites, was known to be thoroughly in vogue. [1])

In the "Manual of Classical Erotology", the learned author states: "It was not without some art, that the patients performed their functions. Their business, however, consisted chiefly in plucking out the hairs, and to know how to ply their haunches.

The patients took care in the first place to entirely remove the hair from all parts of their body [2]); from the lips, arms, chest, legs, the altar of passive lust, the anus; Martial II. 62:

" Pluck out the hair from breast and legs and arms;
Thy rigid member must be free from fur,

---

[1]) Lest some ill-disposed persons should imagine that we have ourselves an admiration for females who clip off the hair from their private parts, we beg leave to state at once that we abhor the practice. In fact, if the truth must be told, we once, with carnal intentions attacked a French housemaid who we believed, was not indifferent to our attentions, and in despite of her protestations to respect her virginity, we rapidly thrust our hand up her petticoats, only to find to our horror that she was clean depilated, wore no drawers, (those incitements to voluptuousness) and had not the slightest hairy appendage to give mysterious charm to the spot.

[2]) Always, however, excepting the head, for they took great care of their head of hair.

Horace (Epode XI. v. 40—43): "Nothing", he says, "will take away his love for Lyciscus, save another love for a plump youth, tying up his long hair".

We know you do this, Labienus, for your lady-love;
But why, Labienus, do this to your anus?"

And again IX, 28:

"While you Chrestus, appear thus with your parts all hairless,
With a mentula like to the neck of a vulture,
A head as shining as a prostitute's buttocks,
With not a hair appearing on your leg,
And with your pallid lips all shorn and bare,
You talk of Curius, Camillus, Numa, Ancus,
Of all hair-covered people that we know.
While you thus spout big words and threatenings
Against theatres and against our times,
Let but some big-limbed man come into sight,
You call him with a nod and take him off...."

And he says, IX, 58:

"Nought is worse used than the rags of Hedylus,
Save one thing, which he can never deny,
His anus, which is worse than Hedylus's rags".

In a similar way he has spoken before of the anus
of Hyllus as more worn by friction than the last
penny of a poor man (II. 51), and Suetonius speaks
similarly of the body of Otho, given to the habits of
a Catamite, and Catullus (XXXIII) reproaches the younger
Vibennius: "You could not sell your hairy buttocks
for a doit."

For the same reason Galba requested Icelus to get
depilated before he was to take him aside. Suetonius,
Galba, Ch. XXII.

"He was very much given to the intercourse between
men, and amongst those he preferred men of ripe age,
exoletes. It is said that when Icelus, one of his old
bed-fellows, came to Spain to inform him of Nero's

death, he, not content with kissing him closely before everyone present, asked him to get at once depilated, and then took him aside with him quite alone. "

Those also depilated their anus, who by favour of a rough head of hair and a bristly beard, tried otherwise to simulate the gravity of the ancient philosophers.

Martial IX. 48.

" Of Democrites, and Zenons and sham Platos,
Of all whose portraits come to us all bearded,
You talk to us as though you were Pythagora's successor,
And from your chin hangs down a thickset beard.
But as a bearded man it is a shame for you
Between your buttocks to receive a rigid member. "

Space will not permit us to dwell upon this subject at great length. We may briefly then point out that not the *" patients "* alone caused themselves to be depilated; men leading an idle, careless life followed the same practice.

" To pluck out the hair, get the hair on the head curled, to drink in the baths to excess, these practices prevail in the city; still they cannot be said to be customary; for nothing of all this is exempt from blame. "

(Quintilian, *Oratorical Institutions*, I, 6.)

On the other hand, to depilate one's armpits was considered as necessary to the cleanliness of the body:

" One man keeps himself tidy, another neglects himself more than is right; one man depilates his legs, another does not depilate even his armpits."
(Seneca, letter, CXIV.)

Even the great Caesar did not disdain this coquetry, Suetonius, J. Caesar, ch. 45;

"He took too much care of his appearance, to the point of not only having his beard removed with nippers, but to get himself shaved and even depilated, for which things he was blamed."

There were people who had women to depilate them. Those women called themselves Ustricules (from *urere*, to burn) as they made use of boiling dropax to burn the hair on the legs and the other parts of the body. Tertullian: "He was so effeminate as to use Ustricules (Pallium, ch. 4.) Saumaise, commenting on this page, p. 284, has punned upon these words, "Formerly the Ustricules served to depilate the legs; now they serve to harass our minds."

The women likewise extirpated the hairs, looking upon the fleece of the pubes as not proper. See Martial, XII, 32.

The Greeks did not disdain this strange practice any more than the Romans. Aristophanes, in *Lysistrata* (V. 89.):—

"My affair will be tidy with the couch-grass pluck'd off." In the "*Frogs*" he speaks of dancing girls barely arrived at puberty beginning to tear off the fur (V. 518-519); in the "*Meeting of the Women*", there is also mentioned a "depilated vulva." (V. 719.) That the Greeks preferred a bare pubes to a furred one, though we may be of a different opinion, is apparent from another passage of Aristophanes in "*Lysistrata*" (V. 151-152), where a smooth pubes is given as a chief incitement to virile ardour:

"If we were to go naked with a smooth pubes, "

our husbands would get brisk and hot for copulation."
As the men employed women to free them of hair,
so women offered their pubes without shame to men
for the same office. Pliny's bile rises at this (Nat.
Hist., XXIX, 8.) "The women are not afraid to show
their pubes. It is but too true, nothing corrupts
manners more than the heart of the medical man."

The Emperors themselves did not shrink from under-
taking this office in the case of their concubines.

(Suetonius, Domitian, ch. 22.)

"It was rumoured, that he was fond of depilating
his concubines himself, and bathed in the midst of
the most infamous courtezans [1])."

ORIENTAL RABELAISIANISM

As throwing additional light upon the subject of
the practise of Depilation in the East, we extract the
following *bon morceau* from Burton's "*Nights*", where
it forms a portion of the story entitled "The man of
Al-Yaman and his Six Slave-Girls." Even with the
exception of the instructive note, this extract has a
fine flavour of Rabelaisian coarseness, combined with
an aptness of phrase probably only to be found in
the *Egyptienne* and her European compeer *la Paris-
sienne*:—

Praised be Allah who created me and beautified

---

[1]) For fuller and more detailed information on this subject,
we would refer the curious reader to Forberg's "*Manual of
Classical Erotology*", where this and sundry other cognate
matters are handled in a scholarly and most masterly manner
and the genuine Latin and Greek texts given to boot.

me and made my embraces the end of all desire, and
likened me to the branch whereto all hearts incline.
If I rise, I rise lightly; if I sit, I sit prettily; I am
nimble-witted at a jest and merrier-souled than mirth
itself. Never heard I one describe his mistress, saying, "my beloved is the bigness of an elephant or
like a mountain long and broad;" but rather, "my
lady hath a slender waist and a slim shape [1]). Furthermore a little food filleth me, and a little water
quencheth my thirst; my sport is agile and my habit
active; for I am sprightlier than the sparrow and
lighter-skipping than the startling.

My favours are the longing of the lover and the
delight of the desirer; for I am goodly of shape,
sweet of smile and graceful as the bending Willow-
wand or the rattan-cane [2]) or the stalk of the basil-
plant; nor is there any can compare with me in
loveliness, even as saith one of me:

> Thy shape with willow branch I dare compare,
> And hold thy figure as my fortunes fair:
> I wake each morn distraught, and follow thee.
> And from the rival's eye in fear I fare.

It is for the like of me that amourists run mad
and that those who desire me wax distracted. If my

---

[1]) Although the Arab's ideal of beauty, as has been seen
and said, corresponds with ours, the Egyptians, (modern) the
Maroccans and other negrofied races like "walking tun-butt"
as Clapperton called his amorous widow.

[2]) Arab. "Khayzar" or "Khayzaran" is the rattan-palm.
Those who have seen this most graceful "palmijuncus" in its
native forest will recognize the neatness of the simile.

lover would draw me to him, I am drawn to him;
and if he would have me incline to him, I incline to
him and against him. But now, as for thee, O fat
of body, thine eating is the feeding of an elephant,
and neither much nor little filleth thee. When thou
liest with a man who is lean, he hath no ease of
thee; nor can he anyways take his pleasure of thee;
for the bigness of thy belly holdeth him off from going
in unto thee and the fatness of thy thighs hindereth
him from coming at thy slit. What goodness is there
in thy grossness, and what courtesy of pleasantness
in thy coarseness? Fat flesh is fit for naught but
the flesher, nor is there one point therein that plead-
eth for praise. If one joke with thee, thou art angry;
if one sport with thee, thou art sulky; if thou sleep,
thou snorest; it thou walk, thou lollest out thy tongue;
if thou eat, thou art never filled. Thou art heavier
than mountains, and fouler than corruption and crime.
Thou hast in thee nor agility nor benedicite, nor
thinkest thou of aught save meat and sleep. When
thou pissest thou swishest; if thou turd thou gruntest
like a bursten wine-skin or an elephant transmogrified.
If thou go to the watercloset, thou needest one to
wash thy gap and pluck out the hairs which overgrow
it; and this is the extreme of sluggishness and the
sign, outward and visible, of stupidity [1]), in short,

---

[1]) This is the popular idea of a bushy "veil of nature" in
women: it is always removed by depilatories and vellication.
When Bilkis, Queen of Sheba, discovered her legs by lifting
her robe (Koran xxvii), Solomon was minded to marry her,
but would not do so till the devils had by a depilatory
removed the hair. The popular preparation (called Núrah)

there is no good thing about thee, and indeed the poet saith of thee:—

"Heavy and swollen, like an urine-blader blown
With hips and thighs like mountain propping piles of stones;
Whene'er she walks in Western hemisphere, her tread
Makes far the Eastern world with weight to moan and groan".

---

consists of quicklime 7 parts, and Zirnik or orpiment, 3 parts: it is applied in the Hammam to a perspiring skin, and it must be washed off immediately the hair is loosened or it burns and discolours. The rest of the body-pile (Sha'arat opp. to Sha'ar = hair) is eradicated by applying a mixture of boiled honey with turpentine or other gum, and rolling it with the hand till the hair comes off. Men, I have said, remove the pubes by shaving, and pluck the hair off the armpits, one of the vestiges of pre-Adamite man. A good depilatory is still a desideratum, the best perfumers of London and Paris have none which they can recommend. The reason is plain: the hair-bulb can be eradicated only by destroying the skin.

BURTON.

See Page 11 of present book for further details.

A BYPATH OF HUMAN PASSION

A BYPATH OF HUMAN PASSION

Captain Sir Richard Francis Burton, the famous Arabic Scholar, Traveller, and Explorer who, in his various Works, has done very much to draw aside the Veil concealing the Curious Mysteries of oriental "Sexuology" has printed some very remarkable Observations on the subject of Pederasty, or Boy-love, which it will not be out of place here to quote—He states [1]:

S ubsequent enquiries in many and distant countries enabled me to arrive at the following conclusions.

1. There exists what I shall call a "Sotadic Zone", bounded westwards by the northern shores of the Mediterranean (N. lat. 43°) and by the Southern (N. lat. 30°). Thus the depth would be 780 to 800 miles including meridional France, the Iberian Penin-

---

[1] Vide the tenth Vol. of the Original Edition of his famous "Nights". These notes on "Pederasty" have not been reproduced in the "Popular Edition" of the "Nights"; a concession made to British Philistinism!

sula, Italy and Grece, with the coast regions of Africa from Marocco to Egypt.

2. Running eastward the Sotadic Zone narrows, embracing Asia-Minor, Mesopotamia and Chaldea, Afghanistan, Sind, the Punjab, and Kashmir.

3. In Indo-China the belt begins to broaden, enfolding China, Japan and Turkistan.

4. It then embraces the South Sea Islands and the New World where, at the time of its discovery, Sotadic love was, with some exceptions, an established racial institution.

5. Within the Sotadic Zone, the Vice is popular and endemic, held at the worst to be a mere peccadillo, whilst the races to the North and South of the limits here defined practise it only sporadically; amid the opprobrium of their fellows, who, as a rule, are physically incapable of performing the operation and look upon it with the liveliest disgust.

Before entering into topographical details concerning Pederasty, which I hold to be geographical and climatic, not racial, I must offer a few considerations of its cause and origin. We must not forget that the love of boys has its noble sentimental side. The Platonists and pupils of the Academy, followed by the Sufis or Moslem Gnostics, held such affection, pure as ardent, to be the beau ideal which united in man's soul the creature with the Creator. Professing to regard youths as the most cleanly and beautiful objects in this phenomenal world, they declared that by loving and extolling the chef-d'œuvre, corporeal and intellectual, of the Demiurgus, disinterestedly and without any admixture of carnal sensuality, they are paying

the most fervent adoration to the Causa causans.
They add that such affection, passing as it does the
love of women, is far less selfish than fondness for
and admiration of the other sex which, however
innocent, always suggests sexuality [1]); and Easterns
add that the devotion of the moth to the taper is
purer and more fervent than the Bulbul's love for
the Rose. Amongst the Greeks of the best ages the
system of boy-favourites was advocated on considerations of morals and politics. The lover undertook
the education of the beloved through precept and
example, while the two were conjoined by a tie stricter
than the fraternal. Hieronymus the Peripatetic strongly advocated it, because the vigorous disposition of
youths, and the confidence engendered by their associ-
ation, often led to the overthrow of tyrannies. Socrates
declared that "a most valiant army might be composed
of boys and their lovers; for that of all men they
would be most ashamed to desert one another." And
even Virgil, despite the foul flavour of "Formosum
pastor Corydon," could write:—

Nisus amore pio pueri.

The only physical cause for the practice which
suggests itself to me and that must be owned to be

---

[1]) Glycon the courtezan in Athen. xiii. 34 declares that
"boys are handsome only when they resemble women"; and
so the Learned Lady in the Nights (vol. V, 160) declares
"Boys are likened to girls because folks say, Yonder boy is
like a girl." For the superior physical beauty of the human
male compared with the female, see the Nights, vol. IV, 15;
and the boy's voice before it breaks excels that of any diva.

purely conjectural, is that within the Sotadic Zone there is a blending of the masculine and feminine temperaments, a crasis which elsewhere only occurs sporadically. Hence the *feminisme* whereby the man becomes patiens as well as agens, and the woman a tribade, a votary of mascula Sappho [1]), Queen of

---

[1]) "Mascula" from the Priapiscus, the over-development of clitoris (the veretrum muliebre, (in Arabic, Abu Tartür) habens cristam), which enabled her to play the man. Sappho (nat. B. C. 612) has been retoilée like Mary Stuart, La Brinvilliers, Marie-Antoinette, and a host of feminine names which have a savour not of sanctity. Maximus of Tyre (Dissert xxiv) declares that the Eros of Sappho was Socratic. and that Gyrinna and Atthis were as Alcibiades and Chermides to Socrates: Ovid, who could consult documents now lost, takes the same view in the Letter of Sappho to Phaon in Tristia ii. 265.

Lesbia quid docuit Sappho nisi amare puellas?

Suidas supports Ovid. Longinus eulogises the ἐρωτικη μανία (a term applied only to carnal love) of the far-famed ode to Atthis:—

(Ille mî par esse videtur***.
(*Heureux! qui près de toi pour toi seule soupire***
Blest as th'immortal gods is he, etc.)

By its love symptoms, suggesting that possession is the sole cure for passion, Erasistratus discovered the love of Antiochus for Stratonice. Mure (Hist. of Greek Literature, 1880) speaks of the Ode to Aphrodite (Frag. I) as "one in which the whole volume of Greek literature offers the most powerful concentration into one brilliant focus of the modes in which amatory concupiscence can display itself." But Bernhardy, Bode, Richter, K. O. Müller and especially Welcker have made Sappho a model of purity, much like some of our dull wits who have converted Shakespeare, that most debauched genius, into a good British bourgeois.

Frictrices or Rubbers. Prof. Mantegazza claims to have discovered the cause of this pathological love, this perversion of the erotic sense, one of the marvellous list of amorous vagaries which deserve, not prosecution but the pitiful care of the physician, and the study of the physiologist. According to him, the nerves of the rectum and the genitalia, in all cases closely connected, are abnormally so in the pathic who obtains by intromission the venereal orgasm which is usually sought through the sexual organs. So amongst women there are tribads who can procure no pleasure except by foreign objects introduced a posteriori. Hence his threefold distribution of Sodomy [1]); Peripheric or anatomical, caused by an unusual distribution of the nerves and their hyperaesthesia; luxurious, when love a tergo is preferred on account of the narrowness of the passage; and (3) the Psychical. But this is evidently superficial: the question is what causes this neuropathy, this abnormal distribution and condition of the nerves [1])?

---

[1]) The Arabic Sahhákah, the Tractatrix or Subigitatrix, who has been noticed in vol. IV, 134. Hence to Lesbianise ($\lambda \varepsilon \sigma \sigma \iota \zeta \varepsilon \iota \nu$) and tribassare ($\tau \varrho \iota \sigma \varepsilon \sigma \vartheta \alpha \iota$); the former applied to the love of woman for woman, and the latter to its mécanique; this is either natural, as friction of the Labia and insertion of the clitoris when unusually developed; or artificial by means of the fascinum, the artificial penis (the Persian "Mayájang"); the patte de chat, the banana-fruit and a multitude of other succedanea. As this feminine perversion is only glanced at in The Nights, I need hardly enlarge upon the subject.

[2]) Plato (symp.) is probably mystical when he accounts for such passions by there being in the beginning three species of humanity, men, women, and men-women or androgyne.

As Prince Bismarck finds a difference between the male and female races of history, so I suspect a mixed physical temperament effected by the manifold subtle influences massed together in the word climate. Something of the kind is necessary to explain the fact of this pathological love extending over the greater portion of the habitable world, without any apparent connection of race or media, from the polished Greek to the cannibal Tupi of the Brazil. Walt Whitman speaks of the ashen grey faces of onanists: the faded colours, the puffy features and the unwholesome complexion of the professed pederast with his peculiar cachectic expression, indescribable but once seen never forgotten, stamp the breed, and Dr. G. Adolph is justified in declaring "Alle Gewohnheits paederasten

---

When the latter were destroyed by Zeus for rebellion, the two others were individually divided into equal parts. Hence each division seeks its other half in the same sex; the primitive man prefers men, and the primitive woman women. C'est beau, but—is it true? The idea was probably derived from Egypt, which supplied the Hebrews with andrognic humanity; and thence it passed to extreme India, where Shiva as Ardhanari was male on one side and female on the other side of the body, combining paternal and maternal qualities and functions. The first creation of humans (Gen. I. 27 was hermaphrodite (= Hermes and Venus) masculum et fæminam creavit eos.—Male and female created he them—on the sixth day, with the command to increase and multiply (ibid. v. 28) while Eve, the woman, was created subsequently. Meanwhile, say certain Talmudists, Adam carnally copulated with all races of animals. Sec. L'Anandryne, in Mirabeau's Erotika Biblion, where Antoinette Bourgnon laments the undoubling which disfigured the work of God, producing monsters incapable of independent self-reproduction like the vegetable kingdom.

erkennen sich einander schnell, oft mit einen Blick."
This has nothing in common with the féminisme
which betrays itself in the pathic by womanly gait,
regard and gesture: it is a something sui generis;
and the same may be said of the colour and look of
the young priest who honestly refrains from women
or their substitutes. Dr. Tardieu, in his well-known work
"Etude médico-légale sur les Attentats aux Mœeurs",
and Dr. Adolph, note a peculiar infundibuliform disposition of the "After", and a smoothness and want
of folds even before any abuse has taken place, together
with special forms of the male organs in confirmed
pederasts. But these observations have been rejected
by Caspar, Hoffmann, Brouardel and Dr. J. H. Henri
Coutagne (Notes sur la Sodomie, Lyon, 1880), and it
is a medical question whose discussion would here be
out of place.

The origin of Pederasty is lost in the night of
ages: but its historique has been carefully traced by
many writers, especially Virey [1]), Rosenbaum [2]) and
M. H. E. Meier [3]). The ancient Greeks who, like the
modern Germans, invented nothing but were great
improvers of what other races invented, attributed the

---

[1]) De la femme, Paris, 1827.

[2]) Die Lustsuche des Alterthum's, Halle, 1839.

[3]) See his exhaustive article on (Grecian) "Paederastie" in
the Allgemeine Encyclopœdie of Ersch u. Gruber, Leipzig,
Brockhaus, 1837. He carefully traces it through the several
states, Dorians, Æolians, Ionians, the Attic cities and those of
Asia Minor. For these details I must refer my readers to
Mr. Meier; a full account of these would fill a volume, not
the section of an essay.

formal apostolate of Sotadism to Orpheus, whose stigmata were worn by the Thracian women:

> —Omnenque refugerat Orpheus
> Fæmineam venerem ;—
> llle etiam Thracum populis fuit auctor, amorem
> ln teneres transferre mares : citraque juventam
> Ætatis breve ver, et primos carpere flores.
>
> Ovid. *Met*. x. 79—85.

Euripides proposed Laïus father of Oedipus as the inaugurator, whereas Timaeus declared that the fashion of making favourites of boys was introduced into Greece from Crete, for Malthusian reasons, said Aristotle (Pol. ɪɪ. 10) attributing it to Minos. Herodotus, however, knew far better, having discovered (ii c. 80) that the Orphic and Bacchic rites were originally Egyptian. But the Father of History was a traveller and an annalist rather than an archaeologist, and he tripped in the following passage (I C. 135) "As soon as they (the Persians) hear of any luxury, they instantly make it their own, and hence, among other matters, they have learned from the Hellenes a passion for boys" ("Unnatural lust" says modest Rawlinson). Plutarch (De Malig, Herod. xɪɪɪ) [1]) asserts with much more probability that the Persians used eunuch boys according to the *Mos Graecia*, long before they had seen the Grecian main.

In the Holy Books of the Hellenes, Homer and Hesiod, dealing with the heroic ages, there is no trace of pederasty. although, in a long subsequent

---

[1]) Against which see Henri Estienne, Apologie pour Hérodote a society satire of XVIth century, lately reprinted by Liseux.

generation Lucian suspected Achilles and Patroclus, as he did Orestes and Pylades, Theseus and Pirithous. Homer's praises of beauty are reserved for the feminines, especially his favourite Helen. But the Dorians of Crete seem to have commended the abuse to Athens and Sparta, and subsequently imported it into Tarentum, Agrigentum and other colonies. Ephorus in Strabo (x. 4 § 21) gives a curious account of the violent abduction of beloved boys by the lover; of the obligations of the ravisher to the favourite ¹) and of the marriage ceremonies which lasted two months. See also Plato Laws I. c. 8. Servius (Ad. Æneid. x. 325) informs us "De Cretensibus accepimus, quod in amore puerorum intemperantus fuerunt, quod postea in Laconas et in totam Græciam translatum est." The Cretans, and afterwards their apt pupils the Chalcidians, held it disreputable for a beautiful boy to lack a lover. Hence Zeus, the national Doric God of Crete, loved Ganymede ²); Apollo, another Dorian deity, loved

---

¹) In Sparta the lover was called ει̇σπνηλας and the beloved as in Thessaly α̇ι̇της.

²) The more I study religions, the more I am convinced that man never worshipped anything but himself. Zeus, who became Jupiter, was an ancient King, according to the Cretans, who were entitled liars because they showed his burial-place. From a deified ancestor he would become a local god, like the Hebrew Jehovah, as opposed to Chemosh of Moab; the name would gain amplitude by long time and distant travel, and the old island chieftain would end in becoming the demiurgus. Ganymede (who possibly gave rise to the old Lat. "Catamitus") was probably some fair Phyrgian boy ("son of Tros") who in process of time became a symbol of the wise man seized by the eagle (perspicacity) to be raised amongst the Immortals;

Hyacinth, and Hercules, a Doric hero who grew to be a sungod, loved Hylas and a host of others: thus Crete sanctified the practice by the examples of the gods and demi-gods. But when legislation came, the subject had qualified itself for legal limitation, and as such was undertaken by Lycurgus and Solon, according to Xenophon (Lac. ii. 13) who draws a broad distinction between the honest love of boys and dishonest (ἀίχιστος) lust.

They both approved of pure pederastia, like that of Harmodius and Aristogiton; but forbade it with serviles, as degrading to a free man. Hence the love of boys was spoken of like that of women (Plato: Phædrus; Repub. vi. c. 19 and Xenophon, Synop. iv. 10) *e. g.*, "There was once a boy, or rather a youth, of exceeding beauty and he had very many lovers"— this is the language of Hafiz and Sa'adi. Æschylus, Sophocles and Euripides were allowed to introduce it upon the stage, for "many men were as fond of having boys for their favourites as women for their mistresses; and this was a fashion in many well-regulated cities of Greece." Poets like Alcæus, Anacreon, Agathon, and Pindar affected it and Theognis sang of a "beautiful boy in the flower of his youth." The statesmen Aristides and Themistocles quarrelled over Stesileus of Teos; and Pisistratus loved Charmus, who first built an altar to puerile Eros, while Charmus loved Hippias, son of Pisistratus. Demosthenes the

---

and the chaste myth simply signified that only the prudent are loved by the gods. But it rotted with age, as do all things human. For the Pederastia of the gods, see Bayle under Chrysippe.

orator took into keeping a youth called Cnosion, greatly to the indignation of his wife. Xenophon loved Clinias and Autolycus; Aristotle, Hermas, Theodectes [1]) and others; Empedocles, Pausanias; Epicurus, Pytocles; Aristippus, Eutichydes, and Zeno with his stoics had a philosophic disregard for women, affecting only pederastia. A man in Athenæus (iv. c. 40) left in his will that certain youths he had loved should fight like gladiators at his funeral; and Charicles in Lucian abuses Callicratidas for his love of " sterile pleasures. " Lastly there was the notable affair of Alcibiades and Socrates, the "sanctus pæderasta" [2]) being violemment soupçonné when under the mantle: non semper sine plagâ ab eo surrexit. Athenæus (v. c. 13) declares that Plato represents Socrates as absolutely intoxicated with his passion for Alcibiades [3]).

[1]) See. Dissertation sur les idées morales des Grecs et sur les dangers de lire Platon. Par M. Audé, Bibliophile, Lemonnyer, Rouen, 1879. This is the pseudonym of the late Octave Delepierre, who published with Gay, but not the Editio Princeps—which, if I remember rightly, contains much more matter.

[2]) The phrase of J. Matthias Gesner, Comm. Reg. Soc. Gœttingen i. I-32. It was founded upon Erasmus' "Sancte Socrate, ora pro nobis", and the article was translated by M. Alcide Bonneau, Paris, Liseux, 1877.

[3]) The subject has employed many a pen, e. g. Alcibiade Fanciullo a Scola, D. P. A. (supposed to be Pietro Aretino—ad captandum?) Oranges, par Juan Wart, 1652: small square 8 vo. of pp. 102, including 3 preliminary pp. and at end an unpaged leaf with 4 sonnets, almost Venetian, by V. M. There is a re-impression of the same date, a small 12 mo. of longer format, pp. 124 with pp. 2 for sonnets; in 1862 the imprimerie Raçon, printed 102 copies in 8°, of pp. IV.-108, and in 1863

The ancients seem to have held the connection impure, or Juvenal would not have written—

Inter Socraticos notissima fossa cinædos,

followed by Firmicus (vii. 14) who speaks of " Socratici pædicones ". It is the modern fashion to doubt the pederasty of the master of Hellenic Sophrosyne, the " Christian before Christianity " ; but such a world-wide term as Socratic love can hardly be explained by the lucus-a-non-lucendo principle. We are overapt to apply our nineteenth century prejudices and pre-

---

it was condemned by the police as a liber spurcissimus atque excrandus de criminis sodomici laude et arte. This work produced " Alcibiade Enfant à l'école ", traduit pour la première fois de l'Italien de Ferrante Pallavicini, Amsterdam, chez l'ancien Pierre Marteau, mdccclxvi. Pallavicini (nat. 1618), who wrote against Rome, was beheaded, æt. 26 (March 5, 1644) at Avignon by the vengeance of the Barberini : he was a bel esprit déréglé, nourri d'études antiques and a memb. of the Acad. Degl' Incogniti. His peculiarities are shown by his " Opere Scelte ", 2 vols 12 mo. Villafranca, mdclxiii ; these do not include Alcibiade Fanciullo, a dialogue between Philotimus and Alcibiades which seems to be a mere skit at the Jesuits and their Péché philosophique. Then came the " Dissertation sur Alcibiade Fanciullo a Scola " traduit de l'Italien de Giambattista Baseggio et accompagnée de notes et d'une post-face par un bibliophile français (M. Gustave Brunet, Librarian of Bordeaux) : Paris, J. Gay, 1861—un 8vo. of pp. 78 (paged) 254 copies. The same Baseggio printed in 1850 his Disquisi-zione (23 copies) and claims for F. Pallavicine the authorship of Alcibiades which the Manuel du Libraire wrongly attributes to M. Girol. Adda in 1859. I have heard of but not seen the " Amator fornaceus, amator ineptus " (Palladii, 1633) supposed by some to be the origin of Alcibiade Fanciullo ; but most critics consider it a poor and insipid production.

possessions to the morality of the ancient Greeks who would have specimen'd such squeamishness in Attic salt.

The Spartans, according to Agnon the Academic (confirmed by Plato, Plutarch and Cicero), treated boys and girls in the same way before marriage: hence Juvenal (xi. 173) uses "Lacedæmonius" for a pathic, and other writers apply it to a tribade. After the Peloponnesian war, which ended in B. C. 404, the use became merged in the abuse. Yet some purity must have survived, even amongst the Bœotians, who produced the famous Narcissus [1]), described by Ovid (Met. iii. 339) :—

> Multi illum juvenes, multæ cupiere puellæ ;
> Nulli illum juvenes, nullæ tetigere puellæ : [2])

for Epaminondas, whose name is mentioned with three beloveds, established a Holy Regiment composed of mutual lovers, testifying the majesty of Eros and preferring to a discreditable life a glorious death.

---

[1]) The word is from νάρκη, numbness, torpor, narcotism: the flowers, being loved by the infernal gods, were offered to the Furies. Narcissus and Hippolytus are often assumed as types of morosa voluptas, masturbation and clitorisation for nymphomania: certain mediæval writers found in the former a type of the Saviour; and Mirabeau a representation of the androgynous or first Adam: to me, Narcissus suggests the Hindu Vishnu absorbed in the contemplation of his own perfections.

[2]) The verse of Ovid is parallel'd by the song of Al-Zàhir-al-Jazari (Ibn Khall, iii, 720).

> Illum impuberem amaverunt mares ; puberem feminae.
> Gloria Deo ! nunquam amatoribus carebit.

Philip's reflections on the fatal field of Chaeroneia
form their fittest epitaph. At last the Athenians,
according to Æschines, officially punished Sodomy
with death; but the threat did not destroy bordels of
boys, like those of Karachi; the Porneia and Porno-
boskeia, where slaves and "pueri venales" "stood",
as the term was, near the Pnyx, the city walls and a
certain tower, also about Lycabettus (Æsch. contra
Tim.); and paid a fixed tax to the state. The pleasures
of society in civilized Greece (I) seem to have been
sought chiefly in the heresies of love—Hetairesis[1])
and Sodatism.

It is calculated that the French of the sixteenth
century had four hundred names for the parts genital,
and three hundred for their use in coition. The Greek
vocabulary is not less copious, and some of its pederastic terms, of which Meier gives nearly a hundred,
and its nomenclature of pathologic love are curious
and picturesque enough to merit quotation.

To live the life of Abron (the Argive) i. e. That
of a πάσχων, pathic or passive lover.

The Agathonian song.

---

[1]) The venerable society of prostitutes contained three chief
classes. The first and lowest were the Dicteriads, so called
from Diete (Crete) who imitated Pasiphaë, wife of Minos, in
preferring a bull to a husband; above them was the middle
class, the Aleutridæ who were the Almahs or professional
musicians, and the aristocracy was represented by the Hetairai,
whose wit and learning enabled them to adorn more than one
page of Grecian history. The grave Solon, who had studied
in Egypt, established a vast Dicterion (Philemon in his
Delphica), or bordel, whose proceeds swelled the revenue of
the Republic.

Aischrourgia = dishonest love, also called Akolasia, Akrasia, Arrenokoitja, etc.

Alcinoan youths, or "non-conformists,"

In cute curandâ plus æquo operata Juventus.

Alegomenos, the "Unspeakable", as the pederast was termed by the Council of Ancyra: also the Agrios, Apolaustus and Akolastos.

Androgine, of whom Ansonius wrote (Epig. lxviii. 15):—

Ecce ego sum factus femina de puero.

Badas and Badizein = clunes torquens: also Batalos = a catamite.

Catapygos, Katapygosyne = puerarius and catadactylium from.

Dactylion, the ring, used in the sense of Nerissa's, but applied to the corollarium puerile.

Cinædus (Kinaidos), the active lover ($\pi o\iota\omega\nu$) derived either from his kinetics or quasi ($\varkappa\grave{\upsilon}\omega\nu$ $\mathring{\alpha}\iota\delta\tilde{\omega}\varsigma$) = dogmodest, also Spatalocinædus (lasciviâ fluens) = a fair Ganymede.

Chalcidissare (Khalkidizein) from Chalcis in Euboea, a city famous for love a posteriori; mostly applied to le léchement des testicules by children.

Clazomenæ = the buttocks, also a sotadic disease, so-called from the Ionian city devoted to Aversa Venus; also used of a pathic.

—et tergo femina pube vir est.

Embasicoetas, prop. a link-boy at marriages, also a "night-cap" drunk before bed, and lastly an effeminate; one who perambulavit omnium cubilia (Catullus). See Encolpius' pun upon the Embasicete in Satyricon, cap. IV.

Epipedesis, the carnal assault.

Geiton lit. "Neighbour" the beloved of Encolpius, which has produced the Fr. Giton = Bardache, Ital. bardascia from the Arab. Baradaj, a captive, a slave; the augm. form is Polygeiton.

Hippias (tyranny of) when the patient of (woman or boy) mounts the agent. Aristoph. Vesp. 502. So also Kelitizein = peccare superne or equum agitare supernum of Horace.

Mokhtheria, depravity with boys.

Paidika, whence pædicare (act) and pædicari (pass); so in the Latin poet:—

> PEnelopes primam DIdonis prima sequatur,
> Et primam CAni, syllaba prima REmi.

Pathicos, Pathicus, a passive, like Malakos (malacus, mollis, facilis), Malchio, Trimalchio (Petronius), Malta, Maltha. and in Horace (Sat. II. 25).

> Malthinus tunicis demissis ambulat.

Praxis = the malpractice.

Pygisma = buttockry, because most actives end within the nates, being too much excited for further intromission.

Phoenicissare (ψοινικίζειν) = cunnilingere in tempore menstruum, quia hoc vitium in Phœnicia generata solebat (Thes. Erot. Ling, Lat.); also irrumer en miel.

Phicidissare, denotat actum per canes commissum

quando lambunt cunnos vel testiculos (Suetonius):
also applied to pollution of childhood.

Samorium flores (Erasmus, Prov. xxiii.) alluding to
the androgynic prostitutions of Samos.

Siphniassare (σιφνιαζειν, from Siphnos, hod. Sifanto
Island) = digito podicem fodere ad pruriginem res-
tinguendam, says Erasmus (see Mirabeau's Erotika
Biblion, Anoscopie).

Thrypsis = the rubbing.

Pederastia had in Greece, I have shown, its noble
and ideal side: Rome however, borrowed her mal-
practices, like her religion and polity, from those
ultra-material Etruscans and debauched with a brazen
face. Even under the Republic, Plautus (Casin. ii, 21)
makes one of his characters exclaim, in the utmost
sangfroid, "Ultro te, amator, apage te a dorso meo!"
With increased luxury the evil grew, and Livy notices
(xxxix, 13), at the Bacchanalia, plura virorum inter
sese quam fœminarum stupra. There where individual
protests, for instance S. Q. Fabius Maximus Servilianus
(Consul U. C. 612) punished his son for dubia castitas;
and a private soldier, C. Plotius, killed his military
Tribune, Q. Luscius, for unchaste proposals. The Lex
Scantinia (Scatinia?), popularly derived from Scanti-
nius the tribune and of doubtful date (B. C. 226?)
attempted to abate the scandal by fine, and the Lex
Julia by death; but they were trifling obstacles to
the flood of infamy which surged in with the Empire.
No class seems then to have disdained these "sterile
pleasures": l'on n'attachait point alors à cette espèce
d'amour une note d'infamie, comme en païs de chré-
tienté, says Bayle under "Anacreon". The great

Cæsar, the Cinædus calvus of Catullus, was the husband of all the wives and the wife of all the husbands in Rome (Suetonius, cap. LII); and his soldiers sang in his praise, Gallias Cæsar subegit, Nicomedes Cæsarem (Suet. cies XLIX.); whence his sobriquet "Fornix Byrthinicus". Of Augustus the people chaunted.

> Videsne ut Cinædus orbem digito temperet?

Tiberius, with his pisciculi and greges exoletorum, invented the Symplegma or nexus of Sellarii, agentes et patientes in which the spinthriae (lit. women's bracelet's) were connected in a chain by the bond of flesh [1]) (Seneca Quæst. Nat.): Of this refinement, which in the earlier part of the nineteenth century was renewed by sundry Englishmen at Naples, Ausonius wrote (Epig. cxix. I).

> Tres uno in lecto: stuprum duo perpetiuntur;

And Martial had said (XII. 43).

> Quo symplegmate quinque copulentur;
> Qua plures teneantur a catena; etc.

Ausonius recounts of Caligula he so lost patience that he forcibly entered the priest, M. Lepidus, before the sacrifice was completed. The beautiful Nero was formally married to Pythagoras (or Doryphoros) and afterwards took to wife Sporus who was first subjected

---

[1]) This and Saint Paul (Romans I, 27) suggested to Caravaggio his picture of Saint Rosario (in the Museum of the Grand Duke of Tuscany), showing a circle of thirty men turpiter ligati.

to castration of a peculiar fashion; he was then named Sabina after the deceased spouse, and claimed queenly honours. The "Othonis et Trajani pathici" were famed; the great Hadrian openly loved Antinous and the wild debaucheries of Heliogabalus seem only to have amused, instead of disgusting, the Romans.

Uranopolis allowed public lupanaria where adults and meritorii pueri, who began their career as early as seven years, stood for hire : the inmates of these cauponæ wore sleeved tunics and dalmatics like women. As in modern Egypt, pathic boys, we learn from Catullus, haunted the public baths. Debauchees had signals like freemasons, whereby they recognised one another. The Greek Skematizein was made by closing the hand to represent the scrotum and raising the middle finger as if to feel whether a hen had eggs, tâter si les poulettes ont l'œuf: hence the Athenians called it Catapygon or sodomite and the Romans digitus impudicus or infamis, the "medical finger" [1]) of Rabelais and the Chiromantists. Another sign was to scratch the head with the minimus —digitulo caput scabere (Juv. ix. 133) [2]). The prostitution of boys was first forbidden by Domitian; but Saint Paul, a Greek, had formally expressed his abomination of Le Vice (Rom. i. 26 ; 1 Cor. vi. 8) and we may agree

---

[1]) Properly speaking "Medicus is the third or ring-finger, as shown by the old Chiromantist verses.

Est pollex Veneris; sed Jupiter indice gaudet,
Saturnus medium; Sol *medicumque* tenet.

[2]) So Seneca uses "digito scalpit caput". The modern Italian does the same by inserting the thumb-tip between the index and medius to suggest the clitoris.

with Grotius (de Verit. ɪɪ c. 13) that early Christianity did much to suppress it. At last the Emperor Theodosius punished it with fire as a profanation, because sacrosanctum esse debetur hospitium virilis animæ.

In the pagan days of Imperial Rome her literature makes no difference betwen boy and girl. Horace naïvely says (Sat. ɪɪ. 119):

> Ancilla aut verna est præsto puer;

and with Hamlet, but in a dishonest sense :—

> —Man delights me not
> Nor woman neither.

Similarly the Spaniard, Martial, who is a mine of such pederastic allusions (xɪ. 46) :—

> Sive puer arrisit, sive puella tibi.

That marvellons satyricon which unites the wit of Molière [1]) with the debaucheries of Piron, whilst the

---

[1]) What can be wittier than the now trite Tale of the Ephesian Matron, whose dry humour is worthy of " The Nights " ? No wonder that it has made the grand tour of the world. It is found in the neo-Phædrus, the tales of Musæus and in the Septem Sapientes, as the " Widow which was comforted ". As the " Fabliau de la Femme qui se fit putain sur la fosse de son mari ", it tempted Brantome and La Fontaine; and Abel Rémusat shows in his " Contes Chinois " that it is well known to the Middle Kingdom. Mr. Walter K. Kelly remarks, that the most singular place for such a tale is the " Rule and Exercise of Holy Dying " by Jeremy Taylor, who introduces it into his chap. v.—" Of the Contingencies of Death and Treating our Dead ". But in those days divines were not mealy-mouthed.

writer has been described, like Rabelais, as purissimus in puritate, is a kind of Triumph of Pederasty. Geiton, the hero, a handsome curly-pated hobbledehoy of seventeen, with his calinerie and wheedling tongue, is courted like one of the sequor sexius : his lovers are inordinately jealous of him, and his desertion leaves deep scars upon the heart. But no dialogue between man and wife in extremis could be more pathetic than that in the scene where shipwreck is imminent. Elsewhere every one seems to attempt his neighbour : a man, alte succinctus, assails Ascyltos ; Lycus, the Tarentine skipper, would force Encolpius, and so forth : yet we have the neat and finished touch (cap. vii) :—
"The lamentation was very fine (the dying man having manumitted his slaves) albeit his wife wept not as though she loved him. *How were it had he not behaved to her so well ?* "

Erotic Latin Glossaries [1]) give some ninety words connected with Pederasty and some, which "speak with Roman simplicity", are peculiarly expressive.

---

[1]) Glossarium Eroticum Linguæ Latinæ, sive Theogoniæ, legum et morum nuptialum apud Romanos explanatio nova, auctore P.P. (Parisiis, Dondey-Dupré, 1826, in-8°) P.P. is supposed to be the Chevalier Pierre Pierrugues, an engineer who made a plan of Bordeaux, and who annotated the Erotica Biblion. Gay writes, " On s'est servi pour cet ouvrage des travaux inédits de M. le baron de Schonen, etc. Quant au chevalier Pierre Pierrugues, qu'on désignait comme l'auteur de ce savant volume, son existence n'est pas bien avérée, et quelques bibliographes persistent à penser que ce nom cache la collaboration du baron de Schonen et d'Éloi Johanneau. Other glossicists, as Blondeau and Forberg have been printed by Liseux, Paris.

"Aversa Venus" alludes to women being treated as boys: hence Martial, translated by Piron, addresses Mistress Martial (v. 44):—

Teque puta, cunnos, uxor, habere duos.

The capillatus or comatus is also called calamistrarus, the darling curled with crisping irons; and he is an Effeminatus, *i. e.* qui muliebra patitur; or a Delicatus, slave or eunuch for the use of the Draucus, Puerarius (boy-lover) or Dominus (Mart. xi. 71). The Divisor is so called from his practice Hillas dividere or cædere, something like Martial's cacare mentulam or Juvenal's Hesternæ occurrere cænæ. Facere vicibus (Juv. vii. 238), incestare se invicem or muruum facere (Plaut. Trin. ii. 437), is described as "a puerile vice", in which the two take turns to be active and passive: they are also called Gemelli and Fratres = compares in prædicatione. Illicita libido is = præpostera seu postica Venus, and is expressed by the picturesque phrase indicare (seu incurvare) aliquem. Depilatus, divellere pilos, glaber, lævis, and nates pervellere are allusions to the Sotadic toilette. The fine distinction between demittere and dejicere caput are worthy of a glossary, while pathica puella, puera, putus, pullipremo, pusio, pygiaca sacra, quadrupes, scarabæus and smerdalius explain themselves.

From Rome the practice extended far and wide to her colonies, especially the Provincia now called Provence. Athenæus (xii. 26) charges the people of Massilia with "acting like women out of luxury"; and he cites the saying "May you sail to Massilia!"

as if it were another Corinth. Indeed the whole Keltic race is charged with Le Vice by Aristotle (Pol. II. 66), Strabo (IV. 199) and Diodorus Siculus (v. 32). Roman civilisation carried also pederasty to Northern Africa, where it took firm root, while the negro and negroid race to the South ignore the erotic perversion, except where imported by foreigners into such Kingdoms as Bornu and Haussa. In old Mauritania, now Marocco [1]), the Moors are notable sodomites; Moslems, even of saintly houses, are permitted openly to keep catamites, nor do their disciples think worse of their sanctity for such licence: in one case the English wife failed to banish from the home "that horrid boy."

Yet pederasty is forbidden by the Koran. In chap. IV. 20. we read; "And if two (men) among you commit the crime, then punish them both," the penalty being

---

[1]) This magnificent country, which the petty jealousies of Europe condemn, like the glorious regions about Constantinople, to mere barbarism, is tenanted by three Moslem races. The Berbers, who call themselves Tamazight (plur. of Amazigh) are the Gaetulian indigenes speaking an Africo-Semitic tongue (See Essai de grammaire Kabyle, etc., par A. Hanoteau, Paris, Benjamin Duprat). The Arabs, descended from the conquerors in our eighth century, are mostly nomads and camel-breeders. Third and last are the Moors proper, the race dwelling in towns, a mixed breed originally Arabian but modified by six centuries of Spanish residence, and showing by thickness of feature and a parchment-colored skin, resembling the American Octoroon's, a negro innervation of old date. The latter are well described in "Morocco and the Moors", etc. (Sampson Low & C°, 1876), by my late friend Dr. Arthur Leared, whose work I should like to see reprinted.

some hurt or damage by public reproach, insult or scourging. There are four distinct references to Lot and the Sodomites in chapters VII. 78; XI. 77-84; XXVI. 160-174 and XXIX, 28-36. In the first the Prophet commissioned to the people says, "Proceed ye to a fulsome act wherein no creature hath foregone ye? Verily ye come to men in lieu of women lustfully." We have then an account of the rain which made an end of the wicked, and this judgment on the cities of the plain is repeated with more detail in the second reference. Here the angels, generally supposed to be three, Gabriel, Michael and Raphael, appeared to Lot as beautiful youths, a sore temptation to the sinners, and the godly man's arm was straitened concerning his visitors because he felt unable to protect them from the erotic vagaries of his fellow townsmen. He therefore shut his doors and from behind them argued the matter: presently the riotous assembly attempted to climb the wall when Gabriel, seeing the distress of his host, smote them on the face with one of his wings and blinded them, so that all moved off crying for aid and saying that Lot had magicians in his house. Hereupon the "Cities" which, if they ever existed, must have been Fellah villages, were uplifted: Gabriel thrust his wing under them and raised them so high that the inhabitants of the lower heaven (the lunar sphere) could hear the dogs barking and the cocks crowing. Then came the rain of stones: these were clay pellets baked in hellfire, streaked white and red, or having some mark to distinguish them from the ordinary, and each bearing the name of its destination, like the missiles which destroyed the host of

Abrahat-al-Ashram ¹). Lastly the "Cities" were turned upside down and cast upon earth. These circumstantial unfacts are repeated at full lengh in the other two chapters; but rather as an instance of Allah's power than as a warning against pederasty, which Mohammed seems to have regarded with philosophic indifference. The general opinion of his followers is that it should be punished like fornication, unless the offenders made a public act of penitence. But here, as in adultery, the law is somewhat too clement, and will not convict unless four credible witnesses swear to have seen rem in re. I have noticed (vol. ι. 211) the vicious opinion that the Ghilman or Wuldan, the beautiful boys of paradise, the counterparts of the Houris, will be lawful catamites to the True Believers in a future state of happiness: the idea is nowhere countenanced in Al-Islam; and although I have often heard debauchees refer to it, the learned look upon the assertion as scandalous.

As in Marocco, so the Vice prevails throughout the old regencies of Algiers, Tunis and Tripoli and all the cities of the South Mediterranean seaboard, whilst it is unknown to the Nubians, the Berbers and the wilder tribes dwelling inland. Proceeding Eastward we reach Egypt, that classical region of all abominations which, marvellous to relate, flourished in closest contact with men leading the purest of lives, models

---

¹) Thus somewhat agreeing with one of the multidudinous modern theories that the Pentapolis was destroyed by discharges of meteoric stones during a tremendous thunder-storm. Possible;— but where are the stones?

of moderation and morality, of religion and virtue. Amongst the ancient Copts, Le Vice was part and portion of the Ritual, and was represented by two male partridges alternately copulating (Interp. in Priapi Carm. xvii). The evil would have gained strength by the invasion of Cambyses (B. C. 524), whose armies, after the victory over Psammenitus, settled in the Nile-Valley, and held it, despite sundry revolts, for some hundred and ninety years. During these six generations the Iranians left their mark upon Lower Egypt and, especially, as the late Rogers Bey proved, upon the Fayyum, the most ancient Delta of the Nile ¹). Nor would the evil be diminished by the Hellenes who under Alexander the great, "Liberator and Saviour of Egypt" (B. C. 332), extinguished the native dynasties: the love of the Macedonian for Bagoas the eunuch being a matter of history. From that time, and under the rule of the Ptolemies the morality gradually decayed; the Canopic orgies extended into private life, and the debauchery of the men was equalled only by the depravity of the women. Neither Christianity nor Al-Islam could effect a change for the better; and social morality seems to have been at its worst during the past century, when Sonnini travelled (A. D. 1717)) The French officer, who is thoroughly trustworthy, draws a dark picture of the widely-spread criminality, especially of the bestiality and the sodomy

---

¹) To this Iranian domination I attribute the use of many Persic words which are not yet obsolete in Egypt. "Bakhshish", for instance, is not intelligible in the Moslem regions west of the Nile-Valley, and for a present the Moors say Hadiyah, regalo or favor.

(chap. xv.) which formed the "delight of the Egyptians." During the Napoleonic conquest, Jaubert in his letter to General Bruix (p. 19) says, "Les Arabes et les Mamelouks ont traité quelques-uns de nos prisonniers comme Socrate traitait, dit-on, Alcibiade. Il fallait périr ou y passer." Old Anglo-Egyptians still chuckle over the tale of Sa'd Pasha and M. de Ruyssenaer, the high-dried and highly respectable Consul-General for the Netherlands, who was solemnly advised to make the experiment, active and passive, before offering his opinion upon the subject. In the present age, extensive intercourse with Europeans has produced, not a reformation but a certain reticence amongst the upper classes: they are as vicious as ever, but they do not care to display their vices to the eyes of mocking strangers.

Syria and Palestine, another ancient focus of abominations, borrowed from Egypt, and exaggerated the worship of androgynic and hermaphroditic deities. Plutarch (De Iside) notes that the old Nilotes held the moon to be of "male-female sex", the men sacrificing to Luna and the women to Lunus [1]), Isis also was a hermaphrodite, the idea being that Aether or Air (the lower heavens) was the menstruum of

---

[1]) Arnobius and Tertullian, with the arrogance of their caste and its miserable ignorance of that symbolism which often concealed from vulgar eyes the most precious mysteries, used to taunt the heathen for praying to deities whose sex they ignored: " Consuistis in precibus Seu tu Deus seu tu Dea, dicere! " These men would know everything; they made God the merest work of man's brains, and armed him with a despotism of omnipotence which rendered their creation truly dreadful.

J

generative nature; and Damascius explained the tenet by the all-fruitful and prolific powers of the atmosphere. Hence the fragment attributed to Orpheus, the song of Jupiter (Air).—

> All things from Jove descend
> Jove was a male, Jove was a deathless bride;
> For men call Air, of two-fold sex, the Jove.

Julius Firmicus asserts that "The Assyrians and part of the Africans" (Along the Mediterranean seaboard?) "hold Air to be the chief element and adore its fanciful figure (imaginata figura), consecrated under the name of Juno or the Virgin Venus. * * * Their companies of priests cannot duly serve her unless they effeminate their faces, smooth their skins, and disgrace their masculine sex by feminine ornaments. You may see men in their very temples, amid general groans, enduring miserable dalliance and becoming passives like women (viros muliebra pati), and they expose, with boasting and ostentation, the pollution of the impure and immodest body." Here we find the religious significance of eunuchry.

It was practised as a religious rite by the Tympanotribas or Gallus [1]), the castrated votary of Rhea or Bona Mater, in Phrygia called Cybele, self-mutilated but *not* in memory of Atys; and by a host of other creeds: even Christianity, as sundry texts show [2]),

---

[1]) Gallus lit. = a cock, in pornologic parlance is a capon, a castrato.

[2]) The texts justifying or conjoining castration are Matt. xviii 8-9; Mark ix. 43-47; Luke xxiii. 29 and Col. iii. 5. Saint Paul preached (1 Corin. vii. 29) that a man should live with

could not altogether cast out the old possession. Here too we have an explanation of Sotadic love in its second stage, when it became, like cannibalism, a matter of superstition. Assuming a nature-implanted tendency, we see that like human sacrifice it was held to be the most acceptable offering to the goddess in the Orgia or sacred ceremonies, a something set apart for peculiar worship. Hence in Rome, as in Egypt, the temples of Isis (Inachidos limina, Isiacæ sacraria Lunæ) were centres of sodomy and the religious practice was adopted by the grand priestly castes from Mesopotamia to Mexico and Peru.

We find the earliest written notices of the Vice in the mythical destruction of the Pentapolis (Gen. xix.), Sodom, Gomorrah (—'Amirah, the cultivated country), Adama, Zeboïm, and Zoar or Bela. The legend has been amply embroidered by the Rabbis, who made the

---

his wife as if he had none. The Abelian heretics of Africa abstained from women because Abel died virginal. Origen mutilated himself after interpreting too rigorously Matth. xix. 12, and was duly excommunicated. But his disciple, the Arab Valerius, founded (A. D. 250) the castrated sect called Valerians who, persecuted and dispersed by the Emperors Constantine and Justinian, became the spiritual fathers of the modern Skopzis. These eunuchs first appeared in Russia at the end of the xith. century, when two Greeks, John and Jephrem, were metropolitans of Kiew; the former was brought thither, in A. D. 1089, by Princess Anna Wassewolodowna and is called by the chronicles Nawjè or the Corpse. But in the early part of the last century (1715-1733) a sect arose in the circle of Uglitseh and in Moscow, at first called Clisti or flagellants which developed into the modern Skopzi. For this extensive subject see De Stein (Zeitschrift für Ethn. Berlin, 1875) and *The Ethnology of the Sixth Sense* by Dr. Jacobus.

Sodomites do every thing *à l'envers : e. g.* if a man were wounded he was fined for bloodshed and was compelled to fee the offender ; and if one cut off the ear of a neighbour's ass he was condemned to keep the animal till the ear grew again. The Jewish doctors declare the people to have been a race of sharpers with rogues for magistrates, and thus they justify the judgment which they read literally. But the traveller cannot accept it. I have carefully examined the lands at the North and at the South of that most beautiful lake, the so-called Dead Sea, whose tranquil loveliness backed by the grand plateau of Moab, is an object of admiration to all save patients suffering from the strange disease " Holy Land on the Brain [1])." But I found no traces of craters in the neighbourhood, no signs of vulcanism, no remains of " metoric stones," the asphalt which named the water is a mineralised vegetable washed out of the limestones, and the sulphur and salt are brought down by the Jordan into a lake without issue. I must therefore look upon the mystery as a myth which may have served a double purpose. The first would be to deter the Jew from the Malthusian practices of his pagan predecessors, upon whom obloquy was thus cast, so far resembling the scandalous and absurd legend which explained the names of the children of Lot by Pheiné and Thamma as " Moab " (Mu-ab) the water or semen of the father, and " Ammon " as mother's son, that is, bastard. The fable would also account for the

---

[1]) See the marvellously absurd description of the glorious " Dead Sea " in the Purchas v. 84.

fissure containing the lower Jordan and the Dead sea, which the late Sir R. I. Murchison used wrong-headedly to call a "Volcano of Depression": this geological feature, that cuts off the river-basin from its natural outlet the Gulf of Eloth (Akabah), must date from myriads of years before there were "Cities of the Plains".

But the main object of the ancient lawgiver, Osarsiph, Moses or the Moseidae, was doubtless to discountenance a perversion prejudical to the increase of the population. And he speaks with no uncertain voice, "Whoso lieth with a beast shall surely be put to death (Exod. xxii. 19): If a man lie with mankind as he lieth with a woman, both of them have committed an abomination: they shall surely be put to death; their blood shall be upon them" (Levit. xx. 13; where v. v. 15-16 threaten with death man and woman who lie with beasts). Again, there shall be no whore of the daughters of Israel nor a sodomite of the sons of Israel (Deut. xxii. 5).

The old commentators on the Sodom myth are most unsatisfactory; e. g. Parkurst s. v. Kadesh. "From hence we may observe the peculiar propriety of this punishment of Sodom and of the neighbouring cities. By their sodomitical impurities they meant to acknowledge the Heavens as the cause of fruitfulness independently upon, and in opposition to Jehovah [1]),

---

[1]) Jehovah here is made to play an evil part by destroying men instead of teaching them better. But, "Nous faisons les dieux à notre image et nous portons dans le ciel ce que nous voyons sur la terre." The idea of Yahweh or Yah is probably Egyptian, the Ankh or ever-living One: the etymon,

therefore Jehovah, by raining upon them not genial showers but brimstone from heaven, not only destroyed the inhabitants, but also changed all that country, which was before as the garden of God, into brimstone and salt that is not sown nor beareth, neither any grass groweth therein."

It must be owned that to this Pentapolis was dealt very hard measure for religiously and diligently practising a popular rite which a host of cities even in the present day, as Naples and Shiraz, to mention no others, affect for simple luxury and affect with impunity. The myth may probably reduce itself to very small proportions, a few Fellah villages destroyed by a storm, like that which drove Brennus from Delphi.

The Hebrews entering Syria found it religionised by Assyria and Babylonia, whence Accadian Ishtar had passed west and had become Ashtoreth, Ashtaroth or Ashirah [1]), the Anaitis of Armenia, the Phœnician Astarte and the Greek Aphrodite, the great Moon-goddess [2]) who

---

however, was learned at Babylon and is still found amongst the cuneiforms.

[1]) The name still survives in the Shajaràt al-Asharà, a clump of trees near the village Al-Ghajar (of the Gypsies) at the foot of Hermon.

[2]) I am not quite sure that Astarte is not primarily the planet Venus; but I can hardly doubt that Prof. Max Müller and Sir G. Cox are mistaken in bringing from India Aphrodite the Dawn and her attendants, the Charites identified with the Vedic Harits. Of Ishtar, in Accadia, however, Roscher seems to have proved that she is distinctly the Moon sinking into Amenti (the west, the Underworld) in search of her lost spouse Izdubar, the Sun-god. This again is pure Egyptianism.

is queen of Heaven and Love. In another phase she was Venus Mylitta = the Procreatrix, in Chaldaic Mauludata, and in Arabic, Moawallidah, she who bringeth forth. She was worshipped by men habited as women and vice versâ; for which reason in the Torah (Deut xx. 5) the sexes are forbidden to change dress. The male prostitutes were called Kadesh the holy, the women being Kadeshah, and doubtless gave themselves up to great excesses. Eusebius (De Bit. Const. III c. 55) describes a school of impurity at Aphac, where women and "Men who were not men" practised all manner of abominations in honour of the Demon (Venus). Here the Phrygian symbolism of Kybele and Attis (Atys) had become the Syrian Ba'al Tammuz and Astarte, and the Grecian Dionæa and Adonis, the anthropomorphic forms of the two greater lights. The site, Apheca, now Wadi al-Afik on the route from Bayrut to the Cedars, is a glen of wild and wondrous beauty, fitting frame-work for the loves of goddess and demigod: and the ruins of the temple destroyed by Constantine contrast with Nature's work, the glorious fountain, splendidior vitro, which feeds the river Ibrahim and still at times Adonis runs purple to the sea [1]).

---

[1]) In this classical land of Venus the worship of Ishtar-Ashtaroth is by no means obsolete. The Metàwali heretics, a people of Persian descent and Shiite tenets, and the peasantry of "Bilád B'sharrah", which I would derive from Bayt Ashirah, still pilgrimage to the ruins, and address their vows to the Sayyidat al-Kabiràh, the Great Lady. Orthodox Moslems accuse them of abominable orgies, and point to the lamps and rags which they suspend to a tree entitled Shajarat all-Sitt—the

The Phœnicians spread this androgynic worship over Greece. We find the consecrated servants and votaries of Corinthian Aphrodite called Hierodouli (Strabo VIII. 6), who aided the ten thousand courtezans in gracing the Venus-temple: from this excessive luxury arose the proverb popularised by Horace. One of the head-quarters of the cult was Cyprus where, as Servius relates (Ad. Æn. II. 632), stood the simulacre of a bearded Aphrodite, with a feminine body and costume, sceptered and mitred like a man. The sexes when worshipping it exchanged habits, and here the virginity was offered in sacrifice: Herodotus (I. c. 199) describes this defloration at Babylon but sees only the shameful part of the custom which was a mere consecration of a tribal rite. Everywhere girls before marriage belong either to the father or to the clan and thus the maiden paid the debt due to the public before becoming private property as a wife. The same usage prevailed in ancient Armenia and in parts of Ethiopia; and Hero-dotus tells us that a practice very much like the Babylonian " is found also in certain parts of the Island of Cyprus: " it is noticed by Justin (XVIII. c. 5) and probably it explains the " Succoth Benoth " or Damsels' booths which the Babylonians transplanted

---

Lady's tree—an Acacia Albida which, according to some travellers, is found only here and at Sayda (Sidon) where an avenue exists. The people of Kasrawàn, a Christian province in the Libanus, inhabited by a peculiarly prurient race, also hold high festival under the far-famed Cedars, and their women sacrifice to Venus like the Kadashah of the Phœnicians. This survival of old superstition is unknown to missionary "Hand-books", but amply deserves the study of the anthropologist.

to the cities of Samaria [1]). The Jews seem very successfully to have copied the abominations of their pagan neighbours, even in the matter of the "dog" [2]). In the reign of wicked Rehoboam (B. C. 975) "There were also sodomites in the land and they did according to all the abominations of the nations which the Lord cast out before the children of Israel" (1 Kings xiv. 20). The scandal was abated by jealous King Asa (B. C. 958) whose grandmother [1]) was high-priestess of Priapus (princeps in sacris Priapi): he "took away the sodomites out of the land (I Kings xv. 12). Yet the prophets were loud in their complaints, especially the so-called Isaiah (B. C. 760) "except the Lord of Hosts had left to us a very small remnant, we should have been as Sodom" (1. 9); and strong measures were required from good king Josiah (B. C. 641) who amongst other things, "brake down the houses of the sodomites that were by the house of the Lord, where the women wove hangings for the grove" (2 Kings

---

[1]) Some commentators understand "the tabernacles sacred to the reproductive powers of women"; and the Rabbis declare that the emblem was the figure of a setting hen.

[2]) "Dog" is applied by the older Jews to the Sodomite, and thus they understand the "price of a dog" which could not be brought into the Temple (Deut. xxiii. 18). I have noticed it in one of the derivations of cinœdus and can only remark that it is a vile libel upon the canine tribe.

[3]) Her name was Maachah and her title, according to some, "King's Mother": She founded the sect of Communists who rejected marriage and made adultery and incest part of worship in their splendid temple. Such were the Basilians and the Carpocratians, followed in the XIth century by Tranchelin, whose sectarians, the Turlupins, long infested Savoy.

K

xxiii. 7). The bordels of boys (pueris alienis adhæ-
severunt) appear to have been near the temple.

Syria has not forgotten her old "praxis." At
Damascus I found some noteworthy cases amongst
the religious of the great Amawi Mosque. As for the
Druses we have Burckhardt's authority (Travels in
Syria, etc., p. 202) "unnatural propensities are very
common amongst them."

The Sotadic zone covers the whole of Asia Minor
and Mesopotamia now occupied by the "unspeakable
Turk", a race of born pederasts [1]); and in the former

---

[1]) A story is told in a Turkish book of "how a boy escaped
from two old men":—"A rich man, named Koran, who was
addicted to going with boys, and a certain Shaykh Nedji
resolved to satisfy their lust on a child.

The Shaykh brought a nice lad into a garden planted with
orange trees; he was a stranger and the son of a *baboutchi*
(slipper maker).

"Come with me," said this young blackguard, "and I will
show you how the *baboutchis* enjoy themselves."

Then he stripped. "I must have him," cried the Shaykh.
With that he drew out his tool, but the old man, who would
have given his life to be able to perform, could not succeed
in his endeavours. He was not of an age to get an erection
suddenly; in spite of all his efforts and his vexation, he could
not penetrate into him.

He then determined to play a cunning trick on Koran.

"My dear Koran," he said, "this boy belongs to me, and I
would not change him for anything in the world. However
I will give him to you on one condition, and that is that you
never b—r him till he is of full age. If you break this
agreement, I shall be informed of the fact, by my knowledge
of alchemy."

With that they went into the garden, and the Shaykh left
them, hid himself, and watched them. As for me,—Koran,—I

region we first notice a peculiarity of the feminine figure, the mammæ inclinatæ, jacentes et pannosæ, which prevails over all this part of the belt. Whilst the women to the North and South have, with local exceptions, the mammæ stantes of the European Virgin [1]), those of Turkey, Persia, Afghanistan and Kashmir lose all the fine curves of the bosom, sometimes even before the first child; and after it the hemispheres take the form of bags. This cannot result from climate only; the women of Marathaland, inhabiting a damper and hotter region than Kashmir, are noted for fine firm breasts even after parturition. Le Vice of course prevails more in the cities and towns of Asiatic Turkey than in the villages; yet even these are infected; while the nomad Turcomans contrast badly in this point with the Gypsies, those Badawin of India.

The Kurd population is of Iranian origin, which

---

pulled out my tool and prepared to perform on the boy. He stooped forward, bared himself, and was ready to receive me. Whilst he was thus placed, I stooped and leaned over him, but I perceived that he was a little bit on one side. "Put yourself straight," I said, "and we will try to bring this job to a satisfactory conclusion."

At that moment he looked behind him, and saw the Shaykh and I guessed why the latter had offered me the boy. The boy being ashamed of being seen, ran away.

Thus did I—Koran—remain with my weapon in my hand, just as my dart was about to hit the bull's eye. This is what happened to me, and this is how a boy escaped the importunities of two old men."

[1]) A noted exception is Vienna, remarkable for the enormous development of the virginal bosom, which soon becomes pendulent.

means that the evil is deeply rooted: I have noted in The Nights that the great and glorious Saladin was a habitual pederast. The Armenians, as their national character is, will prostitute themselves for gain, but prefer women to boys: Georgia supplied Turkey with catamites, whilst Circassia sent concubines. In Mesopotamia, the barbarous invader has almost obliterated the ancient civilisation which is ante-dated only by the Nilotic: the myteries of old Babylon nowhere survive save in certain obscure tribes like the Mandæans, the Devil-worshippers, and the Ali-ilahi. Entering Persia, we find the reverse of Armenia; and, despite Herodotus, I believe that Iran borrowed her pathologic love from the peoples of the Tigris-Euphrates valley and not from the then insignificant Greeks. But whatever may be its origin, the corruption is now bred in the bone. It begins in boyhood, and many Persians account for it by paternal severity. Youths arrived at puberty find none of the facilities with which Europe supplies fornication.

Onanism [1]) is to a certain extent discouraged by circumcision, and meddling with the father's slave-girls and concubines would be risking cruel punishment if not death. Hence they use each other by turns, a "puerile practice" known as Alish-Takish, the Lat. facere vicibus or mutuum facere. Temperament, media, and atavism recommend the custom to

---

[1]) Gen. xxxviii. 2-11. Amongst the classics, Mercury taught the "Art of le Thalaba" to his son Pan, who wandered about the mountains distraught with love for the Nymph Echo, and Pan passed it on to the Pastors. See Thalaba in Mirabeau.

the general; and after marrying and begetting heirs, Paterfamilias returns to the Ganymede. Hence all the odes of Hafiz are addressed to youths, as proved by such Arabic exclamations as' Afaka 'Ilah = Allah assain thee (masculine) [1]): the object is often fanciful but it would be held coarse and immodest to address an imaginary girl [2]). An illustration of the penchant is told at Shiraz concerning a certain Mujtahid, the head of the Shi'ah creed, corresponding with a prince-archbishop in Europe. A friend once said to him, "There is a queastion I would fain address to your Eminence, but I lack the daring to do so;" "Ask and fear not", replied the Divine. "It is this, O Mujtahid! Figure thee in a garden of roses and hyacinths, with the evening breeze waving the cypress-beads, a fair youth of twenty sitting by thy side, and the assurance of perfect privacy. What, prithee, would be the result?" The holy man bowed the chin of doubt upon the collar of meditation; and, too honest to lie, presently whispered, "Allah defend me from such temptation of Satan!" Yet even in Persia men have not been wanting who have done their utmost to uproot the Vice: in the same Shiraz they speak of a father who finding his son in flagrant delict, put him to death like Brutus or Lynch of Galway. Such isolated cases, however, can effect nothing.

---

[1]) The reader of The Nights has remarked how often the "he" in Arabic poetry denotes a "she"; but the Arab, when uncontaminated by travel, ignores pederasty, and the Arab poet is a Badawi.

[2]) So Mohammed addressed his girl-wife, Ayishah, in the masculine.

Chardin tells us that houses of male prostitution
were common in Persia, whilst those of women were
unknown: the same is the case in the present day,
and the boys are prepared with extreme care by diet,
baths, depilation, unguents, and a hosts of artists in
cosmetics [1]). Le Vice is looked upon at most as a
pecadillo and its mention crops up in every jest-book.
When the Isfahan man mocked Shaykh Sa'adi, by
comparing the bald heads of Shirazian elders to the
bottom of a lota, a brass cup with a wide-necked
opening used in the Hammam, the witty poet turned
its aperture upwards and thereto likened the well-
abused podex of an Isfahani youth. Another favourite piece of Shirazian "chaff" is to declare that when
an Isfahan father would set up his son in business
he provides him with a pound of rice, meaning that
he can sell the result as compost for the Kitchen-
garden, and with the price buy another meal: hence
the saying Khak-i-pai kahu = the soil at the lettuce-
root. The Isfahanis retort with the name of a station
or halting-place between the two cities, where, under
pretence of making travellers stow away their riding-
gear, many a Shirazi had been raped: hence "Zin o
takaltu tu bibar" = carry within saddle and saddle-
cloth! A favourite Persian punishment for strangers
caught in the Harem or Gynæceum is to strip and

---

[1]) So amongst the Romans we have the Iatroliptae, youths
or girls who wiped the gymnast's perspiring body with swan-
down, a practice renewed by the professors of "Massage;"
Unctores who applied perfumes and essences; Fricatrices and
Tractatrices or shampooers; Dropacistae, corn-cutters; Alipilarii
who plucked the hair, etc., etc.

throw them and expose them to the embraces of the grooms and negro-slaves. I once asked a Shirazi how penetration was possible if the patient resisted with all the force of the sphincter muscle: he smiled and said, "Ah, we Persians know a trick to get over that; we apply a sharpened tent-peg to the crupper-bone (os coccygis) and knock till he opens." A well-known missionary to the East during the last generation was subjected to this gross insult by one of the Persian Prince-Governors, whom he had infuriated by his conversion mania; in his memoirs he alludes to it by mentioning his "dishonoured person;" but English readers cannot comprehend the full significance of the confession. About the same time, Shaykh Nasr, Governor of Bushire, a man famed for facetious black-guardism, used to invite European youngsters serving in the Bombay Marine, and ply them with liquor till they were insensible. Next morning the middies mostly complained that the champagne had caused a curious irritation and soreness in la parte-poste.

The same Eastern " Scrogin " would ask his guests if they had ever seen a man-cannon (Adami-top); and on their replying in the negative, a grey-bearded slave was dragged in, blaspheming and struggling with all his strength. He was presently placed on all fours and firmly held by the extremities; his bag-trowsers were let down and a dozen peppercorns were inserted ano suo; the target was a sheet of paper held at a reasonable distance; the match was applied by a pinch of Cayenne in the nostrils; the sneeze started the grapeshot and the number of hits on the butt decided the bets. We can hardly wonder at the loose com-duct of Persian women, perpetually mortified by marital pederasty. During the unhappy campaign of 1856-57, in which, with the exception of a few brilliant skirmishes, we gained no glory, Sir James Outram and the Bombay army showing how badly they could work, there was a formal outburst of the Harems; and even women of princely birth could not be kept out of the officers' quarters.

The cities of Afghanistan and Sind are thoroughly saturated with Persian vice, and the people sing,

Kadr-i-kus Aughàn dànad, kadr-i-kunrà Kabuli:
The worth of coynte the Afghan knows: Cabul prefers the
[other chose!

The Afghans are commercial travellers on a large scale, and each caravan is accompanied by a number of boys and lads almost in woman's attire with kohl'd eyes and rouged cheeks, long tresses and henna'd fingers and toes, riding luxuriously in Kajawas or camel-panniers: they are called Kuch-i safari or travelling wives, and the husbands trudge patiently by their sides. In Afghanistan also a frantic debauchery broke out among the women when they found incubi who were not pederasts; and the scandal was not the most insignificant cause of the general rising at

---

[1]) It is a parody on the well-known song (Roebuck 1. sect. 2, no. 1602):

The goldsmith knows the worth of gold, jewellers worth of
[jewelry;
The worth of rose Bulbul can tell, and Kambar's worth his
[lord, Ali.

Cabul (Nov. 1841), and the slaughter of Macnaghten, Burnes, and other British officers.

Resuming our way Eastward we find the Sikhs and the Moslems of the Panjab much addicted to Le Vice, Although the Himalayan tribes to the North and those lying South, the Rajputs and Marathas, ignore it. The same may be said of the Kashmirians who add another Kappa to the tria Kakista, Kappadocians, Ketans and Kilicians : the proverb says,

Agar kaht-i-mardum uftad, az in sih jins kam giri;
Eki Afghan, dovvum Sindi ¹), siyyum badjins-i-Kashmiri:
Though of men there be famine yet shun these three—
Afghan, Sindi and rascally Kashmiri.

M. Louis Daville describes the infamies of Lahore and Laknau where he found men dressed as women, with flowing locks under crowns of flowers, imitating the feminine walk and gestures, voice and fashion of speech, and ogling their admirers with all the coquetry of bayadères. Victor Jaquemont's Journal de voyage describes the pederasty of Ranjit Singh, the " Lion of the Panjab", and his pathic, Gulab Singh, whom the English inflicted upon Cashmir as a ruler by way of paying for his treason. Yet the Hindus, I repeat, hold pederasty in abhorrence, and are as much scandalised by being called Gandmara (anus-beater) or Gandu (anuser) as Englishmen would be. During the years 1843-44 my regiment, almost all Hindu Sepoys of the Bombay Presidency, was station-

---

¹) For "Sindi" Roebuck (Oriental Proverbs Part I. p. 99) has Runbu (Kumboh) a Panjàbi peasant, and others vary the saying ad libitum. See vol. VI. 156.

ned at a purgatory called Bandar Gharra [1]), a sandy flat with a scatter of verdigris-green milk-bush, some forty miles north of Karachi, the head-quarters. The dirty heap of mud-and-mat hovels, which represented the adjacent native village, could not supply a single woman; yet only one case of pederasty came to light, and that after a tragical fashion some years afterwards. A young Brahman had connection with a soldier comrade of low caste, and this had continued till, in an unhappy hour, the Pariah patient ventured to become the agent. The latter, in Arab. Al-Fa'il = the " doer ", is not an object of contempt like Al-Maful = the " done "; and the high caste sepoy, stung by remorse and revenge, loaded his musket and deliberately shot his paramour. He was hanged by court martial at Hyderabad, and, when his last wishes were asked he begged in vain to be suspended by the feet; the idea being that his soul, polluted by exiting " below the waist ", would be doomed to endless trans-migrations through the lowest forms of life.

Beyond India, I have stated, the Sotadic Zone begins to broaden out embracing all China, Turkistan and Japan. The Chinese, as far we know them in the great cities, are omniverous and omnifutuentes: they are the chosen people of debauchery and their syste-matic bestiality with ducks, goats and other animals is equalled only by their pederasty. Kæmpfer and Orlof Torée (Voyage en Chine) notice the public houses for boys and youths in China and Japan. Mirabeau (L'Anandryne) describes the tribadism of their women

---

[1]) See " Sind revisited " i. 133-35.

in hammocks. When Pekin was plundered, the Harems
contained a number of balls, a little larger than the
old musket-bullet, made of thin silver with a loose
pellet of brass inside somewhat like a grelot [1]): these
articles were placed by the women between the labia,
and an up-and-down movement on the bed gave a
pleasant titillation, when nothing better was to be
procured. They have every artifice of luxury, aphrodisiacs, erotic perfumes and singular applications.
Such are the pills which, dissolved in water and applied
to the glans penis, cause it to throb and swell: so
according to Amerigo Vespucci, American women could
artificially increase the size of their husbands' parts [2]).
The Chinese bracelet of caoutchouc studded with points
now takes the place of the "Herrisson", or Annu-
lus hirsutus [3]), which was bound between the glans
and prepuce. Of the penis succedanæus, that imitation
of the Arbor vitæ or Soter Kosmou, which the Latins
called phallus and fascinum [4]), the French godemiché

---

[1]) They must not be confounded with the *grelots lascifs*, the
little bells of gold or silver set by the people of Pegu in the
prepuce-skin and described by Nicolo de Conti who however
refused to undergo the operation.

[2]) Relation des découvertes faites par Colomb etc. p. 137:
Bologna, 1875: also Vespucci's letter in Ramusio (1. 131) and
Paro's Recherches philosophiques sur les Américains.

[3]) See Mantegazza loc. cit. who borrows from the Thèse de
Paris of Dr. Abel Hureau de Villeneuve, " Frictiones per coitum
productæ magnum mucosæ membranæ vaginalis turgorem, ac
simul hujus cuniculi coarctationem tam maritis salacibus
quæritatam afferunt."

[4]) Fascinus is the Priapus-god to whom the Vestal Virgins
of Rome, professed tribades, sacrificed; also the neck-charm in
phallus-shape. Fascinum is the male member.

and the Italians passatempo and diletto (whence our
" dildo ") every kind abounds, varying from a stuffed
" French Letter " to a cone of ribbed horn which looks
like an instrument of torture. For the use of men
they have the " Merkin " [1]), a heart-shaped article of
thin skin, stuffed with cotton and slit with an artificial
vagina: two tapes at the top and one below lash it
to the back of a chair. The erotic literature of the
Chinese and Japanese is highly developed, and their
illustrations are often facetious as well as obscene.
All are familiar with that of the strong man who by
a blow with his enormous phallus shivers a copper
pot; and the ludicrous contrast of the huge-membered
wights who land in the Isle of Women and presently
escape from it, wrinkled and shrivelled, true Domine
Dolittles. Of Turkistan we know little, but what we
know confirms my statement. M. Schuyler in his
Turkistan (1. 132) offers an illustration of a " Batchah "
(Pers. bachcheh = catamite), " or singing boy surrounded by his admirers ". Of the Tartars, Master Purchas
laconically says (v. 419), " They are addicted to
Sodomie or Buggerie ". The learned casuist, Dr.
Thomas Sanchez the Spaniard, had (says Mirabeau in
Kadhésch) to decide a difficult question concerning the
sinfulness of a peculiar erotic expression. The Jesuits
brought home from Manilla a tailed man, whose move-
able prolongation of the os coccygis measured from

---

[1]) Captain Grose (Lexicon Balatronicum) explains " merkin "
as " counterfeit hair for women's private parts." See Bailey's
Dict.. The Bailey of 1764, an " improved edition", does not
contain the word, which is now generally applied to a cunnus
succedanæus.

7 to 10 inches: he had placed himself between two women, enjoying one naturally while the other used his tail as a penis succedanæus. The verdict was incomplete sodomy and simple fornication. For the Islands north of Japan, the "Sodomitical Sea", and the "nayle of tynne" thrust through the prepuce to prevent sodomy, see Lib. II. chap. IV of Master Thomas Caudish's Circumnavigation, and the vol. VI of Pinkerton's Geography translated by Walckenaer.

Passing over to America we find that the Sotadic Zone contains the whole hemisphere from Behring's Straits to Magellan's. This prevalence of "molities" astonishes the anthropologist, who is apt to consider pederasty the growth of luxury, and the especial product of great and civilised cities, unnecessary, and therefore unknown to simple savagery, where the births of both sexes are about equal, and female infanticide is not practised. In many parts of the New World this perversion was accompanied by another depravity of taste—confirmed cannibalism [1]). The forests and campos abounded in game from the deer to the pheasant-like Penelope, and the seas and rivers produced an unfailing supply of excellent fish and shell-fish [2]), yet the Brazilian Tupis preferred the meat of man to every other food.

---

[1]) I have noticed this phenomenal cannibalism in my notes to Mr. Albert Tootle's excellent translation of "The Captivity of Hans Stade of Hesse:" London Hakluyt Society mdccclxxiv.

[2]) The Ostreinas or shell mounds of the Brazil sometimes 200 feet high, are described by me in Anthropologia No. i. Oct. 1873.

A glance at Mr. Bancroft [1]), proves the abnormal development of sodomy amongst the savages and barbarians of the New World. Even his half-frozen Hyper-borians "possess all the passions which are supposed to develop most freely under a milder temperature". (I. 58) The voluptuouness and polygamy of the North American Indians, under a temperature of almost perpetual winter is far greater than that of the most sensual tropical nations" (Martin's Brit. Colonies III. 524). I can quote only a few of the most remarkable instances. Of the Koniagas of Kadiak Island and the Thinkleets we read (I. 81-82). "The most repugnant of all their practices is that of male concubinage. A Kadiak mother will select her handsomest and most promising boy, and dress and rear him as a girl, teaching him only domestic duties, keeping him at women's work, associating him with women and girls, in order to render his effeminacy complete. Arriving at the age of ten or fifteen years, he is married to some wealthy man, who regards such a companion as a great acquisition. These male concubines arc called Achnutschik or Schopans." (The authorities quoted being Holmberg, Langsdorff, Billing, Choris, Lisiansky and Marchand). The same is the case in the Nutka Sound and the Aleutian Islands, "where male concubinage obtains throughout, but not to the same extent as amongst the Koniagas." The objects of "unnatural" affection have their beards carefully plucked out as soon as the face-hair begins

---

[1]) The Native Races of the Pacific States of South America by Herbert Howe Bancroft, London, Longmans, 1875.

to grow, and their chins are tattooed like those of the women. In California the first missionaries found the same practice, the youths being called Joya (Bancroft I. 415 and authorities Palon, Crespi, Boscanaf Mofras, Torquemada, Duflot and Fages). The Comanches unite incest with sodomy (I. 515). In New Mexico, according to Arlegui, Ribas and other authors, male concubinage prevails to a great extent; "these loathsome semblances of humanity, whom to call beastly were a slander upon beasts, dress themselves in the clothes and perform the function of women, the use of weapons being denied them" (I. 585). Pederasty was systematically practised by the peoples of Cueba, Careta and other parts of Central America. The Caciques and some of the head-men kept harems of youths, who, as soon as destined for the unclean office, were dressed as woman. They went by the name of Camayoas, and were hated and detested by the goodwives (I. 773-74). Of the Nahua nations Father Pierre de Gand (alias de Musa) writes. "Un certain nombre de prêtres n'avaient point de femmes, *sed eorum loco pueros quibus abutebantur.* Ce péché était si commun dans ce pays que, jeunes ou vieux, tous étaient infectés; ils y étaient si adonnés que même les enfants de six ans s'y livraient." Ternaux-Campans, Voyages, Série I, tome X. p. 197). Among the Mayas of Yucutan, Las Casas declares that the great prevalence of "unnatural" lust made parents anxious to see their progeny wedded as soon as possible (Kingsborough's Mex. Ant. VIII. 135). In Vera Paz, a god, called by some Chin and by others Cavial and Maran, taught it by committing the act with

221

another god. Some fathers gave their sons a boy to use as a woman, and if any other approached this pathic he was treated as an adulterer. In Yucatan, images were found by Bernal Diaz proving the sodomitical propensities of the people (Bancroft V. 198). De Pauw (Recherches Philosophiques sur les Américains, London, 1771) has much to say about the subject in Mexico generally; in the northern provinces men married youths who, dressed like women, were forbidden to carry arms. According to Gamara there were at Tamalipas houses of male prostitution; and from Diaz and others we gather that the *peccado nefando* was the rule. Both in Mexico and in Peru, it might have caused, if it did not justify, the cruelties of the Conquistadores. Pederasty was also general throughout Nicaragua, and the early explorers found it amongst the indigenes of Panama.

We have authentic details concerning the Vice in Peru and its adjacent lands, beginning with Cieza de Leon, who must be read in the original or in the translated extracts of Purchas (vol. V. 942, etc.), not in the cruelly castrated form preferred by the Council of the Hakluyt Society. Speaking of the New Granada Indians he tells us that " at Old Port (Porto Viejo) and Puna, the deuill so farre prevayled in their beastly Deuotions that there were Boyes consecrated to serue in the Temple; and at the times of their Sacrifices and Solemne Feasts, the Lords and principall men abused them to that detestable filthinesse; " *i. e.* performed their peculiar worship. Generally in the hill countries, the Devil, under the show of holiness, had introduced the practice, for every temple or chief house of adoration kept one or two men or more, who were attired like women, even from the time of their childhood, and spake like them, imitating them in everything; with these, under pretext of holiness and religion, their principal men on principal days had commerce. Speaking of the arrival of the Giants [1]) at Point Santa Elena, Cieza says (chap. LII.) they were detested by the natives, because in using their women they killed them, and their men also in another way. All the natives declare that God brought upon them a punishment proportioned to the enormity of their offence. When they were engaged together in their accursed intercourse, a fearful and terrible fire came down from Heaven with a great noise, out of the midst of which there issued a shining Angel, with a glittering sword wherewith at one blow they were all killed and the fire consumed them [2]). There remained a few bones and skulls which God allowed to bide unconsumed by the fire, as a memorial of this punishment. In the Hakluyt Society's bowdlerisation we read of the Tumbez Islanders being " very vicious ", many of them committing the abominable offence " (p. 24), also " If by the advice of the Devil any Indian commit the abominable crime, it is thought little of and they call him a woman ". In chapters LII and LVIII we find exceptions. The Indians of Huancabamba, " although so near the peoples of Puerto Viejo and

---

[1]) All Peruvian historians mention these giants, who were probably the large-limbed Caribs (Caraibes) of the Brazil: they will be noticed on page 225.

[2]) This sounds much like a pious fraud of the missionaries, a Europeo-American version of the Sodom legend.

Guayaquil, do not commit the abominable sin ; " and
the Serranos or island mountaineers, as sorcerers and
magicians inferior to the coast peoples, were not so
much addicted to sodomy.

The Royal Commentaries of the Yncas shows that
the evil was of comparatively modern growth. In the
early period of Peruvian history the people considered
the crime " unspeakable : " if a Cuzco Indian, not of
Ycarian blood, angrily addressed the term pederast
to another, he was held infamous for many days.
One of the generals having reported to the Ynca
Ccapacc Yupanqui, that there were some sodomites,
not in all the valleys, but one here and one there,
" nor was it a habit of all the inhabitants but only
of certain persons who practised it privately, " the
ruler ordered that the criminals should be publicly
burned alive, and their houses, crops and trees
destroyed : moreover, to show his abomination, he
commanded that the whole village should so be treated
if one man fell into this habit. " (Lib. III, cap. 13.)
Elsewhere we learn, " There were sodomites in some
provinces, though not openly nor universally, but
some particular men and in secret. In some parts
they had them in their temples, because the Devil
persuaded them that the Gods took great delight in
such people, and thus the Devil acted as traitor to
remove the veil of shame that the Gentiles felt for
this crime, and to accustom them to commit in public
and in common. "

During the time of the Conquistadores male concubinage had become the rule throughout Peru. At
Cuzco, we are told by Nuno de Guzman in 1530,

" The last which was taken, and which fought most courageously, was a man in the habite of a woman, which confessed that from a childe he had gotten his liuing by that filthinesse, for which I caused him to be burned. " V. F. Lopez [1]) draws a frightful picture of pathologic love in Peru. In the reigns that followed that of Inti-Kapak (Ccapacc) Amauri, the country was attacked by invaders of a giant race coming from the sea: they practised pederasty after a fashion so shameless that the conquered tribes were compelled to fly (p. 271). Under the pre-Yncarial Amauta, or priestly dynasty, Peru had lapsed into savagery, and the Kings of Cuzco preserved only the name. "Toutes ces hontes et toutes ces misères provenaient de deux vices infâmes, la bestialité et la sodomie. Les femmes surtout étaient offensées de voir la nature frustrée de tous ses droits. Elles pleuraient ensemble en leurs réunions sur le misérable état en lequel elles étaient tombées, sur le mépris avec lequel elles étaient traitées. *** Le monde était renversé, les hommes s'aimaient et étaient jaloux les uns des autres. *** Elles cherchaient, mais en vain, les moyens de remédier au mal ; elles employaient des herbes et des recettes diaboliques qui leur ramenaient bien quelques individus, mais ne pouvaient arrêter les progrès incessants du vice. Cet état de choses constitua un véritable moyen âge, qui dura jusqu'à l'établissement des Incas" (p. 277).

When Sinchi Roko (the xcvth of Montesimos and the xcist of Garcilazo) became Ynca, he found morals at the lowest ebb. " Ni la prudence de l'Inca, ni les

---

[1]) Les Races Aryennes du Pérou, Paris, Franck, 1871.

lois sévères qu'il avait promulguées n'avaient pu extirper entièrement le péché contre nature. Il reprit avec une nouvelle violence, et les femmes en furent si jalouses qu'un grand nombre d'elles tuèrent leurs maris. Les devins et les sorciers passaient leurs journées à fabriquer, avec certaines herbes, des compositions magiques qui rendaient fous ceux qui en mangeaient, et les femmes en faisaient prendre, soit dans les aliments, soit dans la chicha, à ceux dont elles étaient jalouses " (p. 291).

I have remarked that the Tupi races of the Brazil were infamous for cannibalism and sodomy; nor could the latter be only racial, as proved by the fact that colonists of pure Lusitanian blood followed in the path of the savages. Sr. Antonio Augusto da Costa Aguiar [1]) is outspoken upon this point. " A crime which in England leads to the gallows, and which is the very measure of abject depravity, passes with impunity amongst us by the participating in it of all or many *(de quasi todos, ou de muitos)*. Ah! if the wrath of Heaven were to fall by way of punishing such crimes *(delictos)*, more than one city of this Empire, more than a dozen, would pass into the category of the Sodoms and Gomorrahs " (p. 30). Till late years pederasty was looked upon in Brazil as a peccadillo; the European immigrants following the practice of the wild men who were naked, but not, as Columbus said, " clothed in innocence ". One of Her Majesty's Consuls used to tell a tale of the hilarity provoked in a " fashionable " assembly by the open

---

[1]) O Brazil e os Brazileiros, Santos, 1862.

declaration of a young gentleman that his mulatto
" patient " had suddenly turned upon him, insisting
upon becoming agent. Now, however, under the
influences of improved education and respect for the
public opinion of Europe, pathologic love among
the Luso-Brazilians has been reduced to the normal
limits.

Outside the Sotadic Zone, I have said, Le Vice is
sporadic, not endemic: yet the physical and moral
effect of great cities where puberty, they say, is induced
earlier than in country sites, has been the same in
most lands, causing modesty to decay and pederasty
to flourish. The Badawi Arab is wholly pure of Le
Vice; yet San'a the capital of Al-Yaman and other
centres of population, have long been and still are
thoroughly infected. History tells us of Zu Shanatir,
tyrant of " Arabia Felix ", in A. D. 478, who used
to entice young men into his palace and cause them
after use to be cast out of the windows; this unkindly
ruler was at last poniarded by the youth Zerash,
known from his long ringlets as " Zu Nowas ". The
negro race is mostly untainted by sodomy, yet Joan
dos Sanctos [1]) found in Cacongo of West Africa
certain " Chibudi, which are men attyred like women
and behaue themselves womanly, ashamed to be called
men; are also married to men, and esteem that un-
naturale damnation an honor. " Madagascar also delighted in dancing and singing boys dressed as girls.
In the Empire of Dahomey I noted a corps of prostitutes
kept for the use of the Amazon-Soldieresses.

---

[1]) Æthiopia Orientalis, Purchas, ii. 1558.

North of the Sotadic zone we find local but notable instances. Master Christopher Burrough [1]) describes on the western side of the Volga "a very fine stone castle, called by the name Oueak, and adioyning to the same a Towne called by the *Russes*, *Sodom*, *** which was swallowed into the earth by the iustice of God, for the wickednesse of the people". Again; although as a rule Christianity has steadily opposed pathologic love both in writing and preaching, there have been remarkable exceptions. Perhaps the most curious idea was that of certain medical writers in the middle ages: "Usus et amplexus pueri, bene temperatus, salutaris medecina" (Tardieu). Bayle notices (under "Vayer"), the infamous book of Giovanni della Casa, Archbishop of Benevento "De laudibus Sodomiæ" [2]) vulgarly known as "Capitolo del Forno". The same writer refers (under "Sixte IV") that the Dominican Order, which systematically decried Le Vice had presented a request to Cardinal di Santa Lucia that Sodomy might be lawful during three months annually from June to August; and that the Cardinal had written: "Be it done as they demand." Hence the Fæda Veneris of Battista Mantovano. Bayle rejects the history for a curious reason, venery being colder in summer than in winter, and quotes the proverb "Aux mois qui n'ont pas d'R, peu embrasser et bien boire." But in the case of a celibate priesthood such scandals are inevitable: witness the famous Jesuit épitaph "Ci-gît un Jésuit, etc."

---

[1]) Purchas III. 243.

[2]) For a literal translation see 1re série de la Curiosité littéraire et bibliographique, Paris, Liseux, 1880.

In our modern capitals, London, Berlin, and Paris for instance, the Vice seems subject to periodical outbreaks. For many years also, England sent her pederasts to Italy, and especially to Naples, whence originated the term "Il Vizio Inglese". It would be invidious to detail the scandals which of late years have startled the public in London and Dublin, for these the curious will consult the police reports. Berlin, despite her strong flavour of Phariseeism, Puritanism, and Chauvinism, in religion, manners and morals, is not a whit better than her neighbours. Dr. Caspar [1]), a well-known authority on the subject, adduces many interesting cases, especially an old Count Cajus and his six accomplices. Among his many correspondents one suggested to him that not only Plato and Julius Cæsar but also Winckelmann and Platen (?) belonged to the Society; and he had found it flourishing at Palermo, the Louvre, the Scottish Highlands and St. Petersburg, to name only a few places. Frederick the Great is said to have addressed these words to his nephew, "Je puis vous assurer, par mon expérience personelle, que ce plaisir est peu agréable à cultiver." This suggests the popular anecdote of Voltaire and the Englishman who agreed upon an "experience," and found it far from being satisfactory. A few days afterwards the latter informed the Sage of Ferney that he had tried it again, and provoked the exclamation, "Once a philosopher,

---

[1]) His best known works are (2) Praktisches Handbuch der Gerechtlichen Medecin, Berlin, 1860; and (2) Klinische Novellen zur Gerechtlichen Medecin, Berlin, 1863.

twice a sodomite!" The last revival of the kind in Germany is a society at Frankfort and its neighbourhood, self-styled "Les Cravates Noires" in opposition, I suppose, to Les Cravates Blanches of A. Belot.

Paris is by no means more depraved than Berlin or London, but whilst the latter hushes up the scandal, Frenchmen do not: hence we see a more copious account of it submitted to the public. For France of the 17th century consult the "Histoire de la Prostitution chez tous les Peuples du Monde," and "La France devenue Italienne," a treatise which generally follows "L'Histoire Amoureuse des Gaules" by Bussy, Comte de Rabutin [1]). The head-quarters of male prostitution were then in the Champ Flory, i. e., Champ de Flore, the privileged rendez-vous of low courtezans. In the 18th century, "quand le Français à tête folle", as Voltaire sings, invented the term "Péché Philosophique", there was a temporary recrudescence; and after the death of Pidauzet de Mairobert (March 1779), his "Apologie de la Secte Anandryne" was published in L'Espion Anglais. In those days the Allée des Veuves in the Champs-Elysées had a "fief reservé des Ebugors" [2])—"veuve" in the language of

---

[1]) The same author printed another imitation of Petronius Arbiter, the "Larissa" story of Théophile Viaud. His cousin, the Sévigné, highly approved of it. See Bayle's objections to Rabutin's delicacy and excuses for Petronius' grossness in his "Eclaircissement sur les obscénités" (Appendice au Dictionnaire Antique).

[2]) The Boulgrin of Rabelais, which Urquhart renders Ingle for Boulgre, an "Indorser", derived from the Bulgarus or

Sodoms being the maîtresse en titre, the favourite youth.

At the decisive moment of monarchical decomposition, Mirabeau [1]) declares that pederasty was reglementée and adds, "Le goût des pédérastes, quoique moins en vogue que du temps d'Henri III (the French Heliogabalus), sous le règne duquel les hommes se provoquaient mutuellement [2]) sous les portiques du Louvre, fait des progrès considérables. On sait que cette ville (Paris) est un chef d'œuvre de police; en conséquence il a des lieux publics autorisés à cet effet. Les jeunes gens qui se destinent à la profession, sont soigneusement enclassés, car les systèmes règlementaires s'étendent jusque-là. On les examine; ceux qui peuvent être agents et patients, qui sont beaux, vermeils, bien faits, potelés, sont réservés pour

---

Bulgarian, who gave to Italy the term bugiardo—liar. Bougre and Bougrerie date (Littré) from the 13th century. I cannot, however, but think that the trivial term gained strength in the 16th, when the manners of the Bugres or indigenous Brazilians were studied by Huguenot refugees in La France Antartique and several of these savages found their way to Europe. A grand Fête in Rouen on the entrance of Henri II and dame Catherine de Medicis (June 16, 1564 showed, as part of the pageant, three hundred men (including fifty "Bugres" or Tupis) with parroquets and other birds and beasts of the newly explored regions. The procession is given in the four-folding woodcut "Figure des Brésiliens" in Jean de Prest's Edition of 1551.

[1]) Erotica Biblion, chap. Kadésch (pp. 93 et seq.). Edition de Bruxelles with notes by the Chevalier Pierrugues of Bordeaux, before noticed.

[2]) Called Chevaliers de Paille because the sign was a straw in the mouth, à la Palmerston.

les grand seigneurs, ou se font payer très cher par les évêques et les financiers. Ceux qui sont privés de leurs testicules, ou en termes de l'art (car notre langue est plus chaste que nos mœurs) qui n'ont pas le *poids du tisserand*, mais qui donnent et reçoivent, forment la seconde classe : ils sont encore chers, parce que les femmes en usent, tandis qu'ils servent aux hommes. Ceux qui ne sont plus susceptibles d'érection tant ils sont usés, quoiqu'ils aient tous ces organes nécessaires au plaisir, s'inscrivent comme *patients purs*, et composent la troisième classe : mais celle qui préside à ces plaisirs, vérifie leur impuissance. Pour cet effet, on les place tout nus sur un matelas ouvert par la moitié inférieure ; deux filles les caressent de leur mieux, pendant qu'une troisième frappe doucement avec des orties naissantes le siège des désirs vénériens. Après un quart d'heure de cet essai, on leur introduit dans l'anus un poivre-long rouge, qui cause une irritation considérable ; on pose sur les échaubulures produites par les orties, de la moutarde fine de Caudebec, et l'on passe le *gland* au camphre. Ceux qui résistent à ces épreuves et donnent aucun signe d'érection, servent comme patiens à un tiers de paie seulement [1]).

The Restoration and the Empire made the police more vigilant in matters of politics than of morals. The favourite club, which had its mot de passe, was in the Rue Doyenne, old quarter St. Thomas du Louvre ; and the house was a hôtel of the 17th cen-

---

[1]) I have noticed that the eunuch in Sind was as meanly paid, and have given the reason.

tury. Two street-doors, on the right for the male Gynæceum and the left for the female, opened at 4 p.m. in winter and at 8 p.m. in summer. A decoy-lad, charmingly dressed in women's clothes, with big haunches and small waist, promenaded outside; and this continued till 1826, when the police put down the house.

Under Louis-Philippe, the conquest of Algiers had evil results, according to the Marquis de Boissy. He complained without ambages of mœurs Arabes in French regiments, and declared that the results of the African wars was an effroyable debordement pédéras-tique, even as the vérola resulted from the Italian campaigns of that age of passions, the 16th century. From the military, the fléau spread to civilian society, and the Vice took such expansion and intensity that it may be said to have been democratised in cities and large towns; at least so we gather from the Dossier des Agissements des Pédérastes. A general gathering of "La Sainte Congrégation des glorieux Pédérastes" was held in the old Petite Rue des Marais where, after the theatre, many resorted under pretext of making water. They ranged themselves along the walls of a vast garden and exposed their podices; bourgeois, richards and nobles came with full purses, touched the part which most attracted them and were duly followed by it. At the Allée des Veuves the crowd was dangerous from 7 to 8 p.m.: no policeman or ronde de nuit dared venture in it; cords were stretched from tree, to tree and armed guards drove away strangers, amongst whom they say was once Victor Hugo. This nuisance was at length suppressed by the municipal administration.

The Empire did not improve morals. Balls of sodomites were held at n° 8 Place de la Madeleine, where on Jan 2, 1864, some one hundred and fifty men met, all so well dressed as women that even the landlord did not recognise them. There was also a club for Sotadic debauchery called the Cent Gardes and the Dragons de l'Impératrice [1]). They copied the impérial toilette and kept it in the general wardrobe: hence, " faire l'Impératrice " meant to be used carnally. The site, a splendid hôtel in the Allée des Veuves, was discovered by the Procureur-Général, who registered all the names; but, as these belonged to not a few senators and dignitaries, the Emperor wisely quashed proceedings. The club was broken up on July 16th, 1864. During the same year, *La Petite Revue*, edited by M. Loredan Larchey, son of the General, printed an article, " Les échappés de Sodome: " it discusses the letter of M. Castagnary to the *Progrès de Lyon*, and declares that the Vice had been adopted by plusieurs corps de troupes. For its latest developments as regards the *chantage* of the *tantes* (pathics), the reader will consult the last issues of Dr Tardieu's well known Etudes. [2]) He declares that the servant-class is most

---

[1]) Centuria Librorum Absconditorum (by Pisanus Fraxi) 4° p. LX and 593. London. Privately printed, 1879.

[2]) A friend learned in these matters supplies me with following list of famous pederasts. Those who marvel at the wide diffusion of such erotic perversion, and its being affected by so many celebrities, will bear in mind that the greatest men have been some of the worst: Alexander of Macedon.

infected; and that the vice is commonest between the ages of fifteen and twenty five.

The pederasty of The Nights may be briefly distributed into three categories. The first is the funny form, as the unseemly practical joke of masterful Queen Budur (vol. III. 300-306) and the not less hardy jest of the slave-princess Zumurrud (vol. IV. 226). The second is in the grimmest and most earnest phase of the perversion, for instance where Abou Nowas [1])

Julius Cæsar and Napoleon Bonaparte held themselves high above the moral law which obliges common-place humanity. All these are charged with the Vice. Of kings we have Henri III, Louis XIII and XVIII, Frederick II of Prussia, Peter the Great, William II of Holland, and Charles II and III of Parma. We find also Shakespeare (I. xv. Edit. François Hugo) and Molière, Théodore de Beza, Lully (the composer), d'Assoucy, Count Zintzendorff, the Grand Condé, Marquis de Villette, Pierre-Louis Farnèse, Duc de la Vallière, De Soleinne, Count d'Avaray, Saint-Mégrin, d'Epernon, Amiral de la Susse, La Roche. Pouchin, Rochfort Saint Louis, Henne (the Spiritualist), Comte Horace de Viel-Castel, Lerminin, Fiévée, Théodore Leclerc, Cambacérès, Marquis de Custine, Sainte-Beuve and Count d'Orsay. For others refer to the three vols. of Pisanus Fraxi; Index Librorum Prohibitorum (London 1877), Centuria Librorum Absconditorum (before alluded to), and Catena Librorum Tacendorum, London 1885. The indices will supply the names.

[1]) Of this peculiar character, Ibn Khallikan remarks (II. 43), "There were four poets whose works clearly contraried their character. Abu al-Atahiyah wrote pious poems himself being an atheist, Abù Hukayma's verses proved his impotence, yet he was more salacious than a he-goat; Mohammed Ibn Hàzim praised contentment, yet he was greedier than a dog; and Abù Nowas hymned the joys of sodomy, yet he was more passionate for women than a baboon."

debauches the three youths (vol. V. 64-69); whilst in
the third form it is wisely and learnedly disscussed,
to be severely blamed, by the Shaykhah, or Reverend
Woman (vol. V. 154).

To conclude this part of my subject, the éclair-
cissement des obscénités. Many readers will regret
the absence from The Nights of that modesty which
distinguishes "Amadis de Gaul," whose author, when
leaving a man and a maid together, says, "And nothing shall be here related; for these and suchlike things
which are conformable neither to good conscience nor
nature, man ought in reason lightly to pass over,
holding them in slight esteem as they deserve." Nor
have we less respect for Palmerin of England who
after a risqué scene declares, "Herein is no offence
offered to the wise by wanton speeches, or encour-
agement to the loose by lascivious matter." But
these are not oriental ideas, and we must e'en take
the Eastern as we find him. He still holds "Naturalia
non sunt turpia," together with "Mundis omnia
munda;" and, as Bacon assures us the mixture of a
lie doth add to pleasure, so the Arab enjoys the
startling and lively contrast of extreme virtue and
horrible vice placed in juxtaposition.

Those who have read through these ten volumes
will agree with me that the proportion of offensive
matter bears a very small ratio to the mass of the
work. In an age saturated with cant and hypocrisy,
here and there a venal pen will mourn over the "Por-
nography" of The Nights, dwell upon the "Ethics
of Dirt," and the "Garbage of the Brothel"; and will
lament the "wanton dissemination (!) of ancient and

filthy fiction. " This self-constituted Censor morum
reads Aristophanes and Plato, Horace and Virgil,
perhaps even Martial and Petronius, because " veiled
in the decent obscurity of a learned language; " he
allows men Latiné loqui; bnt he is scandalised at
stumbling-blocks much less important in plain English.
To be consistent, he must begin by bowdlerising not
only the classics, with which boys' and youths' minds
and memories are soaked and saturated at schools
and colleges, but also Boccaccio and Chaucer, Shakespeare and Rabelais; Burton, Sterne, Swift and a long
list of works which are yearly reprinted and republished
without a word of protest. Lastly, why does not this
inconsistent puritan purge the Old Testament of its
allusions to human ordure and the pudenda; to carnal
copulation and impudent whoredom, to adultery and
fornication, to onanism, sodomy and bestiality? But
this he will not do, the whited sepulchre! To the
interested critic of the Edinburgh Review (n⁰ 335 of
July, 1886), I return my warmest thanks for his
direct and deliberate falsehoods:—lies are one legged
and short-lived, and venom evaporates [1]). It appears
to me that when I show to such men, so " respectable "

---

[1]) A virulently and unjustly abusive critique never yet injured
its object: in fact it is generally the greatest favour an author's
unfriends can bestow upon him. But to notice in a popular
Review books which have been printed and not published, is
hardly in accordance with the established courtesies of literature.
At the end of my work, I propose to write a paper, 'The
Reviewer Reviewed,' which will, amongst other things, explain
the motif of the writer of the critique and the editor of the
Edinburgh.

and so impure, a landscape of magnificent prospects whose vistas are adorned with every charm of nature and art, they point their unclean noses at a little heap of muck here and there lying in a field-corner.

FINIS.

N. B.—It will be noticed that this Appendix contains several references to Sir Richard Burton's translation of the " *Arabian Nights* ". We deemed it fairer to Sir Richard to give the whole of the article to selecting passages here and there, which standing apart might have easily led to a misconstruction of his *real* meaning.